ACCELERATED LEARNING

IN PRACTICE

Brain-based methods for accelerating motivation and achievement

ALISTAIR SMITH

THE FOLLOWING SCHOOLS, COLLEGES AND OTHER ORGANISATIONS HAVE DIRECTLY OR INDIRECTLY CONTRIBUTED CASE STUDIES TO THIS BOOK.

Acton High School, Acton, London
Bedminster Down School, Bristol
Birley School, Sheffield
Bracken Hill Primary School, Sheffield
Brislington School, Bristol
Byron Wood Primary School, Sheffield
The Castle School, Taunton, Somerset
Cramlington High School, Northumberland
Crispin School, Somerset
Devon LEA
Ealing LEA, London
Erias High School, Colwyn Bay, Clywd
Essex LEA
Firth Park School, Sheffield
Grace Owen Nursery School, Sheffield
Haggerston School, Hackney, London
The Harwich School, Dovercourt, Harwich
Hengrove School, Bristol
Holy Family Primary School, Langley, Berkshire
King Edmund Community School, Yate, South Gloucestershire
Leicestershire LEA
Lutterworth Grammar and Community School, Leicestershire
Mallett Lambert School, Hull
Mirfield Free Grammar, West Yorkshire
The Minster School, Southwell, Nottinghamshire
Ninestiles School, Birmingham
North Lincolnshire LEA
Pen Park School, Bristol
Ralph Allen School, Bath
Sacred Heart RC Secondary School, Southwark, London
Sheffield LEA
Sittingbourne Community College, Kent
Somerset LEA
Somervale School, Midsomer Norton, Bath and North East Somerset
South West Special Schools Headteacher's Conference
St Aidan's School, Carlisle, Cumbria
St George Community School, Bristol
St James Catholic High School, Hendon
St John the Baptist School, Woking, Surrey
Stewards School, Harlow, Essex
Town Farm Primary School, Stanwell, Surrey
Woolwich Polytechnic School, Greenwich
Sir William Nottidge School, Kent
Wadham School, Crewkerne, Somerset
Wilberfoss CE Primary School, York

Published by Network Educational Press Ltd.
PO Box 635
Stafford
ST16 1BF

First Published 1998, Reprinted 2000
© Alistair Smith

Paperback ISBN 1 855 39 048 5
Hardback ISBN 1 855 39 068 X

Alistair Smith asserts his moral right to be identified as the
author of this work.

Every effort has been made to contact copyright holders of materials
reproduced in this book. The publishers apologise for any omissions
and will be pleased to rectify them at the earliest opportunity. Please
see p.253 for a comprehensive list of acknowledgements.

Managing Editor: Sara Peach
Editorial Work by Sara Peach and Carol Thompson
Design by Heather Blackham, HB Designs
Illustration by Oliver Caviglioli

Printed in Great Britain by
MPG Books Ltd, Bodmin, Cornwall

ACCELERATED
LEARNING
IN PRACTICE

Contents

Section Three: The strategies to accelerate learning in the classroom

Section Four: Resources and contacts for accelerated learning in the classroom

How to use this book

This book deliberately sets out to model the practices which its author espouses. The format is structured to help you, the reader, access and retain the information you need to begin to accelerate your own learning or the learning of the students you teach.

The BIG picture is given via the memory map at the beginning of the book. Each section is preceded by a synopsis and reviewed by summary questions. The sections and the content within each section follow the order of the accelerated learning in the classroom cycle. Section One reminds us of the impact new research into the neurology of learning is beginning to have. It carefully links the theory to the accelerated learning in the classroom cycle described elsewhere in my 1996 book of the same name. The substance of the strategies for the classroom teacher lies within Sections Two and Three. In Section Three there is an overview of how schools and colleges can take this forward and there are a number of case studies of successful practice. In Section Four there are further resources and useful contact addresses as well as a glossary of terms.

◆ The introduction summarises the case for a new paradigm for learning and gives an overview of the accelerated learning in the classroom model

◆ Section One outlines the research evidence behind the model recommended throughout the book

◆ Section Two shows how to achieve a positive and supportive learning environment

◆ Section Three takes you through the seven stages of the accelerated learning in the classroom cycle and provides classroom strategies for each stage and 17 ways in which your learning community can take it forward

◆ Section Four provides resources, references and contact addresses

Wherever possible the research sources are quoted in full at the back of the book. I have tried to ensure that the most recent research information has been used to substantiate the model I offer. I offer one caveat. This book does not cover strategies for accessing and using the new information and communications technologies. I acknowledge the impact they are having in both formal and informal learning but I feel it is a specialist area which cannot be covered in any depth within these pages.

In January 1998, I met the developer of 'Photoreading', Paul Scheele. Photoreading is the world's most effective whole brain reading system. A year earlier I had met Howard Berg. A man once described in the *Guinness Book of Records* as the 'World's fastest reader'. Howard Berg uses a method which others have described as Speedreading. This allows him to 'read' 25,000 (twenty-five thousand) words per minute with over 75% comprehension! I commend some of the practices which underlie both Photoreading and Speedreading to you when you begin to use this book:

7

◆ be specific about how you wish to use the information in the book

◆ future-base – by the end of reading this book what outcome do you wish for yourself? – envisage the successful achievement of that outcome

◆ relax

◆ survey the book first – flick through the pages to get a 'feel' for its content and layout – do this quickly and simply scan for visual information and as you do so you will begin to notice certain key words; look at all sections including the index

◆ relax again before 'photoreading' the book – move through a page at a time taking in the visual information from all the page, soften the focus of your eyes so that all the information is available, spend about a second or two on each page

◆ formulate questions for those sections you wish to use before returning to those sections and scanning down the centre of the page, dip into the text for more focused reading, finding cues which will begin to answer your questions

◆ relax again

◆ rapid read those areas of the text which the cues have alerted you to, read for meaning and comprehension at this stage

One of the principles which underlies the success of Howard Berg and others who exhibit mastery over learning skills is that of 'state'. A positive and purposeful state of mind where one is receptive and open to new ideas is essential. Speedreaders have to suspend traditional beliefs about reading being hard work, incremental, assimilated word by word, line by line before the system begins to work for them. They recognise that a state of high-challenge but low-stress – relaxed alertness – is a prerequisite for achievement. I hope that you can approach this book in the same way.

A note on memory mapping

The 'memory map' produced for you summarises the key content of this book. It also provides our second strategy to accelerate learning. I recommend that you take a moment to look through our example and think about how it might help you and your students in the act of learning.

A memory map provides a method of structuring note-taking and thinking which moves away from 'extracting', from 're-working' and from 'rote-rehearsal'. The creation of a memory map is challenging, creative and interpretative. It requires an interaction and understanding of any new information which can be missing from other, more conventional, approaches. Sections One to Four in this book are each preceded by a summary memory map.

In Section Three I describe in detail how to utilise memory mapping techniques and how to develop them from topic and concept webs, trigger charts and priority lists. If you want to know more about the technique turn to page 192 before continuing with the book. You may find it helps to model the process by creating your own memory map of *Accelerated Learning in Practice*.

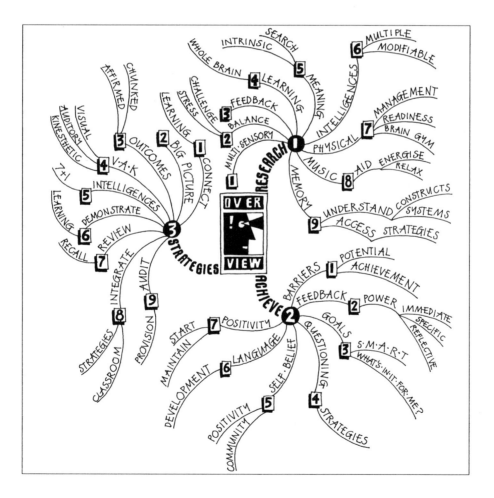

Note: The memory maps included in this book use principles derived from the work of Tony Buzan on mind mapping.

Acknowledgements

This book owes its existence to the overwhelming enthusiasm of educationalists for the ideas described in *Accelerated Learning in the Classroom* and my belief that there is so much more to be discovered, described and shared.

In putting the book together I have had benefit of the driving skills of Rob Bailey, Alan Coveney and Ken Smith. Barbara Teale kept faith and Sara Peach has, once again, taken care of the edit from beginning to end. Oliver Caviglioli's brilliant art work and visual skills bring the book to life and are so much more impressive because he understands the issues under discussion better than most. Kirsty Wallace has been a model of positivity.

Many teachers contributed ideas through their own professional practice. My thanks to you all. A particular thank you to Cris Edgell, the best teacher I ever met, and to Ani Magill, a model Headteacher and more.

Win Wenger has given me fresh insights and inspiration as well as a copy of his new work from Project Renaissance. Paul Scheele wired me to his EEG equipment and Colin Rose has provided inspiration and kind words.

The pursuit of more detailed understanding about accelerated learning and the workings of the brain in learning has led me into a diversity of academic disciplines and research experiences where I very quickly realised that few, if any, individuals are blessed with an informed overview and that the seeming inaccessibility of some of the areas can be both intimidating and a disincentive to push any further. Whilst there is an explosion of quality new research information about the brain, learning and performance, there is so much more yet to be discovered. Some generalisations are therefore necessary.

What I offer in the pages that follow is a model of learning based on my attempt to pull together some of the work evidenced in the fields of cognitive neuroscience and cognitive neuropsychology, human motivational theory and performance psychology, learning theory and school improvement and school effectiveness research. I have also tried to utilise other approaches to understanding human performance, which await the stamp of academic credibility, notably neuro-linguistic programming and transactional analysis.

Inevitably, this uneasy 'mix' will contain flaws, oversights and simplifications and some may not be able to see beyond this. I hope that for those of you who are enthused by the model you find here, it offers some of the excitement and sense of possibility that led me to try and describe it to you.

Whatever you would do or would wish to do, begin it. . . . After a lifetime of being fearful of water, my mother, in her late fifties, learned to swim and taught me that beliefs can limit or liberate. So this is for her.

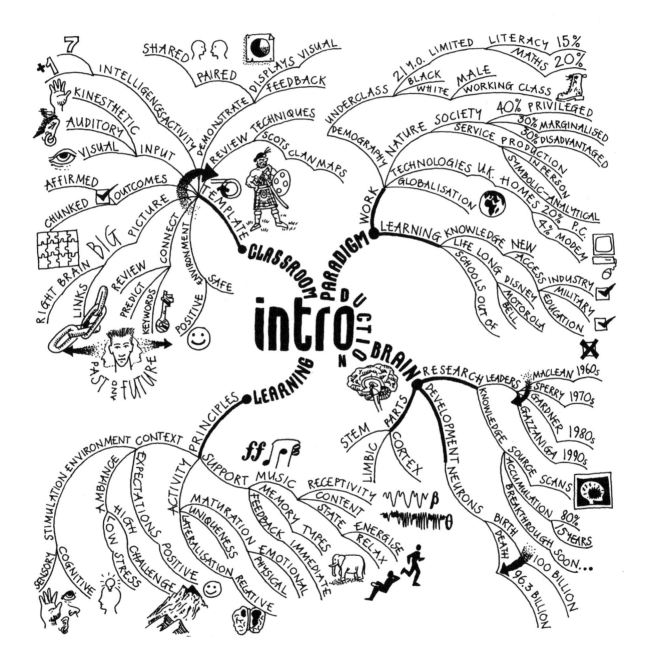

Introduction:

A model of learning

1 A NEW PARADIGM FOR LEARNING

> *In times of change the learners will inherit the earth, while the knowers will find themselves beautifully equipped to deal with a world that no longer exists.*

ERIC HOFFER, quoted IAL Conference
'Unleashing the Brain's Potential', **1997**

A S WE ENTER A NEW CENTURY and the change it heralds, how can we create a society of learners ready to 'inherit the earth'? What sort of young people are going to be best equipped to deal with the only certainty that the millennium guarantees, the certainty of continual change in an uncertain world? What tools will our educational legacy equip them with to meet the challenge? What tools *could* our legacy provide?

To know what the best equipped learner facing the uncertainties of the 21st Century should have, we ought to consider what life in the 21st Century will be like. Sadly, the past is less and less of a guide to what the future holds.

Bill Gates, founder of the Microsoft Corporation, points us to the first principle which must be endorsed: *"In a changing world, education is the best preparation for being able to adapt . . . as economies shift, people and societies which are appropriately educated will tend to do best . . . my advice is to get a good formal education and then keep on learning . . . acquire new interests and skills throughout your life."*

Undoubtedly we must do more to release the potential of learners whom we meet in our schools and colleges. It can be done by equipping them with powerful lifelong learning tools. There are seven compelling reasons why this is necessary and why now is an opportune time to meet the challenge. The following seven factors point the way towards a new paradigm for learning . . .

Demographic factors

> **We are in a post-industrial society where it is impossible for a youngster without skills, without school skills, to get a job with which to support a family.**

LISBETH SCHORR, *Within our Reach: Breaking the Cycle of Disadvantage,* Bantam Doubleday

As employment patterns change world-wide, there is an increasing risk of a recurring cycle of disadvantage with an attendant and growing underclass of young men and women on the periphery of society because they lack the marketable skills to allow them to participate. If the unemployed of the European Union, some 18 million, were to stand side by side, the line would spread halfway around the globe. In the west we are living longer, experiencing more marital breakdown and fractured families and a differential in the success achieved in formal education.

In the UK the number of jobs for low skilled workers fell by 1 million between 1979 and 1990 according to the Institute of Economics and Statistics at Oxford University. During the same period, the number of jobs for skilled workers increased by about 1.5 million. Globalisation has really hurt the unskilled workers and the Institute of Development Studies at Sussex University says that *'90% of the fall in unskilled workers wages – some 20% in the period compared with skilled workers – is because of the growth in international trade.'*

In the UK the Basic Skills Agency has reported that as many as 15% of 21 year olds have limited literacy skills and 20% limited competence in mathematics. Only 50% of those who complete two years of Youth Training in the UK obtain a qualification and 24% complete their training only to become unemployed. Around 50,000 teenagers leave school in the UK each year without any sort of qualification. In summer 1997 these figures were confirmed again and some Headteachers' organisations were describing the 'growth of an underclass'.

In what appears to be a contradiction, standards of educational achievement in the UK are rising and falling at the same time. Don't be socially disadvantaged – particularly if you are black, or white working class and male. In primary schools in England and Wales, boys are ten times more likely to be excluded than girls and in secondary schools they are five times more likely to be excluded. Afro-Caribbean males are six times more likely to be excluded than any other group. Standards appear to be rising faster for groups who can be 'characterised' as 'advantaged'. Standards for groups 'characterised' as 'average' or 'disadvantaged' are also rising but more slowly (*see Barber, c.1*).

According to the UK Secondary Headteachers' Association publication *Boys Can Do Better*, boys in schools don't realise the changing job market and the impact of the technological revolution means that those jobs SHA say they still want – the physical and manual – will not exist. SHA reports that *'in the UK by the year 2000 there will be 300,000 fewer 'male' jobs and 500,000 more 'female' jobs and that by the year 2000 more women than men will be working'*. The people who are missing out are the young, unskilled men – exactly those who are the most prominent group in crime statistics.

Changing nature of work

 Tomorrow's employees will be doing what robots cannot do, which means that their work will call for sophisticated intelligence.

R. N. CAINE, G. CANE, *Making Connections: Teaching and the Human Brain*, ASCD

Will Hutton labels the UK 'the thirty, thirty, forty society', where the bottom 30% are the disadvantaged (unemployed or economically inactive), the next 30% are the marginalised and the insecure, and the final 40% are the privileged in full-time jobs but with less security than in the recent past.

If you should fall into the 40%, then you may expect to encounter a changed workplace. Three trends are emerging. The retention by companies of a core of highly skilled and trained people employed full-time with the rest working in short-term project groups, part-time, seasonally or to meet short-term demand. Some seasonal work, particularly in the leisure and catering industries. Self-employed individuals who market and sell their skills and are recruited on temporary and task-specific contracts.

What some economists are calling 'the new service society' is made up of three broad categories of work emerging around the world. They are routine production services, in-person services and symbolic-analytical services. Routine production services involve manufacture and include repetitive low skill tasks performed by low and mid-level managers or, in countries where labour costs are high, robots. Each industrial robot introduced replaces three to four jobs and, on average, pays for itself in 12 months. Robotisation in the next ten years will mean that seven million jobs will be eliminated. According to John Naisbitt, author of *Megatrends 2000*, *'90% of new jobs are in companies with under 50 people.'* Increasingly we see the move from big to small and more franchising, autonomous profit centres, out-sourcing and direct-marketing. Employees will need to be more adaptable, resourceful and independent.

Bill Gates's company Microsoft had a market value at the end of 1996 of $85.5 billion and net fixed assets of just $930 million. The remarkably low valuation of fixed assets is because Microsoft's worth is tied up in the knowledge, the technical expertise and the intellectual capital of its staff. The August 1997 edition of *Management Today* describes 'knowledge management' as the next big idea. In the US the proportion of knowledge workers will have risen from 17% to 59% over the course of this century, with those involved in handling material things halved to 41%. The trend is set to continue.

Impact of new technologies

The new government has made it abundantly clear that education is its top priority. Education is the key to creating a society which is dynamic and productive, offering fairness to everyone. It is the key to building the information society – and we are regarding the development of children's Information and Communication technology skills as the fourth 'R', a basic skill as important as literacy and numeracy.

BARONESS BLACKSTONE, EDUCATION MINISTER,
DFEE Press Release 29/July/97

The world is becoming one gigantic information exchange. In many developed countries the home will become the vital centre of work, education and entertainment. Instant communication is the dominant technology. A single fibre optic cable used to carry 80,000 – now it can carry 10 million. At times more than 1 billion people tune in their television sets to watch the same event. More than 50 million people from 160 countries are now able to engage in a dialogue with each other over the internet. Doctors can video conference with patients sitting in surgeries hundreds of miles away. Students can enrol to take degrees at universities in a different continent and follow interactive courses without leaving their homes.

Previously the Microsoft Corporation were quoted as measuring power by one ratio: personal computers per household. In April 1998 they were quoted as measuring power in networks per capita. That is, how broadly and deeply a country has taken its PCs and linked them together into networks within companies, schools and entertainment sources and then tied them into the Internet and the World Wide Web. A further measure is 'bandwidth – the capacity of cable, telephone lines and fibre optics to carry digital information. John Chambers, President of Cisco Systems, the US company making the black boxes connecting the Internet around the world, says *'the Internet Revolution will change how people live, work, play and learn. Jobs and power will gravitate to those societies with most networks and bandwidths because those countries will find it easier to gather, tap and deploy knowledge in order to design, invent, manufacture, communicate, educate and entertain.'*

In the UK, figures from the OECD show that in 1995 only 20% of British households had a PC and only 4% had a modem allowing access to the Internet or other services. DFEE figures show that primary schools in the UK have an average of 13 computers each and a student/computer ratio of 13:1. Secondary schools have on average 96 computers each and a student/computer ratio of 9:1. Some 25% of schools are connected to the Internet and over 30% of UK teachers have undergone more than one IT training course.

The gap between information technology 'haves' and 'have nots' remains a cause of serious concern. According to Motorola, IT 'haves' tend to be in social groups ABC1, aged between 16 and 44, in full-time employment and working on average 43.7 hours per week. Without direct government intervention, the Community Development Foundation report 'The Net Result', funded by IBM, argues that people with low incomes or who are unemployed are *'unlikely to be able to access information technologies'*. The report sees access to on-line information as *'not a luxury but vital to playing an active role in society'*.

Globalisation

> **In the coming century there will be no national products or technologies, no national corporations, no national industries. There will no longer be national economies . . . all that will remain rooted within national borders are the people who comprise a nation. Each nation's primary assets will be its citizen's skills.**

ROBERT REICH, *The Work of Nations*, Vintage Books

In June 1997 the Canadian Government and the World Bank organised a summit in Toronto, Canada. The summit, attended by 1500 representatives from all over the world, looked at the interaction between technology, knowledge and world change. It pointed up the significance of the Internet and its potential for creating a new divide between those who have the technology and the skills to access it and those who don't.

In an age when over a billion people can simultaneously watch a television event like the funeral of Diana, Princess of Wales, the concept of the 'global village' has come home. Multinational companies have global marketing and communications strategies. Universities and colleges offer their programmes around the world. Satellite technology allows instant communication across the globe. Information can be accessed and sent in seconds. The entire contents of the Encyclopaedia Britannica can be sent via optical fibre and satellite technology from Auchtermuchty, Scotland to Auckland, New Zealand in less than a second. The pace of life is accelerating and the globe is shrinking.

New knowledge about learning

> The world didn't need Isaac Newton to know that apples fall off trees. It did need Newton to give us a general theory that explains why apples fall off trees ... knowing why leads to other discoveries, new applications and further refinement ... We are beginning to understand why some teachers are effective and to see that there is more to teaching than literacy skills, subject-matter competence, and domain independent teaching skills.

J. T. BRUER, *Schools for Thought: A Science of Learning in the Classroom*, MIT Press

An often quoted statistic is that 80% of what we know about the brain and its design for learning has been accumulated in the last 15 years. Perhaps for the first time there is an opportunity for educators to benefit from the work of the neuro-scientists, the quantum physicists and the chaos and complexity theorists working towards a global brain theory.

Robert Sylwester, a conference keynote speaker at the 1997 International Alliance for Learning Conference 'Unleashing the Potential of the Brain', shared his view that within ten years there will be a global brain theory which will be the equivalent of $E=MC^2$ or the discovery of DNA. The truth is that brain research is now developing at an incremental and frightening pace. A parallel and less heartening truth is that the formal education system in the UK is responding to this at a frighteningly slow pace.

Why is it that new knowledge about learning, about motivation, self-esteem and intelligence is not being applied in our classrooms? Why is it that this information and the learning tools which accompany it can be available to 3M, the Disney Corporation, IBM, Proctor & Gamble – each of whom has accelerated learning training programmes – and hundreds of other multinationals world-wide, but not feature as part of the regular repertoire of classroom teachers in this country?

Lifelong learning

> The world our kids are going to live in is changing four times faster than our schools.

DR WILLARD DAGGETT, International Centre for Leadership and Education, USA.

> The rationales for lifelong learning are in the main windy generalisations which are twenty years old; what are needed now are new mechanisms to finance lifelong learning for all and a coherent strategy.

PROFESSOR FRANK COFFIELD, *Can the UK Become a Learning Society?*

If there are four ages of educational man, they are: the age of formal education; the age of work and training; the age of healthy retirement and the age of infirmity. For the first time the age of healthy retirement is becoming longer than the age of work and training. If we don't enthuse people about lifelong learning before the third age what sort of experience can they expect?

19

Multinational investment also leads to a displacing of the knowledge and skills into the local workforce. Sir Geoffrey Holland, in a speech given at the South West Education Show in the UK in July 1997, quotes a Chief Executive Officer of a Multinational Corporation as saying, *'when we relocate we have 48 Education systems we can choose from.'*

Recognising that knowledge is a scarce resource, many companies have established their own in-house universities. Examples include the Disney Corporation, Motorola, Arthur Andersen, Bell and, in the UK, companies like Rover provide a wide range of educational opportunities. One significant differentiating factor in all of this is the difference between the supply and demand sides. How do we create a culture where people actually want to learn? With £100 million of public money spent so far on the competency based National Vocational Qualification (NVQ), previously unpublished research has revealed that of the 878 NVQ's available in the UK in 1996, 330 have never been completed and one person only has completed a further 50 (*Sunday Times*, August 24th, 1997).

In the UK, one-sixth of those starting university courses drop out before completion; one-half of the 80% who stay on in full-time further education fail to achieve any accredited certification. Will investment and capital move towards areas where the desire to learn is most evident? If so, it may not be moving to the UK! Teaching how we learn will become more important than what we learn.

The UK Confederation for British Industry has recognised that youngsters currently in secondary age education are likely to experience eight or more changes of employment in their adult working lives. They will have more chance of retaining employment if they enter the job market later and find employment which comes with further training. Amongst the key skills they have identified are: team-working, interpersonal and communication skills, competence in IT, numeracy, literacy and problem-solving.

The extent of neural networking in early life is an indicator of the likely capacity to handle complex problem-solving after childhood. Dryden and Voss quote research which suggests that 50% of one's ability is developed in the first four years with 80% by the age of eight. Martha Pierson of Baylor College of Medicine is quoted in Kotulak (1996) as saying *'it's just phenomenal how much experience determines how our brains get put together . . . you can't suddenly learn to learn when you haven't first laid down the basic brain wiring . . . that's why early education is so important.'*

In the UK, Colin Rose and his team at Accelerated Learning Systems collaborated with a Local Education Authority to develop materials for pre-school children and their parents known as 'Fundamentals' and a programme called 'Headstart' to be used with children, parents and teachers. In 1997 Headstart had 25,000 homes and this was only six months after its launch. Endorsed by the National Confederation of Parent Teacher's Associations, Headstart sends an age-related pack out to the child at home twice a term for six years. In the pack there is a magazine which is structured to cover a breadth of learning topics and develop multiple and emotional intelligence, an activity book, an interactive video, a parent newsletter and a parent skills paper.

Learning out of schools

Schools were designed for another time, and for another purpose. In a period of 'whole systems change' it is no longer enough to talk of transforming the schools. We have to consider the whole of a young persons learning experience. Inevitably this will mean transforming the way we treat young people, both inside and outside school.

JOHN ABBOTT, *Learning Makes Sense*, Education 2000

Some commentators have attempted to show that we are moving towards an age where, in the developed nations, knowledge itself is wealth. The industrial revolution is described as having instigated a period where, increasingly, the family ceased to be the unit where children were inducted into adulthood and into learning. Learning and working began to be divorced and learning ceased to be based on daily experience and the workplace and became more and more abstract. It became the property of teachers and an academic elite. Looking at industrial and productivity revolutions world-wide, there is perhaps a pattern to the progressive way humans have applied knowledge. The application of human endeavour and initiative to the development of machinery and industrial engineering in the 18th and 19th Centuries. A similar inventiveness applied to the organisation of labour and to productivity in the late 19th and 20th Centuries. Now, at the beginning of the 21st Century initiative, energy and knowledge itself is being applied to knowledge. People make money and secure prosperity by dealing in ideas.

Despite the trends elaborated above, should you visit a school today the chances are the school will look much like it may have done 40 years ago. One could argue that schools in this country are based on a Prussian model of orthodoxy, rigidity and Puritanism where distractions were minimised and learning was about consumption. Windows were built high up, desks were secured in rows and everyone was drilled with the same experience. In addition to the classroom looking much the same as it did 40 years ago, the school day and the mode of delivery of the content which that day offers is similar to that of 100 years ago. There are clearly demarcated timings in which instruction is offered. Attendance is compulsory within a given chronological age frame. Progression is age rather than ability related. Choice is limited and access at some stages is restricted.

In many large corporations we can see that internal structures and work practices are having to be changed to get the best out of their staff. In terms of 'knowledge management' the American company 3M has established internal 'communities of enquiry' where employees work together on complex problems, the 15% rule, which allows employees to spend that amount of time on their own projects, and the governing principle that 25% of company turnover must come from products introduced in the last four years. This has meant that 3M scientists in hundreds of divisions all over the world have been working together in problem-solving teams to produce an endless stream of new products 'sometimes based on new knowledge, more often by combining existing knowledge in different and creative ways'.

More and more organisations are recognising that they need to invest in their people and question inherited orthodoxies. 'The Learning Organisation' has displaced Total Quality Management and Process Re-Engineering as the mantra for the millennium. The orthodoxy of trimming staff development and training budgets in times of adversity is being replaced with the view that we train our way out of a crisis. The April 1998 Human Resource Development Conference of the UK Institute of Personnel and Development contained seminars on Creativity, Emotional Intelligence, Accelerated Learning, Coaching and the Intelligent Organisation. Schools, organised traditionally in strict hierarchies, are also beginning to change some of their internal structures to match changing expectations and delivery patterns. Schools will have to change more to prepare learners for life beyond formal education. In formal schooling we see more specialist college functions, community learning centres for lifelong learning, Personal Education Plans, Interactive technology links and a desire to involve parents and community more.

As more and more parents engage in portfolio working, including working from home, the spread of interactive technologies into the home may become more widespread. Sales of 'self-help' primers for Key Stage tests and academic exams in high street shops continue to rise healthily. Interest in the home schooling movement grows. How far are we away from parents in some families working alongside their teenage sons and daughters at home pursuing interactive distance learning programmes supported by parent tutors, purpose-bought resources and enrolment on challenging university level programmes?

How much longer will it be before we see schools where the curriculum offered is completely modularised and where learners build up modular credits with the portfolio recorded on a smart card and where modules can be taken in a negotiated individual package and completed at different points irrespective of chronological age? Schools where the day is chunked into three blocks with evening sessions available for students and within the community for leisure and interest pursuits and additional modular work. Schools where learning takes place over five – shorter – terms with shorter breaks in between and where teachers guide, facilitate and instruct, learning support staff provide expert knowledge on access and use of inter-active technology, and others provide administrative backing. Schools which connect through interactive technology with other 'learning-hubs' out in the community and beyond.

In 1994, for the first time ever, there were more CD-ROM encyclopaedias sold world-wide than print based ones. In a world where knowledge is doubling every two to three years in almost every occupation we see increasing awareness that adaptability, personal resourcefulness, the capacity to work in teams and to solve problems produces lifelong learning skills which will change the educational emphasis from what is known and learned to how one knows and learns. The former is short term and ultimately disabling; the latter lifelong and empowering.

Professor Frank Coffield in arguing for a co-ordinated strategy to develop a learning society in the UK says that we need to abandon the idea that further investment in education and training, 'will of itself make the UK economically successful or socially cohesive' and that the Government's priorities need to change from 'Education, Education and Education' to 'Employment and Education, the Economy and Education'. Pointing out the paucity of views on what is an appropriate theory of learning, he also laments the fact that *'too many teachers in schools and tutors in universities whose core business is learning show little interest in the process and teach in ignorance of recent advances'*. On raising standards in education he describes a situation where, *'too many students learn to do school in the same way prisoners learn to do time,'* and concludes *'if the aim is to raise standards in education, we should concentrate on the process of learning and teaching in classrooms not on management or mission statements.'*

The imperative to improve the quality of what happens in every classroom requires a more positive, more considered, more structured approach. The model described in this book is offered as a considered and structured approach based on a theory of learning which utilises recent advances. Perhaps we stand on the edge of what Thomas Kuhn would have called a 'paradigm shift'?

2 THE ACCELERATING LEARNING IN THE CLASSROOM CYCLE

 The National Curriculum reforms build on an assumption that if only we get the definition of content right then standards of learning will rise. It is important to challenge this assumption and to claim that the practical means by which the learning process is transacted between teachers and learners is also of vital importance. In recent years attention to pedagogy and methodology has been sacrificed in the struggle to write programmes and install new content.

P. WHITAKER, *Managing to Learn,* **Cassell plc**

THE ACCELERATED LEARNING IN THE CLASSROOM MODEL is a means of helping teachers in classrooms raise student motivation and achievement by providing proven lifelong learning skills based on an understanding of how we learn rather than an expedient preoccupation with what we learn.

The Accelerated Learning Cycle described here has seven stages. Each stage and its place in the cycle is of equal importance. A further pre-stage – the supportive learning environment – is a constant, and operates like a guide-rail keeping the Accelerated Learning Cycle running true.

The Accelerated Learning Cycle is illustrated on the next page . . .

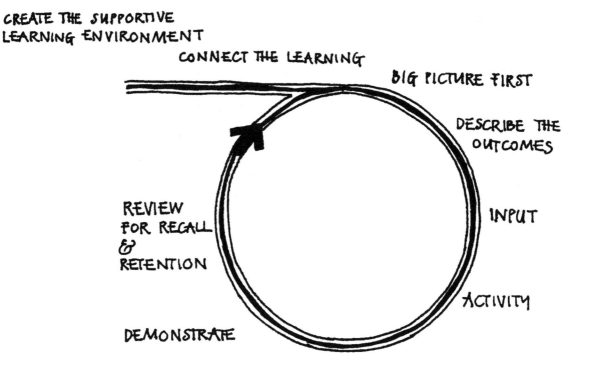

CREATE THE SUPPORTIVE
LEARNING ENVIRONMENT

CONNECT THE LEARNING

BIG PICTURE FIRST

DESCRIBE THE
OUTCOMES

INPUT

ACTIVITY

DEMONSTRATE

REVIEW
FOR RECALL
&
RETENTION

Some of the interventions one might expect to see at each stage of the cycle are outlined below. The cycle is not intended to be mechanistic and dutifully followed. It does, however, offer a consideration of the importance of process in learning. Attention to process and appropiate process interventions shifts thinking away from content and 'coverage'.

PRE-STAGE Create the supportive learning environment

A positive and supportive learning environment characterised by high teacher and learner expectation is a necessary constant for any learning to take place

◆ the learner must be free from anxiety or stress and be challenged

◆ whilst learning they are in a 'resourceful' physical state

◆ the elements of the BASIS model of building and maintaining positive self-esteem are in place

◆ the teacher communicates high expectations positively and provides consistent 'educative' feedback

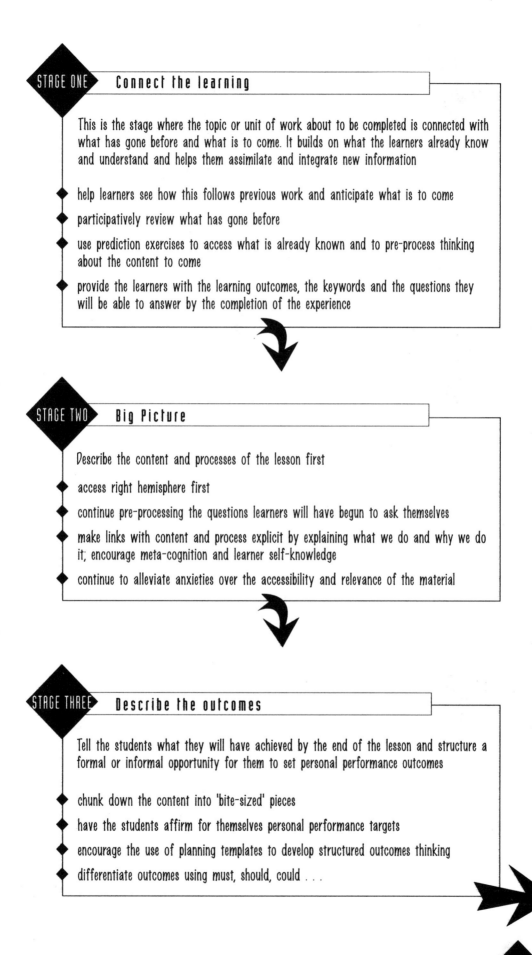

STAGE ONE ▸ Connect the learning

This is the stage where the topic or unit of work about to be completed is connected with what has gone before and what is to come. It builds on what the learners already know and understand and helps them assimilate and integrate new information

◆ help learners see how this follows previous work and anticipate what is to come

◆ participatively review what has gone before

◆ use prediction exercises to access what is already known and to pre-process thinking about the content to come

◆ provide the learners with the learning outcomes, the keywords and the questions they will be able to answer by the completion of the experience

STAGE TWO ▸ Big Picture

Describe the content and processes of the lesson first

◆ access right hemisphere first

◆ continue pre-processing the questions learners will have begun to ask themselves

◆ make links with content and process explicit by explaining what we do and why we do it; encourage meta-cognition and learner self-knowledge

◆ continue to alleviate anxieties over the accessibility and relevance of the material

STAGE THREE ▸ Describe the outcomes

Tell the students what they will have achieved by the end of the lesson and structure a formal or informal opportunity for them to set personal performance outcomes

◆ chunk down the content into 'bite-sized' pieces

◆ have the students affirm for themselves personal performance targets

◆ encourage the use of planning templates to develop structured outcomes thinking

◆ differentiate outcomes using must, should, could . . .

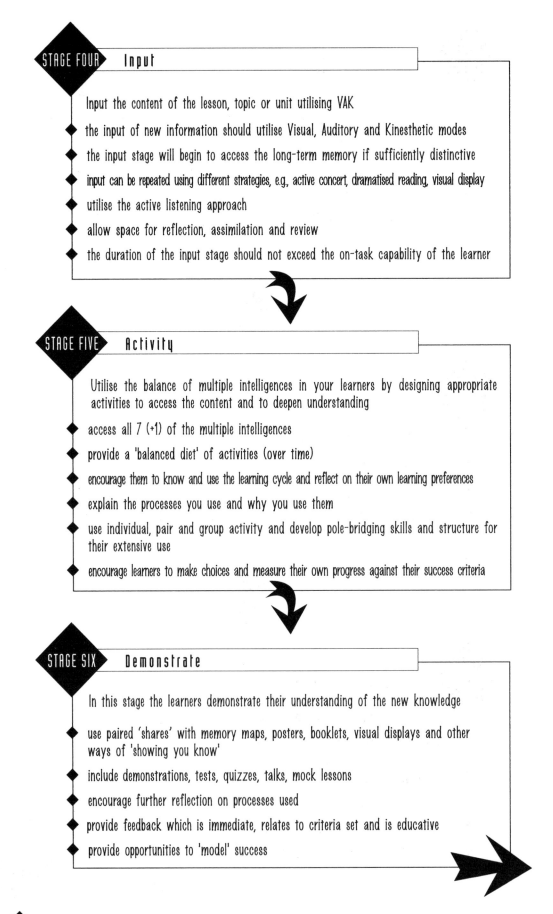

STAGE FOUR Input

Input the content of the lesson, topic or unit utilising VAK

- the input of new information should utilise Visual, Auditory and Kinesthetic modes
- the input stage will begin to access the long-term memory if sufficiently distinctive
- input can be repeated using different strategies, e.g., active concert, dramatised reading, visual display
- utilise the active listening approach
- allow space for reflection, assimilation and review
- the duration of the input stage should not exceed the on-task capability of the learner

STAGE FIVE Activity

Utilise the balance of multiple intelligences in your learners by designing appropriate activities to access the content and to deepen understanding

- access all 7 (+1) of the multiple intelligences
- provide a 'balanced diet' of activities (over time)
- encourage them to know and use the learning cycle and reflect on their own learning preferences
- explain the processes you use and why you use them
- use individual, pair and group activity and develop pole-bridging skills and structure for their extensive use
- encourage learners to make choices and measure their own progress against their success criteria

STAGE SIX Demonstrate

In this stage the learners demonstrate their understanding of the new knowledge

- use paired 'shares' with memory maps, posters, booklets, visual displays and other ways of 'showing you know'
- include demonstrations, tests, quizzes, talks, mock lessons
- encourage further reflection on processes used
- provide feedback which is immediate, relates to criteria set and is educative
- provide opportunities to 'model' success

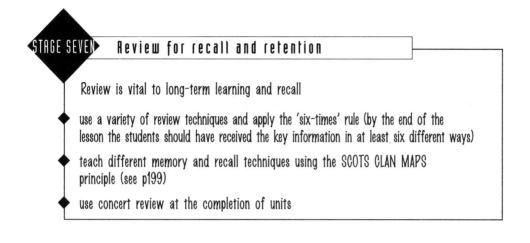

STAGE SEVEN ▶ Review for recall and retention

Review is vital to long-term learning and recall

◆ use a variety of review techniques and apply the 'six-times' rule (by the end of the lesson the students should have received the key information in at least six different ways)

◆ teach different memory and recall techniques using the SCOTS CLAN MAPS principle (see p199)

◆ use concert review at the completion of units

In the Accelerated Learning Cycle we move the learner through the cycle quickly ensuring throughout that a positive and supportive learning environment is in place.

③ NINE PRINCIPLES FOR BRAIN-BASED LEARNING

Our schools . . . are not ineffective because they do not know what happens at synapses or the chemistry of neurotransmitters, but rather because they have yet to address the brain as the organ for learning, and to fit instruction and environment to the 'shape' of the brain as it is increasingly well understood . . . the brain has modes of operation that are natural, effortless, effective in utilising the tremendous power of this amazing instrument. Coerced to operate in other ways, it functions as a rule reluctantly, slowly and with abundant error.

L. A. HART, *The Human Brain and Human Learning,*
Addison Wesley Longman

MUCH IS MADE IN THE POPULAR PRESS and elsewhere about conditions which are antagonistic to learning. Large classes, lack of resources, crumbling school buildings, behaviour problems, hyperactivity, short attention spans, poor diet, too much television, no positive role models and inadequate parental support have all been focused upon in recent years. Whilst it would seem that there is general consensus about what inhibits learning, there doesn't seem to be a corresponding clarity about the optimal conditions for learning.

The situation has led in recent years to many crude caricatures of the teacher's role in facilitating the learning experience. Here in the UK, fighting from opposite corners have been so-called 'traditionalists' espousing whole-class teaching strategies and 'progressives' favouring pupil-centred small-group discovery methods. Advocates of interactive whole-class teaching have cited examples from the successes of Pacific Rim countries such as Taiwan and suggested their methods could be usefully transplanted here. Opponents have accused this lobby of cherry-picking, of denying the contextualising factors and of pandering to politicians with a mind to cost benefit. Time and again the popular press point to declining literacy and numeracy scores as evidence that 'trendy' methods have failed our children. In reality, neither extreme if pursued inflexibly guarantees improvement and in the preening that has surrounded this debate, no one has been offering a considered model based on an understanding of how we learn. Much of our recent concerns have focused on outcomes. Furthermore, those outcomes have been measured on a narrow range of human activity, i.e., what can be measured in performance by paper and pencil tests completed in timed, stress-conditions.

When we look at prevailing models of learning such as those described in the University of London, Institute of Education's 1996 summary paper 'Effective Learning', we recognise the characteristics of the dilemma immediately. The paper begins with a preamble that the reader may be 'disappointed' with the attempts to define learning. What follows is a useful, if tentative summary of prevailing models, followed by a series of open questions for the reader to reflect upon. One comes away feeling fed but not nourished; aware of the essential ingredients but not how to blend them together.

If there was an emerging consensus around the characteristics of effective learning, would some of the hysteria which leads to artificial polarisations around classroom strategies disappear? Where ought one to look for such consensus? Many of the published views from the discipline of educational theory remain tentative, circumscribed by the limits of what is achievable through pragmatic research methods and therefore are cautious about offering a holistic model. Robert Sylwester describes the situation in the following way, *'Educators have never had the scientists' freedom to patiently wait for the research technology to catch up with their curiosity . . . we became a profession of behaviourists, whether we liked it or not.'*

Perhaps a good and useful starting point is to apply the NLP (Neuro Linguistic Programming) presupposition adapted from Korzybski that 'the map is not the territory'. How we perceive the world is not how the world is. It is only one perceptual position. Change your map and you change your experience. If it is possible to look at the dilemma from a range of perspectives then perhaps we can begin to uncover a more useful set of models. The disciplines which inform and surround research into the brain and learning begin to offer a more solid foundation here. Whilst our understanding of the human brain and all its complexity is as yet immature, there is enough emerging consensus around the brain and learning, the brain and memory, emotional learning and human resourcefulness for learning to provide some guiding principles against which to test such models summarised in published research such as *Effective Learning*.

On the next page I summarise what some of the most recent published scientific research tells us about the optimum conditions for learning. I follow this by outlining some of the most significant breakthroughs in recent brain research and then go on to describe ways to begin to apply the new knowledge to classrooms.

NINE PRINCIPLES FOR BRAIN-BASED LEARNING

◆ The brain develops best in environments with high levels of sensory stimulation and sustained cognitive challenge. Such enriched environments produce a greater number of dendritic branches, and hence connections, between neurons.

◆ High challenge but low threat. Learning environments must be perceived to be 'safe'. The mid-brain floods with electrochemical activity under conditions of perceived threat. Higher order thinking functions and memory are inhibited by such conditions. Low self-esteem and lack of self-belief contribute to such a 'survival' response.

◆ Feedback. The brain thrives on immediacy of feedback, on diversity and on choice. When learners engage in what is described as 'pole-bridging', improvements in reasoning powers are dramatic.

◆ Relative lateralisation. There is a synergy with left and right hemisphere learning. Whilst there may be differences in hemispherical function, we now know that this is relative, functions can be compensated for and developed, and that both hemispheres are engaged in simultaneous parallel processing.

◆ Expectations shape outcomes. The search for meaning is innate. Once engaged in a learning outcome we cannot stop the brain processing for meaning. Learning takes place at both conscious and unconscious levels. Motivation accelerates once the learner adopts a positive, personal learning goal.

◆ Uniqueness. Each brain has a high degree of plasticity, developing and integrating with experience in ways unique to itself. There may be different types of intelligence and intelligence is modifiable. Only diversity in teaching and learning can begin to accommodate this.

◆ Physiology and emotional learning. Learning and maturation cannot be separated. Nor can the physical readiness or 'state' of the learner and learning. The emotions direct conscious attention. One cannot isolate the cognitive from the affective. We must therefore pay attention to physical and emotional 'state' in our learning environments.

◆ Music aids learning. The most recent research suggests that music can aid learning in three ways. It can energise or relax — hence altering the individual's 'state' or readiness for learning. It can carry content. It makes the neural networks more receptive for learning.

◆ Types of memory. There may be different types of memory involving different memory pathways in the brain. In this area we know specific and successful strategies for improving recall of information without yet knowing how the brain does it!

4 THE BRAIN AND ITS CONSTRUCTION FOR LEARNING

> *The education profession is now approaching a crossroads. We can continue to focus our energies on the careful observation of external behaviour ... or we can join the search for a scientific understanding of the brain mechanisms, processes, and malfunctions that affect the successful completion of complex learning tasks.*

ROBERT SYLWESTER, *A Celebration of Neurons: An Educator's Guide to the Human Brain,* ASCD

AN OFTEN QUOTED STATISTIC is that 80% of our knowledge about the brain and how it learns has been accumulated in the last 15 years. The scientists who study the brain have benefited from improvements in available technology so that it is now possible to use non-invasive techniques such as PET scans and Functional MRI to observe the patterning of brain activity in various problem-solving situations. Scientists involved in brain research have also derived models from other fields such as chaos and complexity theory, the genetic basis of consciousness, neural Darwinism, linguistics, physical anthropology and cognitive psychology.

It has reached a point where no one researcher can retain an overview of published research and within the 18 month period before the first publication of this book there were at least six major works published on the brain and learning. As one keynote speaker at a major international conference entitled 'Unleashing the Brain's Potential' (International Alliance for Learning Conference, San Antonio, Texas, 1997) stated, within the next ten years there will be a breakthrough in mind-brain research and learning *'which will have a significance similar to the discovery of the theory of relativity or of DNA earlier this century'.*

For those with a professional interest in learning and the conditions which can inhibit or accelerate that process it is an exciting time. What follows in this chapter is a summary for teachers, learners or parents of the 'architecture and the archaeology' of the brain as we currently understand it.

With the texture of a ripe avocado, weighing about three and a half pounds and about the size of your two fists pushed together, the brain is a creamy mass of cells which is mundane in appearance and tantalisingly complex in function.

This slippery bundle of tissue is responsible for one's thoughts, memories, feelings, 'feelings' about feelings, impulses and movements. In recent years various models of the brain's architecture have been proposed. In the 1960s Paul MacLean offered a model which was based on three layers, a hierarchy of function and separate, if inter-related, areas specialising in survival, emotional and rational behaviours. In the 1970s Roger Sperry received a Nobel Prize for his work on the 'split brain'. In the 1980s Howard Gardner proposed a model of seven (now eight) different types of intelligence processed through different brain areas. More recently Gazzaniga, who worked with Roger Sperry, suggested that our brain is divided into a vast number of interconnected clusters of neurons, which 'module' together to process complex cognitive functions.

Paul MacLean's model of the triune brain suggested that the development and organisation of our brains reflected evolutionary necessity. The brain stem or reptilian brain being the earliest part to develop and the part of the brain we share with reptiles and other mammals. Sitting atop the brain stem is a system of highly interconnected areas of functional specialisation called the limbic system. And 'plonked' on top again, split left and right into hemispheres which are connected by a bundle of fibres, is the neo-cortex –

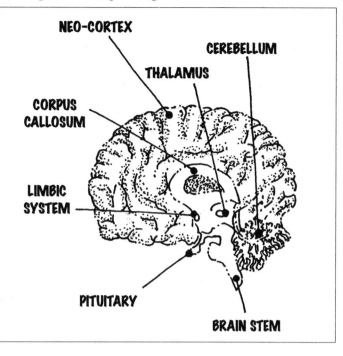

colloquially referred to as the 'thinking cap'. These areas, in MacLean's model, interact but retain some functional specialisation. Summarised, the brain stem is largely responsible for survival behaviours and motor functions; the limbic system with filtering sensory data, with emotional arousal and with long-term memory; the neo-cortex with higher order cognitive functioning.

The attraction of the triune brain model is that it is easily understood. Educationalists can use the model to describe, and thus account for, observed behaviours. Nowadays most modern brain researchers would not describe the brain in such a segmented way. Their emphasis is on integration, simultaneous processing, plasticity, and relative lateralisation. That said, it is of value to look upon it as an archetype for more subtle interpretations of brain function in learning.

In Paul MacLean's model the brain stem is responsible for monitoring motor functions and survival behaviours. It is the part of the brain which 'kicks in' to assume responsibility under conditions of 'threat'. For educationalists the significance of this lies in the contention that a climate of anxiety and unmanageable stress produces all of these 'survival' behaviours and these are antagonistic to higher order thinking and learning generally.

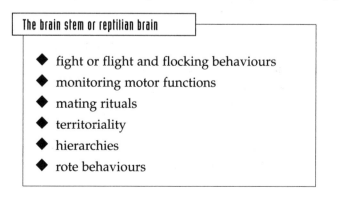

The brain stem or reptilian brain

- ◆ fight or flight and flocking behaviours
- ◆ monitoring motor functions
- ◆ mating rituals
- ◆ territoriality
- ◆ hierarchies
- ◆ rote behaviours

31

Above the brain stem and wrapped around it like the hood of a large mushroom sitting on its stalk is the limbic system. The limbic system has, since MacLean's model was first introduced, been the focus of a great deal of research. It continues to be. Popular contemporary books such as those by Goleman, Calvin and Greenfield, which I refer to later, describe some of the more sophisticated views about this area of the brain and its role in learning, emotions and memory. Wenger points out that the limbic system is 10,000 times faster in processing than the cortex. It should be of no surprise that emotions act as a sentinel at the gate of learning, directing attention to what is deemed significant. In MacLean's model he argues that the limbic system monitors the following functions.

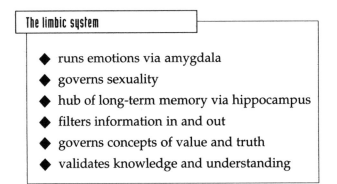

The limbic system

- ◆ runs emotions via amygdala
- ◆ governs sexuality
- ◆ hub of long-term memory via hippocampus
- ◆ filters information in and out
- ◆ governs concepts of value and truth
- ◆ validates knowledge and understanding

It can be seen that this area of the brain plays an important part in assigning value to an experience and hence filtering it in to conscious attention, or out. Increasingly, it is being recognised that the emotions are actively engaged in all aspects of this filtering process and like other functional areas of the brain they can, to some extent, be 'schooled'. Wrapped across both brain stem and limbic system is the cortex. It is the cortex which, operating in conjunction with the older parts of the brain, allows us to engage in higher order thinking, the identification and creation of meaning and long-term planning. The cortex, its size and its use, separates us from other creatures in the animal kingdom. It is split front and back and left and right. It contains the areas associated with some language and movement functions as well as other sensory specialisms.

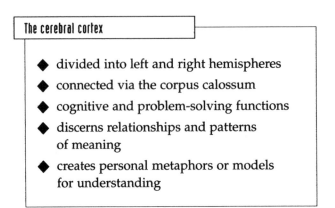

The cerebral cortex

- ◆ divided into left and right hemispheres
- ◆ connected via the corpus calossum
- ◆ cognitive and problem-solving functions
- ◆ discerns relationships and patterns of meaning
- ◆ creates personal metaphors or models for understanding

The brain processes information simultaneously with both hemispheres of the upper cortex involved. It is not true to say that a given hemisphere is exclusively responsible for certain functions. The term that is now used is 'relative lateralisation'. In other words, the brain is asymmetrical. It is believed that the left hemisphere remains predominant, that it processes information sequentially and the right randomly but that both hemispheres are integrated into all problem-solving.

Movement is imperative in development and, some now argue, in learning. Like a puppeteer pulling strings, the brain sends signals that make the muscles contract and move the body. Two strips of grey matter across the top of the brain – the motor cortices – control the muscles on either side of the body. The motor cortex situated on the left hemisphere controls movement of the right side of the body, while the motor cortex on the right hemisphere controls movement of the left side of the body. The different sets of muscles in each part of the body have their own motor control patch. The larger the area of the cortex, the greater the degree of precision of control. Areas like the hand, mouth and feet have greater amounts of the cortex devoted to them. Co-ordinated cross-lateral movements involving both sides of the body thus connect left and right hemispheres and contribute to neural networking across the brain.

Different areas of the cortex have specialist functions. Depending on plasticity, on gender and on the developmental maturity of the brain some of these functions will be relative and capable of replication in other areas of the brain. Marian Diamond has given us a metaphor for this relative lateralisation of function by describing it as 'holographic'.

So what is happening in the brain when we encounter a new experience and begin the process of learning?

When healthy, we are born with a full complement of brain cells – some 100 billion – yet no new cells, known as neurons, develop thereafter. Connections between neurons are what is important. After birth we proceed to lose neurons at a rate of about 100,000 per day. Excess alcohol, drugs, chronic illness or stress increases this rate. Nevertheless if we should struggle through to 100 years of age we will still be left with 96.35 billion brain cells in place! What matters, is not the total number of neurons, but the connections between them. Increases in growth between neurons occurs as a consequence of a stimulating environment. The greatest changes, occur in the first 10 years.

During the first years of life, the brain undergoes a series of extraordinary changes. Starting shortly after birth, a baby's brain, in a display of biological exuberance, produces trillions more connections between neurons than it can possibly use. Then, through a process that resembles Darwinian competition, the brain eliminates connections, or synapses, that are seldom or never used. The excess synapses in a child's brain undergo a draconian pruning, starting around the age of ten or earlier, leaving behind a mind whose patterns of emotion and thought are, for better or worse, unique.

Fertile Minds: How a Child's Brain Develops, TIME MAGAZINE, January, 1997

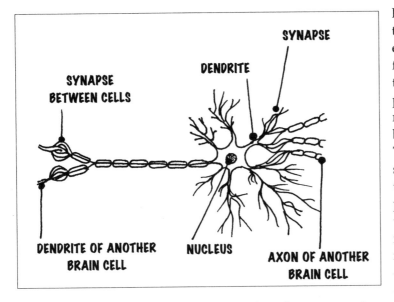

Each neuron connects to others through its axon. The axon has end points which look like fronds and which connect to the dendrites, or receiving points, on neighbouring neurons. The connections are both electrical and chemical. The more frequent the stimulation the more likely that a chemical sheathing process called myelination will take place. Myelination increases the speed with which neurons can connect with each other. Each neuron is connected to hundreds of others by synapses which can be anything from one to a thousand in total. Networks are made through imitation, repeated movement, accumulated experience, memory and response to current needs. A process of 'trimming' takes place constantly and it's a case of use it or lose it. Well-used connections encourage further development and sophistication in that particular part of the network. The difference in density between a newborn's neural network and a two year old's is remarkable.

Neurotransmitters are chemicals which are secreted at the synapse. The presence of such chemicals facilitates the formation, maintenance and strength of the connective patterns of synapses and neurons. Generally speaking they fall into two broad categories of effect: they are either excitatory or inhibitory. Individual neurotransmitters have predictable physiological effects and groups of neurotransmitters have predictable behavioural effects.

Learning is defined as the establishment of new networks. According to Gary Lynch of the University of California, it is the density of the brain as measured by the quantity of synapses, that distinguishes 'greater from lesser mental capacity'.

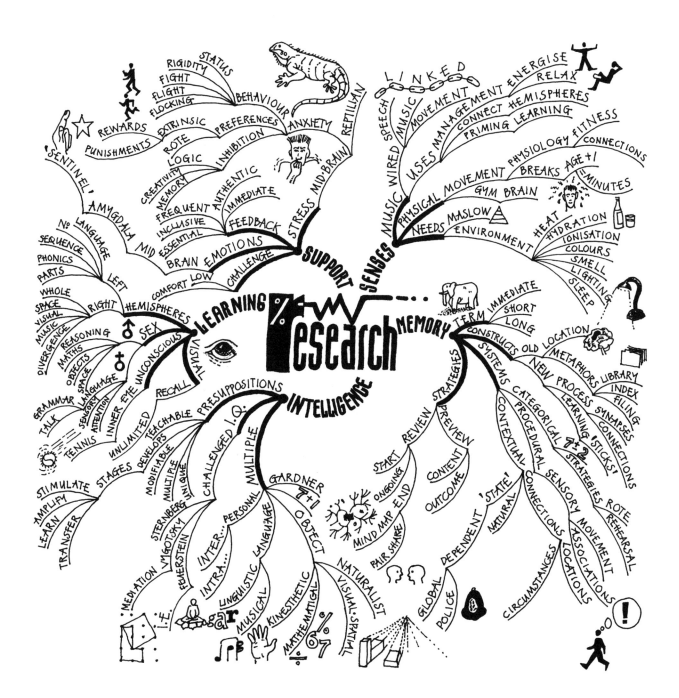

Preview of Section One:

What the most recent brain research tells us about learning

IN SECTION ONE YOU WILL LEARN HOW:

1 multi-sensory stimulation and sustained mental and physical challenge develops lifelong networks of connections in the brain

2 environments and learning experiences characterised by uncertainty, anxiety and stress inhibit meaningful learning

3 immediate, educative feedback improves learning

4 learning experiences which integrate different areas of the brain are the most valuable

5 embedding questions triggers the brain's pattern-seeking tendency

6 we can begin to access and develop different types of 'intelligence'

7 emotional and 'physical' states can help or hinder the process of learning

8 the brain responds to aural stimuli and to music

9 we can naturally store and retrieve information

Section One:
What the most recent brain research tells us about learning

1 MULTI-SENSORY STIMULATION

> *Deprived of a stimulating environment, a child's brain suffers. Researchers at Baylor College of Medicine, for example, have found that children who don't play much or are rarely touched develop brains 20% to 30% smaller than normal for their age.*

Fertile Minds: How a Child's Brain Develops,
TIME MAGAZINE, 2nd October, 1997

A KEY QUESTION WHICH WILL CONTINUE TO PERPLEX educationalists is the extent to which hereditary or environmental factors influence and shape brain development. Heredity and environment interact to produce neural networks which are complex and appear chaotic. Ligands are the basic body-wide units of a language used by cells to communicate with each other, associate with feelings, thoughts and learning behaviours and power our unique learning systems. The complex interaction of feelings, thoughts and learning behaviours shape personality characteristics and contribute to learning preferences and perhaps to learning styles.

So use it or lose it! The more we use our brain as we age, the more we encourage it to grow. With high levels of stimulus and challenge there are higher ratios of synapses (connections) to neurons. More synapses means more routes for higher order cognitive functioning. The optimal conditions for synaptic growth would include multiple complex connective challenges where, in learning, we are actively engaged in multi-sensory immersion experiences. Frequency of immediate feedback and opportunity for choice allows us to rehearse alternative strategies.

Marian Diamond's 1988 work described how an enriched environment where there was high sensory stimulation developed synaptic structures (connections between neurons) throughout the life span and into old age. We know that there is a proliferation of connections between neurons in the early years and that there are optimal 'windows' for developing sensory and motor functions which, if missed, can inhibit or remove the possibility of that development occurring.

The work of the British Institute for Brain Injured Children has shown that compensatory physical motor stimulation at a later stage in life can lead to remarkable developments in children who had previously been designated severely learning disabled and indeed 'beyond hope'. Their work utilises co-ordinated patterned physical movement which goes some way to compensate for the absence of such movements in what would have been the optimal developmental 'window' earlier in life.

> **The institute challenges the myth that brain injuries are untreatable, using a pioneering programme of sensory stimulation. Each child is given an individual programme in which his or her parents are trained. The secret lies in exercises repeated daily, often for months on end . . . Some exercises involve three volunteers and a technique called patterning designed to replicate the development of movement in a 'normal child' through rhythmic movement of the limbs.**

THE OBSERVER, 4th May, 1997

Various parts of the brain develop at various rates. The neo-cortex, the part most actively engaged in higher cognitive processing, is fully developed between the ages of 16 and 25. However, the brain does not develop in an even continuum; it develops in spurts and plateaux. There may be as much as 18 months' developmental difference in the brains of youngsters of the same age in early teens. Researchers such as Alkon (1992) believe that experiences in the critical development periods of early childhood create neural networks and consistent neurological expectations which in turn create and reinforce behaviours, prejudices, fears and psychoneurological beliefs.

Lennenberg's work on supplies of minerals in the body demonstrated identified spurts of development corresponding to the presence of neurotransmitters (natural neural growth factors). He demonstrated their significance to walking and talking at around age two; reading, mathematical computation and writing at around age six; and abstract reasoning at around age twelve. After this third spurt and because of the 'trimming' process it becomes harder to learn foreign languages. Precisely at the point where in the UK it becomes compulsory!

2 LEARNING, CHALLENGE AND STRESS

> *Under stress the indexing capacities of the brain are reduced and the brain's short-term memory and ability to form permanent new memories are inhibited.*

JACOBS AND NADEL, quoted from R. N. Caine and G. Cane,
Making Connections: Teaching and the Human Brain, **ASCD**

> *While rote learning can be accomplished under a good deal of threat . . . pattern discrimination and the more subtle choices . . . suffer severe inhibition. So does the use of oral language and any form of symbol manipulation . . . The inescapable point emerges, cerebral learning and threat conflict directly and completely.*

L. A. HART, *The Human Brain and Human Learning,* **Addison Wesley Longman**

40

THE BRAIN RESPONDS BEST IN CONDITIONS OF HIGH CHALLENGE with low stress, where there is learner choice and regular and educative feedback. Multi-path, individualised and thematic learning with the mental work of engaged problem-solving enriches the brain. So does novel challenge and real-life experience.

The enemy of learning is stress. The optimal conditions for learning include a positive personal learning attitude where challenge is high and anxiety and self-doubt is low.

In the 1950s Dr Paul MacLean gave us his model of the triune or three-part brain and how the brain responded to stress. When challenge becomes unmanageable for a learner, stress develops. With stress comes a change in the chemical and electrical activity in the brain. Survival behaviours assume priority over logical and creative thinking, long-term planning and flexibility. We see the hardening of fight or flight responses, staying with the safe and familiar, anxiety over personal belongings and space. In these circumstances a student who is stressed cannot learn.

It is important to draw a distinction between challenge and stress. Stress includes both fear and anxiety and results from the desire to terminate or escape from a real or imagined negatively reinforcing experience. It coincides with a physiological change which, if not relieved, is harmful to the body and to health. When stress occurs we resort to fight, flight or flocking behaviours. The mid-brain floods with electro-chemical activity and higher order cognitive functioning associated with the neo-cortex is displaced. In stress we experience:

◆ constriction of the arteries with a rise in blood pressure – the heart rate goes from one to five gallons pumped per minute

◆ activation of the adrenal gland assisting in the release of adrenalin and cortisol into the system to help us run and endure physical pain

◆ enlargement of the vessels to the heart

◆ constriction of vessels to the skin and digestive tract

Ira Black in *Information in the Brain: A Molecular Perspective,* MIT Press, reports that such stress responses *'of thirty to ninety minutes can result in a 200 to 300% increase in enzyme activity for twelve hours to three days and in some cases for up to two weeks.'* For many young learners whose lives are ones of constant stress, the classroom and the relationship with you as classroom teacher may be the only still point at the centre of a torrid existence.

41

The mid-brain is responsible for what have been labelled 'reptilian' behaviours. If a learner is experiencing stress or what is called 'induced learner anxiety' because of beliefs – real or imagined – about his or her ability to perform, then don't be surprised to see the physiological responses listed above coincide with some or all of the following behaviours (Caine, Cane and Cromwell, *Mindshifts: A Brain-based Process for Restructuring Education*, Zephyr Press)

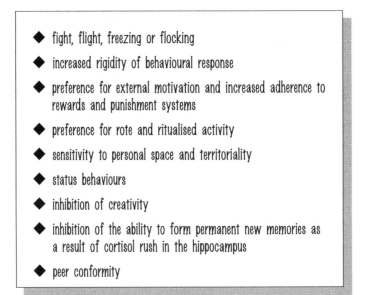

- ◆ fight, flight, freezing or flocking
- ◆ increased rigidity of behavioural response
- ◆ preference for external motivation and increased adherence to rewards and punishment systems
- ◆ preference for rote and ritualised activity
- ◆ sensitivity to personal space and territoriality
- ◆ status behaviours
- ◆ inhibition of creativity
- ◆ inhibition of the ability to form permanent new memories as a result of cortisol rush in the hippocampus
- ◆ peer conformity

Kotulak, in his book *Inside the Brain*, argues that stress turns on genes that leave a memory trace of a bad feeling and goes on to suggest that *'when reinforced, the feeling magnifies and the person "learns" to be difficult, depressed even epileptic.'* Environments where risk-taking is possible, is encouraged and is safe, presuppose accelerated learning. We are not talking of the obvious threat imposed by the overbearing attitude of some teachers but the pervasive background of fear which can characterise schooling inside and outside classrooms. Fear of authority, fear of the institution, fear of loss of independence, fear of failure, fear of physical confinement, fear of behavioural control within a confined physical space.

(since) virtually all academic and vocational learning heavily involves the neo-cortex, it becomes plain that the absence of threat is utterly essential to effective instruction. Under threat, the cerebrum downshifts – in effect, to a greater or lesser extent, it simply ceases to operate.

L. A. HART, *Human Brain and Human Learning*, Addison Wesley Longman

The Equal Opportunities Commission and MORI in England and Wales carried out some interesting research (described later in this book) involving 15 and 16 year olds. It pointed to the fear of psychological intimidation, ahead of physical bullying, amongst their prime safety concerns in schools and schooling. The Elton Report on Discipline in Schools suggested that *'schools which rely heavily on punishments to deter bad behaviour are likely to experience more of it.'* Recent research into the brain and learning consistently points to the significance of creating an atmosphere of high challenge but low stress – what Lozanov called 'relaxed alertness'.

For many learners the comfort zone is where they prefer to be. They will happily copy out sections of text in a masquerade of note-taking. Younger learners will *'copy out in rough, copy it out in neat, draw a coloured border around it, highlight the keywords in primary colours, draw you a picture'*. But rote, repetitive comfort zone activity is not where real learning takes place. To engage in more complex forms of learning may require persistence amidst ambiguity and uncertainty. Doll (1989) pointed out that this can be and can be made 'positively exciting'. For teachers it is a matter of taking learners beyond their comfort zone without undue threat.

Goleman, in his seminal book *Emotional Intelligence: Why it can matter more than IQ*, (1996) popularises the work of Joseph LeDoux on the brain and the primacy of the emotions. He describes the central role of the amygdala, which is part of the mid-brain, in routing signals to different areas of the brain including the neo-cortex. The amygdala plays a powerful role in acquiring, developing and retaining emotional responsiveness.

In essence his thesis is that emotions have primacy in responding to sensory data and thus emotion can overwhelm rational thought: sensory data is routed via an emotional response system before passing to the rational.

He describes the amygdala as an 'emotional sentinel' – *'the amygdala is the specialist for emotional matters . . . if the amygdala is severed from the rest of the brain, the result is a striking inability to gauge the emotional significance of events . . . the amygdala acts as a storehouse of emotional memory, and thus of significance itself; life without the amygdala is a life stripped of personal meanings.'*

In arguing the case for a separate emotional intelligence from an understanding of neuroscience, Goleman goes on to describe the significance of self-knowledge and belief systems and the ability to defer immediate gratification and set purposeful personal goals. He argues for the 'schooling of the emotions' and goes on to show the impact of what is called learned optimism and chart the consequences and possible costs of 'emotional illiteracy'. His work provides a powerful argument for the key presuppositions underlying the accelerated learning in the classroom model:

◆ create a positive, supportive learning environment

◆ recognise the significance of limiting beliefs on performance

◆ build and maintain positive self-esteem

◆ develop the inter- and intra- personal intelligences

◆ encourage the setting of personal performance targets

◆ recognise that external motivation systems – merits, points, stickers – are temporary and will mean less as learners mature

◆ build and use affective vocabulary to allow young learners, particularly boys, to reflect meaningfully on the connections between behaviour, response and outcomes

◆ develop reflective and meta-cognitive thinking as part of regular review activity

3 FEEDBACK AND CHOICE IN LEARNING

 There is no failure, only feedback.

NLP operating principle

Good teaching should provide opportunities for students to take increasing responsibility for their own work.

OFSTED Guidelines

AN UNDERLYING PREMISE OF ACCELERATED LEARNING is that given health, given the motivation, connection to a positive personal outcome and access to useful strategies, we can all learn. This does not mean we can all learn in the same way and to the same outcome but we can learn new skills and understandings and we can all be able to transfer them into new contexts.

As learners we will have different personal preferences for the strategies we use. These may vary by task and context but they will tend to show a consistency over time. Depending on our degree of self-knowledge and the opportunity to reflect on our own learning preference and compare with others, we may or may not become aware of exactly what our own preferred strategies are.

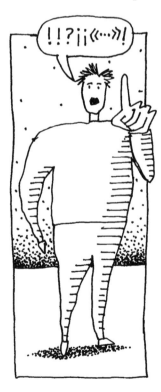

As teachers we may or may not be aware of our own personal learning preferences. We may or may not be aware that such preferences will influence our teaching. We may assume that how we make sense of and interpret data is how everyone makes sense of and interprets data. We may assume that the way we construct and reconstruct reality is how everyone does it. This is an unhelpful state of mind for the creation of powerful learning environments because our tools for understanding the preferred learning strategies of students in our classes are very limited. Our best option is to recognise that only a variety of approaches, reinforced by regular review and the opportunity for students to learn about their own learning, will guarantee accessing all.

Do our students have any clue as to why they are learning what they are learning? Do we encourage them to be aware of the processes of learning? Do we utilise the positive power of peer feedback? Is our feedback frequent? Is it educative?

Positive reinforcement and carefully chosen words change the structure of the brain. An amine called serotonin plays a critical role in self-concept and self-esteem. Serotonin is one of a number of neurotransmitters in the brain which allows connections between neurons to be made. Serotonin is excitatory and is associated with sleep, appetite, pain and mood. It keeps aggression in line. The presence of serotonin encourages the electrical 'jump' across the synapse when connections are made. Where there is immediate positive reinforcement, such as the recognition of a challenge met or a task successfully achieved, serotonin is released simultaneously into the brain and intestines inducing a positive 'gut-feeling', a sense of well-being and security. This feeling coincides with the chemical conditions for enhanced neural networking and higher order thinking.

Reduced levels of serotonin are associated with clinical depression, loss of memory and low self-esteem and, according to Oliver James, are found in people with the lowest status. Commercial drugs such as Prozac temporarily compensate for low levels of serotonin. Chocolate and alcohol have similar short-term effects. However, the continued absence of serotonin and other neurotransmitters can lead to impaired neural networking.

> **A recent Medical Research Council study reported that only 10% of low serotonin amongst depressives is caused by genes ...it is the social environment which is crucial**

OLIVER JAMES, *London Observer*, June 8th, 1997

So reinforce success without dramatising failure! If you want to continue to build healthy brains, catch the students being successful and let them know it! There is evidence that positive reinforcement impacts on the cellular structure of the brain strengthening the hippocampus and amygdala, which are both associated with the emotions and memory. Harsh words and excess of stress can cause arrhythmia and the degeneration of neurons in the hippocampus. Indeed, as explained earlier in this section, under undue stress or anxiety, the mid-brain floods with chemicals prioritising survival behaviours of fight or flight, making creative problem-solving, long-range planning and careful judgement impossible.

Research conducted by Hart, by Barzakov, by Schon and by Druckman and Swets points towards some key characteristics of giving and receiving feedback in the learning process.

Hart suggests that frequent and immediate feedback will help learners *'find out whether their pattern extraction and recognition is correct or improving'*. The best feedback is also real rather than classroom based. So, in language learning it would be the feedback gained in successfully using the language with native speakers. In communications, it would be the ability to successfully make that telephone call to sell space in the school magazine. In science, the successful completion of a planned and researched experiment.

Suggestopaedic researchers such as Win Wenger recommend a strategy called 'pole-bridging' to help boost thinking and intelligence. This involves different areas of the brain in processing information as a task is undertaken. The brain connects information left and right, front and back simultaneously and this process can be encouraged deliberately by talking about or 'externalising' the experience as you do it. Wenger says, *'We go from regions of the brain weaving a tighter relationship and as you get more of what you reinforce,*

45

cumulatively, permanently you reinforce more and more onto line with immediate verbal consciousness those more distant regions of the brain, together with their resources and intelligence.'

Note-taking which involves context as well as content works because of this 'pole-bridging' phenomenon. The fundamental psychological principle of 'you get more of what you reinforce' suggests that if we encourage learners to notice, pay attention to and in some way respond to their own immediate perceptions, however transitory, the behaviour of being perceptive is reinforced. Neurologically, this tightens underlying firing patterns between 'families' of neurons; weaving tighter relationships between regions of the brain. Wenger says that the *'most powerful way to support development of the brain and intelligence is to enrich and clarify feedback on the person's own actions'*. This should be done in the here and now, and externally. Encourage the transmission of this external feedback on internal processing symbolically: *'storyboard your thinking'*, *'draw associated images – annotate and explain them'*, *'what metaphors come immediately to mind?'*

Learners who describe what they are doing aloud as they do it, who reflect on their engagement with the task and their changing motivation, who speculate and hypothesise, achieve dramatically improved results. One commentator (Jensen, 1995) describes the outcomes of documented studies by Wenger as providing intelligence *'gains from one to three points per hour of pole-bridging practice'* with some having *'increased intelligence up to 40 points in 50 hours of work'*.

A simple strategy to improve performance is to add language to doing. Have students describe aloud what they are doing as they do it. Encourage them to reflect on what has been done – aloud – and speculate on what is to come.

Both Barzakov in his work on 'educative' feedback and Schon in work on the reflective practitioner, see feedback as an essential part of a learning loop. Barzakov says that learners need educative feedback in a practical, evaluative and non-threatening form. Teachers would use phrases such as 'what might happen if you were to . . .?', 'In what other ways might this work?' 'How will you start to improve upon this?' 'What do you now know that you didn't before?' 'How might this best be taught to someone else?' The reflective practitioner learns through a cycle of plan, do and review – with review informing improvement and change. Through this process learners are being encouraged to incorporate inquiry and evaluation into their everyday working practice and thus into their thinking. It becomes a 'learned' approach where improvement depends on reflective analysis

At Grace Owen Nursery School, Sheffield, a 'High Scope' style day was introduced in 1994/95. Children plan their activities, do what they have planned and review what they have done in small groups. The school describes the project as vital in raising achievement and say that children know far more about the classroom and even the youngest children thrive on it.

Sheffield School improvement handbook

According to Druckman and Swets, peer feedback has as much, or more, influence as teacher feedback in obtaining lasting performance results. Excess of teacher feedback can be perceived as demotivating if it is too discouraging or 'plastic' or if it is too effusive. Apparently, the approval or disapproval of one's peers is the best reinforcer. This is contradicted by the pragmatic findings of some recent classroom research which points up the sensitivities young learners, particularly adolescents, have about peer feedback.

> **The most demotivating aspect was when teachers warned children in advance that they would not be able to mark their work. The obvious reaction was, 'why on earth should we bother to do it if it's not going to be marked?' Children also find it unpleasant and thankless to mark other children's work. They want teacher advice and approval. They do not like other children knowing how good or bad they are at their work.**

LONDON BOROUGH OF CROYDON, *Pupil Motivation Research*, BRMB International

We will vary in the degree in which we are convinced by Druckman and Swets but we can extract and apply the common principles on feedback:

◆ make it immediate, specific and educative

◆ make it authentic wherever possible

◆ the more often the better

◆ remove it from threat and sanction

◆ involve the learner, peers and others

◆ make it an essential part of a learning cycle

Make action-planning more than a termly ritual! The brain thrives on feedback – feedback that is educative and that can be acted upon. The brain also thrives on purpose. When we set ourselves a positive personal goal which has purpose for us, our brains actively filter data on behalf of the fulfilment of that goal. This would appear to be one of the functions of the reticular system – filtering and diverting data.

Goal- and target-setting activities in schools should be brain-compatible. This would mean harnessing the power of positive visualisation.

Some of the major research findings on visual 'intelligence' suggest that the mind naturally thinks in images and that the most basic mental process is the ability to visualise (Samuels and Samuels) and that the mind can programme and re-programme itself through visual images. Visual information is more readily accessed than semantic information and forms an 'inner guidance system' determining and controlling one's behaviour.

47

> **Since the mind also operates by the process of inference, the mere creation of a mental image, similar to the real object, will cause it to react as if faced by the actuality. The image of an imagined object has mental effects that are in some ways very similar to the image of an object that is actually perceived ... If one is able to imagine something to be true, part of the mind appears to accept that imagined outcome as reality.**

W. HARMAN and H. RHEINGOLD, *Higher Creativity*, JP Tarcher

A changed image can lead to a changed behaviour (Boulding, 1966) but it is an internal process. No other person can change those images and the process of selection for you. This is where affirmations become powerful: when a positive and desired state is created or recreated through a chosen visual image accompanied by a spoken message. Harmon of the Institute of Noetic Sciences, USA, (1986) suggests that *'whatever is vividly or energetically imagined or visualised by the mind, the brain believes to be true and current reality.'*

For action-planning to be more than the hollow exchange of banalities, encourage personal performance targets which are realisable and which do not make comparisons with others and in which a successful positive outcome can be visualised.

4 WHOLE BRAIN LEARNING

> *fitful, irreverent, indulging at times in the grossest profanity (which was not previously his custom), manifesting but little deference for his fellows, impatient of restraint or advice when it conflicts with his desires, at times pertinaciously obstinate, yet capricious and vacillating.*

Physician's notes on Phineas Gage, 1848, R.H.S. Carpenter, *Neurophysiology* (*Third edition*,) Edward Arnold, Hodder & Stoughton Educational

STARTING A SHORT SECTION ON WHOLE BRAIN LEARNING WITH A STORY about Phineas Gage exploits a pun which although awful, is also instructive.

Phineas Gage was an American Mining engineer who, in 1842, was tamping down dynamite with an iron crowbar when the dynamite exploded and the bar shot through his left cheek and out his skull removing most of the frontal cortex of his brain. Gage survived and made a subsequent and precarious living out of exhibiting himself, fragments of his skull and the iron bar for many years afterwards. He also precipitated a rush of medical experiments on brain lesions and helped initiate a trend towards lobotomy which did not end until the 1960s. Gage's skull is in the Smithsonian Museum in Washington. The remarkable thing about Gage was that, despite the trauma of losing 30% of his brain, his intellectual capacities were, according to his physician, 'apparently undiminished'. He endured a profound personality change but was able to continue to reason cognitively much as before.

Work with aphasics has from early times helped in an appreciation of hemispheric functions. Dr Samuel Johnson (1709–84) left us a vivid account of what it is like to suffer a stroke.

> **I went to bed, and in a short time waked and sat up. I felt a confusion and indistinctness in my head that lasted, I suppose, about half a minute. I was alarmed, and prayed God, that however he might afflict my body, he would spare my understanding. This prayer, that I might try the integrity of my faculties, I made in Latin verse. The lines were not very good: I made them easily and concluded myself to be unimpaired in my faculties ... Soon after I perceived that I had suffered a paralytick stroke and that my speech was taken from me. Though God took my speech he left me my hand. In penning this note, my hand, I knew not how nor why, made wrong letters.**

Phineas Gage & Dr. Samuel Johnson, R.H.S. Carpenter, *Neurophysiology (Third Edition)*, Edward Arnold, Hodder & Stoughton

Just as we have a preferred hand, a preferred ear and a preferred eye we have a preferred or dominant hemisphere. After more than 20 years of research and from a database of over 500,000 people, Ned Hermann, creator of the Hermann Brain Dominance Instrument (HBDI), suggests that 30% of this is genetically determined and the balance of 70% or so determined by life experience. Neurophysiological studies have consistently confirmed this. In 96% of right-handed people it is the left hemisphere which dominates. In 65% of left-handed people it is the right hemisphere which dominates. The Hermann Brain Dominance Instrument predicts whether an individual will have a right or left hemispheric preference and whether they favour cerebral or limbic processing. The prediction model, which Hermann describes as a 'metaphor', allows individuals to reflect on their dominant patterns and think of, and plan for, alternative developmental strategies.

In September 1997, Richard Wiseman of the University of Hertfordshire persuaded Yorkshire Television to help him with a simple hemispheric test involving viewers of the 'Tonight' programme. Presenter Carolyn Hodge told viewers she never had a pet when she was a child because she had asthma, then she said she loved pets and viewers were invited to guess whether she was telling the truth. There were over 5,000 calls with 1,564 left handers and 3,342 right handers. More than 72% of the right handers guessed correctly but only 66% of left handers guessed correctly. Apparently she had a guinea pig in her childhood. Professor Wiseman explained the consistency of the results *'right handers tend to use the left hemisphere of the brain which is where linguistic information is processed ... lots of the clues in the clips were to do with language ... when the presenter was lying, there was little detail; when she was telling the truth there was lots of detail.'*

49

Most brains are asymmetric. In 66% the left hemisphere is larger than the right. There are differences in functional specialisms and dominance between left and right hemispheres and also in the processing of information and completion of tasks. The complexity of function and the fact that the brain is plastic, highly interconnected, situational and iterative should not be forgotten when we consider relative lateralisation. Summarised below are some of the recognised specialisations.

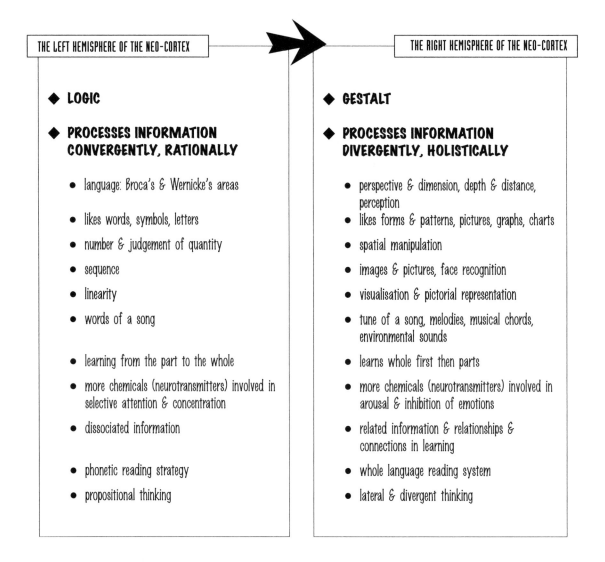

THE LEFT HEMISPHERE OF THE NEO-CORTEX

◆ **LOGIC**

◆ **PROCESSES INFORMATION CONVERGENTLY, RATIONALLY**

- language: Broca's & Wernicke's areas
- likes words, symbols, letters
- number & judgement of quantity
- sequence
- linearity
- words of a song
- learning from the part to the whole
- more chemicals (neurotransmitters) involved in selective attention & concentration
- dissociated information
- phonetic reading strategy
- propositional thinking

THE RIGHT HEMISPHERE OF THE NEO-CORTEX

◆ **GESTALT**

◆ **PROCESSES INFORMATION DIVERGENTLY, HOLISTICALLY**

- perspective & dimension, depth & distance, perception
- likes forms & patterns, pictures, graphs, charts
- spatial manipulation
- images & pictures, face recognition
- visualisation & pictorial representation
- tune of a song, melodies, musical chords, environmental sounds
- learns whole first then parts
- more chemicals (neurotransmitters) involved in arousal & inhibition of emotions
- related information & relationships & connections in learning
- whole language reading system
- lateral & divergent thinking

A recipe for accelerating learning is to use strategies which connect left with right. Give the BIG picture first then chunk down. Pair students to have them describe in words (left) their learning map, graphs or charts (right). Have students visualise the desired outcome or learning goal (right) first before describing it orally (left). The strategies described in detail later in this book continue to pay attention to the synergy of left and right connection.

There is evidence that *concrete* words are stored differently in the brain from *abstract* words. Concrete words may be stored within the visual system whereas abstract words may be stored via a semantic system. Concrete nouns produce mental images more readily than abstract nouns. For example 'potato' is more concrete than 'vegetable' which is more concrete than 'food' which is more concrete than 'nourishment'. The word 'potato' is easier to remember than 'nourishment'. Visual information is processed via the right hemisphere whilst linguistic information is predominantly via the left hemisphere.

Concrete words may be better remembered because they are recalled by left and right hemispheres. Left for the pattern of sounds and right for the visual image. You can see the object as you say the word.

The capacity to store and recall visual information is almost unlimited. Tests done with control groups and 10,000 pictures showed that a 90% recognition level was possible and that this was retained up to three months after seeing the pictures only once (quoted Higbee, 1996). Many studies have found that pictures of objects are remembered better than verbal descriptions of the objects. Jensen, in his book *Superteaching*, claims that visual display placed above eye level in the classroom and sited so it can be read from anywhere in the room will reinforce long-term recall by as much as 70%.

Patients who have had split-brain surgery often experience an inability to dream. Dreaming is a process involving visual imagery and so some investigators have speculated that it might be the responsibility of the right hemisphere. Split-brain patients are also reported as having a deficit in the ability to associate names with faces. The left hemisphere matches by function and the right by appearance. Interestingly, child and adult dyslexics consistently showed reversed or different hemisphere asymmetry with only 10% to 50% of dyslexics having a larger left hemisphere than right. This may say something about the visual processing difficulties associated with dyslexia.

Different styles of music stimulate different hemispheres of the brain. According to research reported by Robertson (1993) and cited by Odam, *'different styles of music will demand a more right or left brain approach both from the composer and the listener.'* He goes on to give the examples of Gorecki, Part and Taverner accentuating right brain function through the use of tonality, concord and intuitive processes which cause strong emotional reactions in listeners, and the work of Boulez, Birtwhistle or Maxwell Davies conversely engaging the listener at an objective and intellectual level through its basis in left-brain processes – arhythmic and atonal properties and dissonance.

Consider this simple experiment. With a mixed group of males and females set up two tasks. In the first ask the whole group to run through the alphabet mentally and count the number of letters, including the letter 'e', that when pronounced contain the sound 'ee'. Next, ask the group to run through the alphabet mentally and count the number of letters that, when written as capitals, contain curves. In both instances the task is done in the head with no writing, speaking or physical manipulation! Which is harder?

The answer depends on whether you are male or female! Males are better with the shape task; females with the sound task. Why?

Male and female brains differ in some ways. These differences begin before birth and partly explain different behavioural patterns. Significant differences occur in the architecture of the brain (where functions are located), the chemistry of the brain (the presence of different levels of excitatory and inhibitory chemicals) and the interactivity of the brain (the capacity of different functional areas to communicate with each other, especially in times of high arousal).

Male and female brains differ in ways which include hemispheric organisation. To generalise, female brains communicate more effectively across the hemispheres. The corpus callosum which connects left and right is proportionately heavier, is thicker and has more fibres in female brains than in male brains and is less susceptible to shrinkage with age. Functional specialisms are more widely diffused in female brains. It is suggested therefore that women are better communicators – particularly under high levels of challenge – and are better at multi-tasking and in accessing intuitive experiences. Male brains are more specialised. They are more susceptible to permanent damage from strokes, especially with age, and are more likely to exhibit brain abnormality.

Lansdell's early work confirmed that language and spatial abilities are more bilateral in females than in males. In a piece of research by Witelson, reported in Springer and Deutsch, the number of neurons per unit volume in the auditory cortex was 11% greater in the brains of women in the sample than those of the men. In the auditory area women had more neural capacity to manipulate language.

Women are more attuned to detecting subtle changes of mood and body language: the left hemisphere develops earlier in baby girls than in baby boys. Girls speak earlier but are also more likely to have better internal connections to areas of the brain associated with language functions. Some researchers suggest therefore that emotional 'centres' are better linked to language functions. Baby boys will be better at an earlier age at manipulating themselves and objects through space. For most boys the right hemisphere – associated with depth perception, perspective and conceptualising spatial manipulation – develops earlier than in girls.

Some reported gender differences of interest to educationalists include those summarised in the table opposite.

MALES	FEMALES
◆ are better at spatial reasoning	◆ are better in grammar and vocabulary
◆ talk later (usually by age of four years)	◆ talk earlier (99% by three years)
◆ have right hemisphere larger than left	◆ have left hemisphere larger than right
◆ talk and play more with inanimate objects	◆ read character and social cues better
◆ solve mathematical problems non-verbally	◆ talk whilst solving mathematical problems
◆ are three times more likely to be dyslexic	◆ are less likely to be dyslexic or myopic
◆ have better general mathematical ability	◆ have better general verbal ability
◆ are better at blueprint reading	◆ have better sensory awareness
◆ enrol in more remedial reading (4:1)	◆ perceive sounds better & sing in tune more
◆ require more space	◆ are slower to anger
◆ favour right ear	◆ listen with both ears
◆ are less at ease with multi-tasking	◆ handle multi-tasking more easily
◆ have shorter attention span	◆ have longer attention span
◆ are more frequently left-handed	◆ proportionately right- and left-handed
◆ differentiated hemispheres – hence right for mathematics and spatial skills, left for language	◆ less marked differentiation between hemispheres
◆ corpus callosum thinner and with fewer fibres	◆ corpus callosum thicker relative to brain size
◆ corpus callosum shrinks 20% by age 50	◆ corpus callosum doesn't shrink
◆ reacts to pain slowly	◆ tolerates long-term pain better
◆ high tolerance of pain	

Based on Moir A., Jessell, D.,
*Brain Sex: The Real Difference Between Men and Wome*n
Michael Joseph, Penguin Books.

Like many of the generalisations that have emerged about boys and girls, relative performance and possible differences in preferred learning styles between boys and girls, this list should be treated with caution and, where possible, reflected upon in the light of other research reported on the brain and learning elsewhere in this book. In brain research, like other areas of research, critical journals do not tend to report 'no difference' findings. Outcomes which are controversial if possibly tenuous are more attractive to editors!

There is a synergy of connections which comes with the attempt to create 'whole brain' learning. Whether or not there is such a thing as whole brain learning aside, teachers should heed the lessons from above and:

◆ be aware that your hemispheric preference — right or left — is not everyone's and challenge your own mental maps about the correct way to do things

◆ present your material in ways which stimulate left and right brain and engage the senses; utilise visual display to reinforce learning points

◆ aim for a balance of left and right hemisphere activity in classroom lessons and within individual pieces of work which you set

◆ avoid rigid adherence to everyone doing the same thing at the same time; encourage learners to challenge themselves by doing some activities which feel uncomfortable

◆ engage the emotions through role-play, empathising activities, discussion and debate

5 LEARNING TO LEARN — THE PERSONAL SEARCH FOR MEANING

What we are discovering is that beneath the surface of awareness, an enormous amount of unconscious processing is going on.

CAMPBELL, *The Improbable Machine*

Since the brain is indisputably a multipath, multimodal apparatus, the notion of mandatory sequences, or even of any fixed sequences, is insupportable. Each of us learns in a personal, highly individual, mainly random way . . . That being the case, any group instruction that has been tightly, logically planned will have been wrongly planned for most of the group, and will inevitably inhibit, prevent or distort learning.

L.A. HART, *The Human Brain and Human Learning*, **ADDISON WESLEY LONGMAN**

THE HUMAN BRAIN OPERATES by 'simultaneously going down many paths' and thus thrives on an input-rich environment. The brain, for Hart, is fundamentally and before all else a pattern detecting device.

We assimilate information constantly through our senses. Visually we process about 100 million bits of data per second. We shift the focus of attention of our eyes about 100,000 times per day – we are not designed to sit head-locked in front of computer or TV screens! We process about 30,000 bits of auditory information per second and a staggering excess of 10 million bodily tactile bits per second.

54

It goes without saying that we are not consciously aware of most of these data! Herbert, in his book *The Elemental Mind*, suggests we consciously process only 15–50 bits of data per second. We assimilate much more than we ever consciously understand. We filter out information which is deemed useless from conscious attention, only filtering in that which is useful or helps us with survival. Learning from this stream of data only emerges in the conscious with some delay, or, in the interim, it influences motives and decisions. Thus we remember what we experience, not just what we are told.

Guy Claxton, in his 1997 book *Hare Brain, Tortoise Mind*, quotes research conducted by Pittman and Bornstein in 1989 to show how unconscious factors influence decision-making. Two candidates were to be interviewed for a job as a research assistant. There was one post and the staff interviewing were given the job specification and the applications. One candidate was strong in computing but poor in writing and the other was the opposite. Before the study each interviewer had taken part in a short experiment on visual perception where, amongst others, one of the candidates had had his photograph flashed up with the accompanying word GOOD five times for an exposure of four milliseconds. This time is far too short for any conscious impression to be registered, yet it turned out that staff were twice as likely to choose the person whose face had been presented to them. In justifying their choice they would go on to argue, not about the candidates, but about whether computing or writing skills were more useful.

by permission of Fourth Estate Ltd. from *Hare Brain, Tortoise Mind: Why Intelligence Increases When You Think Less* by Guy Claxton© 1997

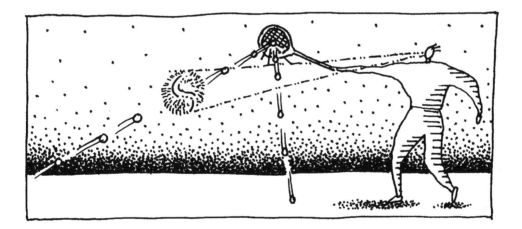

In 1997 research at the University of St Andrews in Scotland looked at the possibility of an 'inner eye' which guided a response to external stimuli outside of conscious attention. The examples given in a BBC Radio interview of July 1997 included top tennis players who, in returning a serve delivered at 110mph or more, cannot possibly see the path of the ball in flight from the server's racket, follow it, set up a return shot and hit it whilst in conscious attention throughout. The 'inner eye' may be a facility which allows an immediate and finely tuned response based on the anticipated delivery but without entering into the stages of a considered and therefore conscious response. Top athletes such as tennis players may have a highly developed facility which allows them to see and respond whilst also consciously planning their next move.

We acquire information. We take it in, but there is no conscious attention paid to it. Nevertheless it influences and shapes decisions, motives and attitudes. In the light of this we can see the significance of creating environments and relationships which are what Lozanov calls 'suggestive'. In other words they are supportive of positive learner success by implication. Physical environments suggest a degree of concern to extend the learning beyond the duration of lessons and are positive and welcoming. Psychological environments are similarly safe, positive and supportive.

We can also see the importance of allowing opportunities for learners to assimilate and integrate new information before moving on. Regular breaks with non-competing stimuli followed by opportunities to re-engage with the material through participative review activities allow the brain to continue to process for meaning.

Both Daniel Goleman in his book *Emotional Intelligence – Why it Matters More than IQ* and Eric Jensen in *Completing the Puzzle* point to recent research which shows that our *'brain decides to think, talk and act before we have any conscious knowledge of it'* and that the *'unconscious mind constitutes over 99% of our learning'*.

6 THE MULTIPLICITY AND MODIFIABILITY OF INTELLIGENCE

> *The IQ movement is blindly empirical. It is based simply on tests with some predictive power about success in school and, only marginally, on a theory of how the mind works. There is no view of process, of how one goes about solving a problem: there is simply the issue of whether one arrives at a correct answer . . . the tasks featured in the IQ test are decidedly microscopic, are often unrelated to one another and seemingly represent a 'shotgun' approach to the assessment of human intellect. The tasks are remote, in many cases, from everyday life.*

HOWARD GARDNER, *Frames of Mind: The Theory of Multiple Intelligences*, **Fontana**

WE CONTINUE TO LABOUR UNDER THE MISCONCEPTION that intelligence is a fixed entity; that it is unvarying; that it can be given a meaningful general measure through combinations of paper and pencil tests, completed in timed conditions.

In schools, too often the labels which can come with some testing regimes – 'not bright enough', 'limited ability' – overlook that what is often being rewarded is an ability under timed, paper and pencil test conditions to use language and a person's skill in defining and using words, knowing facts about the world and in finding connections and differences among verbal concepts. Much of the information required to operate successfully in such tests requires knowledge gained in a specific social and educational milieu.

How is it that a boy or a girl who when in school can perform weakly in formal academic work which requires the ability to organise and motivate oneself, assimilate and integrate new information, plan ahead, prioritise, and apply concepts in a variety of different concepts, can, despite this apparent failure, take themselves off carp fishing at the weekend, journey by three buses, take their own equipment and food, identify the best site by the pond, construct the rods, bait the hooks, and feed the swim and tease the fish until it's caught? Is there not some intelligence or talent in there somewhere?

Professor Michael Howe of Exeter University, in a 1997 review of research covering more than 50 years, shows that intelligence testing is so unreliable that even people recognised as geniuses could have a low IQ score. Interviewed about his book *IQ in Question*, he is quoted as saying, '*IQ tests could be valid as the basis for examinations such as the 11 Plus because the skills highlighted were those required for academic education. But this did not mean that all-round intelligence was being measured or that a person's IQ would not change.*'

The work of leading scholars has challenged the previously cherished notion that intelligence is a single entity which resists development beyond certain prescribed levels. Key figures in this field include Sternberg, Vygotsky and Reuven Feuerstein who, with Jacob Rand, pioneered work on cognitive modifiability through cognitive mediation and created a structure for developments such as 'thinking skills'. They showed that 'intelligence' could be modified and thus expanded and developed.

The CASE (Cognitive Acceleration through Science Education) Project developed by Adey, Shayer and Yates at King's College, London adopts these beliefs about the teaching of thinking skills and is based on the premise that, '*at some time between the ages of about 12 and 18, many people's thinking goes through a qualitative change, something like shifting up a gear . . . whereas in the early teens the student is still using concrete operational thinking, later adolescents are more likely to be able to use formal operational thinking.*' The materials they have developed have produced significant success not only in the subject in which they are used but also in other academic areas.

Benjamin Bloom's point-by-point, structured taxonomy of the logical and emotional domains of the mind's engagement with thinking produced a template for teachers to construct learning experiences. Machado of the Ministry of Intelligence, Venezuela, suggested that intelligence was a basic human right and can be taught. Sternberg of Yale developed his 'triarchic theory' of intelligence, which identifies mental processes of various intelligences, practical ways these processes are applied in everyday life and how they can be transferred into new situations. David Perkins of the Harvard School of Education argues for the 'reflective intelligence' as the '*greatest hope for an all-round improvement in people's intelligent behaviour.*' In his book *Hare Brain, Tortoise Mind*, Guy Claxton, visiting Professor at the University of Bristol, makes a strong case for intuition and for a mode of problem-solving and thinking which allows space for the unconscious to intervene. Howard Gardner headed the movement to suggest that intelligence may be multiple. It is his work which the accelerated learning in the classroom model draws directly from.

Howard Gardner identified three categories of intelligence, with different types of intelligence within each category. He arrived at his personal-related, language-related and object-related categories after studying problem-solving in different cultures around the world and spending years working with adults and children, some of whom were 'gifted' and some of whom had suffered brain damage. His work at the Boston University School of Medicine led to the identification of eight criteria for the existence of these intelligences.

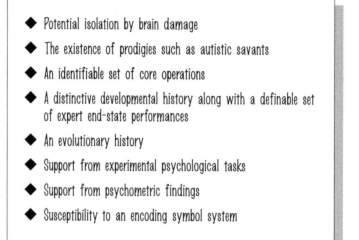

- ◆ Potential isolation by brain damage
- ◆ The existence of prodigies such as autistic savants
- ◆ An identifiable set of core operations
- ◆ A distinctive developmental history along with a definable set of expert end-state performances
- ◆ An evolutionary history
- ◆ Support from experimental psychological tasks
- ◆ Support from psychometric findings
- ◆ Susceptibility to an encoding symbol system

Using these criteria as the backbone for his research, Gardner identified seven different intelligences and later an eighth. They are as follows:

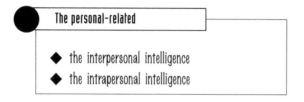

The personal-related

- ◆ the interpersonal intelligence
- ◆ the intrapersonal intelligence

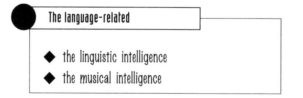

The language-related

- ◆ the linguistic intelligence
- ◆ the musical intelligence

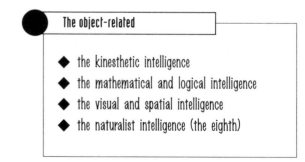

The object-related

- ◆ the kinesthetic intelligence
- ◆ the mathematical and logical intelligence
- ◆ the visual and spatial intelligence
- ◆ the naturalist intelligence (the eighth)

The presuppositions about 'intelligence' we operate in our accelerated learning in the classroom model described in this book include the following facts:

● **Each person is born with a unique blend of intelligences**

Because of the different life experiences we all have some of these intelligences will develop strongly, others slightly and some not at all. Cultural and social variables and the nature of learning encounters will speed or slow this process.

● **Intelligence is a multiple phenomenon**

There are many ways in which individuals make sense of the world and their part in it and there are many ways in which this understanding can be expressed.

● **Teachers can intervene to modify the intelligence of students**

Teachers can play a significant part in removing some of the barriers that hinder the development of an intelligence whilst utilising strategies to develop that intelligence.

● **Intelligence will develop in stages**

For our purposes we have created a model which recognises four stages in the development of an intelligence (discussed in Section Three).

  – stimulate

  – amplify

  – learn and understand

  – transfer and effect

● **Thinking can be taught**

Metacognition: learning about learning and the structured use of tools and techniques, including the questioning strategies and the templates provided with this book to aid this process, will help learners develop thinking skills.

In the ways in which our brains access, respond to, and integrate new experience, we are all unique. Each brain has a high degree of plasticity, developing and integrating with experience every moment in ways unique to itself. As you read this, your brain adds to its store of experience and alters itself.

An informed diversity in teaching and learning can begin to accommodate all of this.

⑦ PHYSICAL READINESS FOR LEARNING

> *Our kids don't have very good attention spans, which means that more than ten minutes of talking to them is actually quite redundant, which in itself promotes good learning because you have to think of other ways of promoting learning rather than trying to pass over information from the front.*

South Bristol Teacher, reported in Bath University,
Departments Adding Significant Value, **1994**

> *Unless learners are in the appropriate learning state, it's time to stop everything and start changing their states.*

E. JENSEN, *Completing the Puzzle: A Brain-Based Approach to Learning,* **Turning Point**

THE BRAIN IS LESS THAN 2.4% of body weight yet it accounts for 20% of energy consumption at rest. To do this it needs oxygen and of all the organs in the body the brain is the greediest in fuel consumption. If it does without oxygen for just a few minutes it begins to die. If you are teaching in an airless room on a hot summer's afternoon with the students immobilised behind desks, then forget about them learning anything!

It doesn't need a neurologist to remind us about meeting basic needs before learning can begin. Abraham Maslow taught us that there is a 'hierarchy of needs' wherein lower level needs must be met before needs on the higher level can begin to be met. He characterised it as a pyramid where movement to the next elevation required the previous level of need to have been satisfied.

**SELF-
ACTUALISATION NEEDS**
To develop our talents in order to
realise our full potential

SELF-ESTEEM AND COMPETENCE NEEDS
To achieve: to gain approval and recognition from others
for our achievements and to be able to trust in our abilities

BELONGING AND LOVE NEEDS
To love and be loved: to have positive relationships in which we are accepted
and to feel that we are valued

SAFETY NEEDS
To feel safe, secure, out of danger or threat and to have confidence that we will not be
harmed physically or psychologically

PHYSIOLOGICAL NEEDS
To have the food, clothing, shelter, sleep, exercise and physical space and comfort we need to survive

Maslow, a psychologist, argued that no matter what level we are currently operating on, all our energy will continually be drawn to any lower level for which we perceive an unmet need. For classroom teachers the message is simple: students will not learn best when they are hungry, tired, too hot, too cold or too confined. Pay attention to the physical state of the learners in your class and intervene where possible if these factors are getting in the way.

Get them out from behind those desks! We are not designed to sit slumped behind a piece of wood for an hour and ten minutes at a time, nor are we designed to sit for three hours in front of a television screen or a computer terminal! Physical movement enhances learning! If you can learn or rehearse a new topic with accompanying movement, it is more likely to be remembered. Furthermore, as you become more practised in a particular series of movements, the brain changes its structure. Concert pianists use their brains differently from amateurs. Top sports players, like top musicians, use fewer brain cells than amateurs attempting the same moves and the cells used are more specifically located. Learning is underpinned by physical changes in neural pathways. Visualising or imagining the movements can have a similar effect. Mental rehearsal prepares the brain for learning.

> **Mobility, even simply standing up, can boost learning. Dr Max Vercruysen of the University of Southern California discovered your body's posture affects learning. His research showed that, on the average, standing increased heartbeats. That sends more blood to the brain, which activates the central nervous system to increase neural firing. Researchers found that on the average, there's a 5–15% greater flow of blood and oxygen to the brain when standing. Psychologically, he says, standing up also creates more attentional arousal and the brain learns more.**
>
> E. JENSEN, *Completing the Puzzle: A Brain-Based Approach to Learning,* Turning Point

Physical activity, besides strengthening heart and muscles, improves the flow of blood to the brain and increases the connections between neurons. The cerebellum, responsible for movement, contains over half of the brain's neurons with more specific pathways into the rest of the brain than any other system. The simple expedient of insisting on rotating seating arrangements literally provides a different perspective of the classroom experience. Shea and Hodges did research to determine the effects of different types of seating – formal and informal – in the classroom. Shea found that students who preferred informal seating arrangements – comfortable chairs and choice of when to use them – performed significantly better in comprehension tests.

Highs and lows are how we are. In daytime we switch hemispherical dominance on cycles of roughly 90 minutes. In classroom lessons different learners will be on different stages within their natural cycle.

The idea of 'brain gym' is now less easy to deride when presented with evidence of links between movement and thinking skills. One of the most talked about ways of linking movement to brain development involves co-ordinating the left and the right sides of the body. For most of the population the right side of the brain will control many of the motor functions of the left side of the body and vice-versa. Physical activity with co-ordinated cross-lateral responses will develop neural pathways across the two sides of the brain.

Build-in frequent breaks and opportunities to reflect on the learning throughout lessons. Work on a rough guide of chronological age plus one. Thus 12 year olds should come out of task for some form of reflection activity every 13 minutes or so. Use such opportunities to build-in review of content. Apply the six times rule – for new content the learners should have encountered at least six times and in six different ways by the end of the lesson. Without review, recall can drop by as much as 80% within 24 hours. The model recommended is

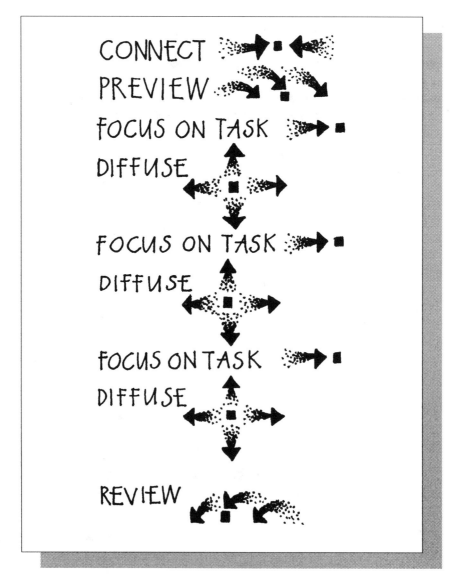

Connecting is about accessing the previous related learning experience before giving the overview or BIG picture then onto task whatever that may be but patterned by frequent short and purposeful breaks known as 'diffusions'. Each diffusion space is an opportunity for physical stretching or brain gym with informal review activities, then back onto task. The brain needs time to assimilate new information, to integrate it and to begin to make sense of it.

In addition to physical movement and a multi-sensory immersion learning environment, it is worth noting in summary what some researchers have found out about the environment and learning. Here is a selection. Read with caution! If you can apply the information do so . . .

◆ **Heat:** Overheating causes a decrease in all-round performance level in tasks requiring concentration, accuracy, physical dexterity and sensory acuity.

◆ **Hydration:** Dehydration leads to inattention, drowsiness and poor learning performance. The fluid to electrolyte balance in the body is adversely affected by dehydration and by some high sugar drinks. Put water fountains back in corridors and staff rooms.

◆ **Ionisation:** The more negatively charged the better. With emissions from smoke, dust, smog, pollutants, chemicals and heating systems the air becomes highly electrified with positive ions. Ionised air raises serotonin levels and stabilises alpha rhythms in the brain. Robert Ornstein reports that rats exposed to negative ionisation grew a 9% larger cerebral cortex.

◆ **Colours:** In *Color and Human Response*, Faber Birren listed the different tendencies of human response to various colours:

> **red** – good for creative thinking, short-term high energy
> **green** – good for productivity, long-term energy
> **yellow/orange** – conducive to physical work, exercise, positive moods
> **blue** – slows pulse, lowers blood pressure, helps study and concentration
> **light colours** – provides minimum disruption across all moods and mental activity

Use light blue for worksheets! White paper with black print is more disruptive to smooth eye patterns.

◆ **Smell:** Females are more sensitive to odours than males. Most odours disrupt sleep: the heart rate increases and brain waves quicken. Smell, according to Charles Wysocki of the Monell Chemical Sense Centre in Philadelphia is the only one of the five senses with direct linkage to the limbic system. Associate an experience with a smell and it is remembered for life! Lavender-chamomile scents reportedly reduce stress; lemon, jasmine and cypress induce a positive attitude. Gary Schwartz of the University of Arizona reports that within one minute, spiced apple scents yield more relaxed brain waves and an average drop in blood pressure of five millimetres per person (quoted Howard).

◆ **Sleep:** Milk products stimulate melatonin production which improves sleep. Simple sugars and fats decrease the oxygen supply to the brain, which decreases alertness and makes you sleepy. More physical interventions in the afternoon teaching slots! The amount of sleep we require is directly related to our body weight! People who nap consistently live longer and show a 30% lower incidence of heart disease. Visualisation techniques have proved to be a big help in reducing or eliminating nightmares.

◆ **Lighting:** London conducted research on lighting and classrooms in 1988. Some 160,000 youngsters were involved in his research. He found that on leaving primary school aged 11, over 50% of the students had developed deficiencies related to classroom lighting. Students who were in classrooms having full-spectrum lighting missed only 65% of the schooldays missed by others in classrooms. He said, *'ordinary fluorescent light has been shown to raise the cortisol level in the blood, a change likely to suppress the immune system'.*

Finally, in terms of physical readiness, be aware that in learning there are 'ah-ha' moments and 'ha' moments. There are occasional 'aaah' moments but there aren't enough 'ha-ha' moments!

Laugh! In his 1989 book, *Head First: the Biology of Hope*, Norman Cousins describes how tests of problem-solving ability yield better results when they are preceded by laughter. Laughter results in an increased number of immune cells and immune cell proliferation, an increased respiratory facility and increased endorphins. He says, *'laughter has a way of turning off posterior hypothalmic activity and freeing the cerebral cortex for stress free activity'.* One of the most useful physical movements in the learning environment might be the belly laugh! Ha Ha!

8 THE MUSICAL IMPULSE AND LEARNING

> *It is concluded that with careful choice of music and its mode of presentation, one can intentionally either impede or maximise learning of tasks having hemispheric lateralisation.*

MCFARLAND AND KENNISON, *CSU Journal of General Psychology 1988* [quoted Odam]

IN AN EXPERIMENT ON FOETAL LEARNING before and after birth conducted in Northern Ireland in 1991, it was reported that *'newborns who had been exposed to the theme tune of a popular TV programme during pregnancy exhibited changes in heart-rate, number of movements and behavioural state 2-4 days after birth. These effects could be attributed to pre-natal exposure alone and not to post-natal exposure or a genetic disposition, and were specific to the tune learned.'* The babies' mothers had all been watching the Australian soap 'Neighbours' during pregnancy! The babies had learned the tune!

Babies *in utero* can respond to the frequency of the mother's voice six weeks before birth. Researchers at Cornell found in a published study from 1996 that four-month-old babies displayed anxiety symptoms when excerpts of Mozart were chopped up and played out of sequence. Virtually every child is born with the capacity to recognise most of the 100 sounds which, when combined together, can formulate any of the 6,000 or so world languages.

Just as we are neurologically wired for movement, we are also wired for speech and music. Immediately after birth, psychomotor control patterns and the appreciation of melody and concomitant aural awareness of rhythmic structure becomes established in the brain. Music teachers who work with the very young utilise movement in their work: much early years music education is inseparable from movement education.

Get out the gramophones! With older learners, whose learning has become more subject to formality and external structure, music and its use in learning generates great controversy. Poor research with limited controls and ill-defined purposes has threatened to close minds on this topic.

Music and movement aid learning and recall. George Odam, in his book *The Sounding Symbol*, points out the link between psychomotor learning and hemisphericity

> **The best performers commit a great deal of what they do to their long-term memories, learning not through a process of logical analysis but through a combination of repetitive movement and right-brain properties of contour and aural perception. Student candidates in formal harmony examinations could often be observed 'playing' on an imaginary keyboard on the exam room desk in order to solve the best part-writing in the set task, because they had learnt the procedures as movements and overall shapes. Only when they made these movements were they then able to subject them to cognitive analysis. Since the right brain does not respond to analysis, indeed does not recognise it, it stores shapes and procedures in their entirety. Such students had learnt to create an aural perception of appropriate sounds internally through movement.**

Reproduced with the permission of Stanley Thornes Publishers Ltd. from *The Sounding Symbol: Music Education in Action*, first published in 1995

Music and speech combined also aids learning and recall. During speech reception the left hemisphere of the brain becomes highly active and the right minimally so. When listening to music the right side becomes highly active with the left less so. Current research by Dr Steven Brown of The University of East Anglia shows that the separate hemispheres of the brain react differently to different types of music. The left hemisphere is stimulated by sevenths and seconds and by discords. The right is stimulated by octaves, fourths, fifths and by concordant sounds. There is also evidence to show that scientists and musicians utilise the hemispheres of the brain differently.

Music students, according to Chesson (1993), use similar right and dominant hemispheric processing mechanisms for problem-solving as science students but *'musicians are more likely to use an integrated processing mode than science students. Science students are more likely to use left processing mode.'* In other words whilst the scientists will tend to favour a logical, sequential and ordered problem-solving approach (left hemisphere dominant), musicians are more likely to use whole-brain, problem-solving approaches.

Following pioneering work by Georgi Lozanov and others, notably Lynn Dhority in the USA, music has been used in carefully chosen ways in accelerated learning language classes throughout the world for many years. Neither Lozanov in the early 1970s nor others such as Dhority later had the access to such sophisticated research outcomes on hemisphericity and music that we have, yet they seemed to understand the positive effects of its use in learning. Amongst the ways in which it is used are managing or creating a 'mood' to which the learners will align themselves. Dhority describes how he discovered this quality.

I began to experiment with playing intentionally background classical music at a barely audible level and noticing how it helped group attunement and rapport, how it provided a cohesive element, notably lacking when it was not there.

LYNN DHORITY, *The ACT Approach: The Use of Suggestion for Integrative Learning,*
Gordon & Breach, MIT Press

Music is also used in ways which include what are called the first, or active, concert and the second, or passive, concert. The active concert involves the teacher reading the text – in language classes this is in the target language – whilst dramatic and emotionally engaging music is played. This occurs after students have been given 'the BIG picture' and before detailed work occurs. The voice 'surfs' the music, rising and falling appropriately, whilst the students follow the text. The text will have target language and translation side by side. The music creates emotional associations and simultaneously connects left and right brain. The pieces preferred by Dhority include works by Brahms, Rachmaninoff, Beethoven, Tchaikovsky and Haydn.

By keeping a diary of lessons it became obvious very early on in the study that the greater quality of learning was with 8X. The way they approached lessons was significantly more positive than 8Y, they settled down to tasks much quicker at the beginning of lessons which I feel was a reflection of how it started, with up-beat music playing in the background and greeting the pupils as they arrived having a remarkable effect. The lessons thus got off to a positive start with 8X, with very few of the annoying factors that can disrupt the start of any lesson. . . . Once the music faded out and stopped they knew it was time to become focused, whereas the start of the lessons with 8Y were a direct contrast and much more stressful for teacher and pupils.

ROGER GILBERT, KING EDMUND COMMUNITY SCHOOL, YATE, M.ED. RESEARCH

The passive concert occurs as a 'suggestive' review towards the end of the learning session. The material presented is the same as the active concert but the method and intended outcome differ. The method, here, is for the students to settle into a state of 'relaxed awareness' whilst listening to slower pieces of music such as some Baroque pieces with less personal, rigorously structured qualities. Students do not follow the text but listen to the music, whilst the teacher reads the text naturally, guided *'not by the music but by the semantics and context of the text'* (Lynne Dhority). The passive concert is a concluding, ritualised activity intended to encode and sublimate the material into the brain.

In a separate experiment (Rauscher, University of California, 1993), subsequently and successfully repeated, test scores of students who learned new material whilst listening to pieces from Mozart, rose consistently and significantly when tested with the music playing and also, though slightly less successfully, when tested with no music. Shaw and Leng at the University of Southern California at Irvine published in Neuroscience letters in 1997 research conducted with 74 college students which showed that performance in spatial-temporal reasoning tests – manipulation of shapes, understanding of symmetry, proportional reasoning and mental imagery – improved after students had been listening to ten minutes of a Mozart piece. EEG scanning showed that the effect did show signs of carry over. Work with three year olds and piano keyboard training showed an improvement in spatial-temporal tasks and object assembly above the 85th percentile. In a further tightly controlled experiment with patients diagnosed as showing early symptoms of Alzheimer's Disease, playing 12 minutes of Mozart before a spatial manipulation task showed improvements of over 300%.

In summary, we can look to work done at the University of Irvine, California, reported at the 1997 International Alliance for Learning Conference, 'Unleashing the Brain's Potential', which suggests that music can aid learning in the following three ways.

Music can energise or relax. It thus becomes a classroom management tool. The teacher uses it to help achieve an appropriate receptiveness for learning.

Music also acts as a carrier. Connecting the left and right hemispheres of the brain. Content learned to a rhythm or with an accompanying tune is more readily recalled. The music carries' the content. Try reciting 'Happy Birthday' or 'Twinkle Twinkle Little Star' without lapsing into the rhythm of the accompanying song! This is the principle upon which the accelerated learning idea of the passive concert works. Simultaneously listening to music with a beat of 60 to 70 beats per minute – some Baroque music, for instance, whilst also listening to a spoken summary of key learning points can activate the brainwave pattern most closely associated with maximum recall of information. The music carries the content whilst also helping the learner stay in the optimum state for learning.

Music can prime the neural networks for learning. Weinberger's research on the auditory cortex claims to show that music 'primes' the neural networks for learning (quoted IAL Conference, 1997). Performance scores in abstract reasoning tasks suggested that certain pieces of music stimulated the brain by rehearsing a 'firing pattern' in the neural pathways.

Many of the teachers I have worked with in the UK now use music in their classrooms. Perhaps it also presupposes an existing supportive relationship beforehand. Their use of it is skilled and judicious. Here are some of the ways to use music to enhance learning:

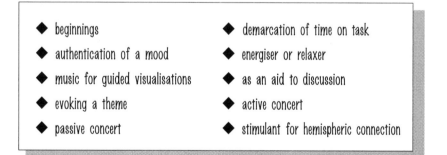

- ◆ beginnings
- ◆ authentication of a mood
- ◆ music for guided visualisations
- ◆ evoking a theme
- ◆ passive concert
- ◆ demarcation of time on task
- ◆ energiser or relaxer
- ◆ as an aid to discussion
- ◆ active concert
- ◆ stimulant for hemispheric connection

In Section Four I list some of the pieces of music which can be used for each of the above moments.

As a postscript it is interesting to note that when the *New York Times* picked up and reported the results of Shaw and Leng's work on Mozart and maths, the CD of the piece they had used – Mozart's Sonata for two Pianos in D Major – sold out in every Boston music shop within the day!

HOW WE STORE AND RETRIEVE INFORMATION USING THREE MEMORY SYSTEMS

> *You can read the same material again and again without it entering your long-term memory. Memorising material needs to be more active. You need to seek out the meaning, think it through and structure it in the way you feel is most relevant.*

NICK MIRSKY, *The Unforgettable Memory Book*, BBC Worldwide Limited

> *Think memory process rather than location.*

W. CALVIN, *How Brains Think: Evaluing Intelligence Then and Now*, Wiedenfield & Nicholson, Orion Publishing

HOW IS IT THAT ONE CAN WALK from one room in the house to another to collect something, arrive in the room, forget what you've come for and have to go back to the original room before you remember?

Memory research has developed considerably in the last ten years. Whereas it used to be believed that memories were stored in specific areas of the brain and memory was regarded as accessing or re-exciting fixed sites, nowadays it is more likely to be described as a process which is both creative and inexact. The neurologists describe memory as learning that sticks. New synapses are formed and old connections are strengthened.

Metaphors for memory have tended to reflect the prevailing technology of the age. Memory does not, however, operate like a reference library, index-card system, filing-cabinet or computer database. It is more complex. It is driven by perceived need, context, associations, the intensity and nature of the original experience and perhaps by the individual's preferred representational system. Memories are constructed from neural pathways that fire together in what Susan Greenfield calls a 'patterned neural assembly'. Such patterns are never the same as we constantly elaborate, modify and interpret.

A more useful metaphor for memory is that of the school fire drill. When the alarm sounds the students organise themselves from different lessons and from different places in or out of the building, at different speeds, in different degrees of readiness and with different individuals present or absent on the day. When the classes are assembled they are in roughly the same order but with subtle differences. With memory, the stimulus – the fire alarm – precipitates a convergence of associated and connected strands of information which come together. The strands of information are like the individual students milling around with some awareness of how they work together to achieve the overall aim. The combination will be different in subtle ways each time dependent on the nature and the 'urgency' of the stimulus. It's never the same.

According to this particular model new learning becomes integrated into a patterning process and with each new integration the base reference points change. We integrate the memory of the memory. In teaching we build on the learner's prior knowledge and models of understanding irrespective of whether these are formally 'correct' or 'incorrect'.

Antonio Damasio, in his book *Descartes' Error*, shows how, as we are presented with new learning, the brain recalls past experience and references this to base data from different areas of the brain simultaneously. New information can thus be integrated into and thus change neural networks, so giving us an enriched template of experience. He says, '*Some circuits are remodelled over and over throughout the lifespan, according to the changes an organism undergoes. Other circuits remain mostly stable and form the backbone of the notions we have constructed about the world outside.*'

Hannaford (1995) says that the reorganisation of base patterns becomes long-term memory and that '*we continue to elaborate and modify the patterning throughout our lives*'. The model of memory which scientists are moving towards is one which is characterised by patterning, associations and context. Hannaford argues that the base patterns are 90% in place by five years of age. The capacity to memorise seems to be fully developed by eight years of age. At this point we are able to recall one unit of information for every 100 we receive. A key point for educationalists here is to recognise the significance of teaching thinking and memory skills early.

Now that we have an understanding of how memory works at a neural level we ought not to forget the practical purpose of this book. Teachers need answers to the following questions about memory.

◆ What's the best way to remember complex information?

◆ How much information can be remembered by students at any one time?

◆ How can we improve students' capacity to remember?

◆ What is the ideal time spent on studying for recall?

◆ How much time should be spent on review?

Two models of memory are helpful here. The first describes the difference between immediate, short-term and long-term memory. The second three systems that operate within immediate, short- and long-term memory are categorical, procedural and sensory and contextual memory. In the prevailing research model, forming a memory can be described with a sheep pen metaphor.

You round up the sheep – *capturing them in the immediate memory*. Your sheepdogs chase them into a holding pen as you open and close a gate – *you capture them in the short-term memory*. You then transfer them into a larger, more secure pen, again as you open and close another gate – *you capture them in the long-term memory*. The round up is like the immediate memory with the sheepdogs acting like prompts or stimuli for recall. The holding pen is like short-term memory and has flaws. The fencing may be in disrepair and, without more careful attention, the sheep may struggle out and need rounding up again. The permanent pen is like long-term memory. Once in, the sheep remain there. All you need to do is remember where the location of the pen is in the landscape.

Immediate memory is a capturing process where thousands of pieces of data can be held for two seconds or less. Here new information pushes out the old unless the old has conscious attention paid to it. The emotions, personal belief systems, context and perceived need direct conscious attention.

Short-term memory is like a holding pen but with gaps in the fencing. The hippocampus, sitting within the limbic system, appears to act as a gatekeeper, selecting chunks of data to remember. A chunk of information is defined as an unfamiliar array of pieces of information. Without conscious attention for a period of at least eight seconds or without rehearsal in an appropriate mode, information can be lost to short-term memory. The sheep escape through gaps in the fence. Try to remember a ten-digit telephone number when you have placed your telephone book more than eight seconds away from your telephone and you will know what I mean! Strategies for recall help transfer the memory from the inadequate and temporary pen into the longer-term permanent pen.

Long-term memory involves a significant chemical response in the brain. The neurotransmitters epinephrine and norepinephrine, associated with arousal, are released and act like memory fixatives. James McGaugh, a psychobiologist at the University of California, showed that rats with low levels of epinephrine had poorer recall ability but when injected with epinephrine their ability to recall information to help them perform tasks improved. When we have strong experiences, epinephrine seems to tell the brain to hold the information. Here again what seem to matter in directing the brain to hold the information are the emotions and the level of emotional arousal, personal belief systems, the context in which the information is apprehended and the perceived need for retaining it.

To get information into *long-term memory* be aware of the natural ways in which the brain assigns significance to experience. Here there is a hierarchy of memory systems. Sometimes described as categorical or semantic memory, procedural memory and contextual memory.

Categorical or semantic memory involves rehearsing information through an emphasis on content rather than context. Repetition, rote rehearsal and drilling are features of this recall system. Work done by George Miller in 1956 clearly demonstrated that there were limits to the amounts of information which could be retained by adults using this method. His famous seven plus or minus two formula also applies to younger learners: the younger the learner the fewer the chunks able to be retained. For adults the maximum amount of information which can be retained without chunking or categorising will be nine units.

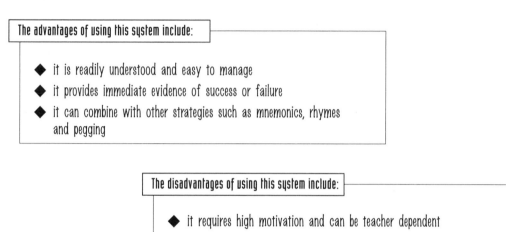

The advantages of using this system include:

◆ it is readily understood and easy to manage
◆ it provides immediate evidence of success or failure
◆ it can combine with other strategies such as mnemonics, rhymes and pegging

The disadvantages of using this system include:

◆ it requires high motivation and can be teacher dependent
◆ it is short-term without regular rehearsal
◆ it is context free and usually difficult to access and transfer
◆ it is chunk limited and may require skill in categorising

Procedural memory is sometimes called sensory memory and involves learning through sensory interaction, particularly movement. It requires little extrinsic motivation and generates physical associations. Research into the role of movement in learning shows that the density and number of neural pathways between the cerebellum – responsible for balance and some motor movement functions – and the cortex is proportionately greater than any other localised system and that movement plays a very important part in learning.

The advantages of using this system include:

◆ it is 'brain-compatible' with minimal extrinsic motivation
◆ information is readily accessed and not necessarily limited by time
◆ it is not chunk dependent or dependent on an ability to categorise

The disadvantages of using this system include:

◆ sensory associations and opportunities for creating them are difficult in classrooms without preparation

◆ it may need to interact with other methods of reinforcement so that a teacher can assess whether learning has occurred

◆ some experiences are more difficult to readily recreate via a sensory approach; some classroom subjects will, by their nature — e.g., philosophy — challenge the teacher to create opportunities for procedural or sensory learning

Contextual memory is based on associative connections between location and circumstances in which the information or experience is accessed. It is natural and requires little extrinsic or intrinsic motivation. Sometimes described as state dependence this type of memory system is used by police forces all over the world to stimulate recall. *'People recall information more readily when they can remember the state in which they learned that information'* (Howard). By state I don't mean Ohio or Nebraska, but the physical circumstances and the immediate environment. Research cited by Goleman and by Howard demonstrated that groups performed better in memory test when they 're-created' the context of the original learning.

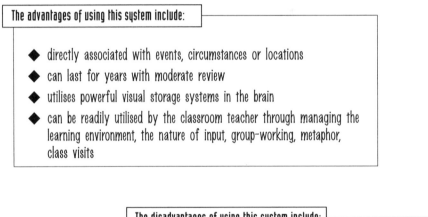

The advantages of using this system include:

◆ directly associated with events, circumstances or locations
◆ can last for years with moderate review
◆ utilises powerful visual storage systems in the brain
◆ can be readily utilised by the classroom teacher through managing the learning environment, the nature of input, group-working, metaphor, class visits

The disadvantages of using this system include:

◆ requires imagination and detailed pre-planning by teacher
◆ poor at details over long-term unless connected with other systems
◆ best achieved when new knowledge is built on thematically from what is already known and understood

We acquire one or two bits of information per second during concentrated study. Decision theorist Herbert Simon says it takes about eight seconds of attention for a new 'bit' to be added to short-term memory. Our average brain capacity is 2.8×10^{20} bits or approximately ten million volumes of books at a thousand pages each.

Jensen (1995), reporting work by Pieron, describes the optimal time on task as *'chronological age plus one or two'*. So for ten year olds the optimal time would be eleven or twelve minutes on task followed by an interval for reflection or review. For adults a maximum of twenty-five minutes before some sort of physical break and/or review activity.

The ideal study pattern may be one of **preview-focus-diffuse-focus-diffuse-focus-diffuse-review**. Time spent on focus is age dependent. The younger the learner the shorter the focus time and the longer the time taken to review and integrate the new information.

Research conducted with fifteen year olds who were asked to recall combinations of nonsense syllables demonstrated that what mattered most in recall was not time on the task but what was done in that time. Time spent on review was as valuable as time spent on reading the new material

% of time reading	% of time on review	Average no. of syllables recalled
100%	0%	65
80%	20%	92
60%	40%	98
40%	60%	105
20%	80%	137

Reproduced with permission of Accelerated Learning Systems Ltd.

A simple maxim is to apply the 'six-times rule'. By the end of the teacher-student involvement with the topic the student ought to have encountered the key learning points in at least six different ways. This could be in or out of the formal classroom, before, during or after the topic is covered in a lesson.

To optimise recall teachers should:

◆ at the beginning of a course go over the content and describe the processes you will use to teach the content

◆ with a new unit of work detail the learning outcomes, specify the key words that learners will be able to spell and explain, and provide the questions they will be able to answer

◆ start each lesson with a review of what's gone before and a preview of what's to come

◆ use open questions to pre-process for student answers and to provoke extended thinking

◆ during the lesson build-in regular, spaced opportunities for students to review

◆ utilise the review, input and memory techniques advocated throughout this book

◆ at the end of the lesson pack up early and go over the material, preview the next lesson

- ◆ at the end of the unit go over it asking students to memory map the key content; get the students to pair share and then test each other
- ◆ at the end of each term spend the last lessons going over the material and highlighting key points

Certain principles of memory can be used to guide us to useful review and recall tools for students. They are best summarised as the SCOTS CLAN MAPS model of memory and are described in detail in Section Three.

◆ SECTION ONE: REVIEW

1 If, as is suggested in this section, sustained mental and physical challenge alongside multi-sensory stimulation develop neural networks in the brain, what are the implications for learning environments? What might parents do to enrich the learning environments of infants?

2 The enemy of learning is stress. What may contribute towards learner 'stress' in classrooms? In what ways could classroom teachers help students manage such stressors?

3 In what ways might 'pole-bridging' be considered the most effective feedback?

4 How, within the course of a learning experience, could a teacher utilise 'left' and 'right' hemisphere approaches?

5 Some researchers describe the brain as a 'pattern seeking and producing instrument'. How might a classroom teacher exploit this function within a lesson?

6 If there are different types of intelligence what are the possible implications for classroom practice?

7 How might physical 'breaks' be used to keep learners in the optimal state for learning?

8 List some possible benefits and potential pitfalls of using music in classrooms.

9 How might memory and recall tools be integrated into classroom lessons?

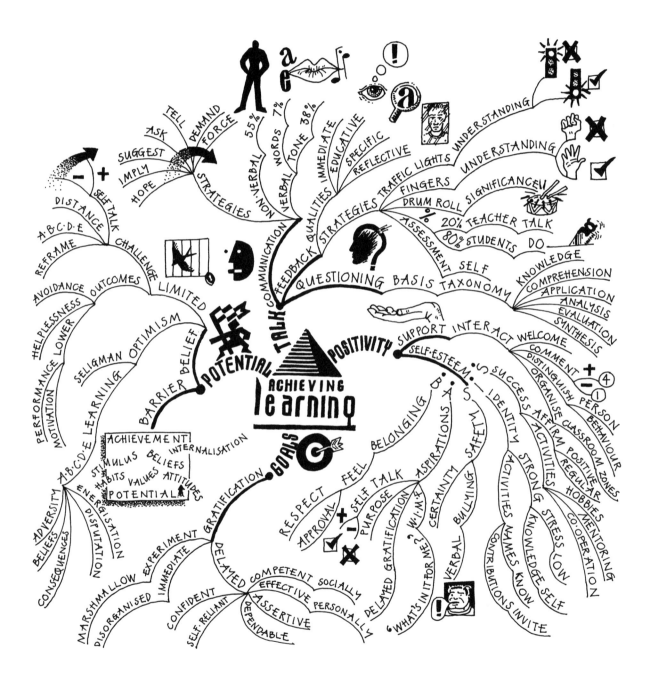

Preview of Section Two:

Creating a positive learning attitude and an achievement culture

IN SECTION TWO YOU WILL LEARN:

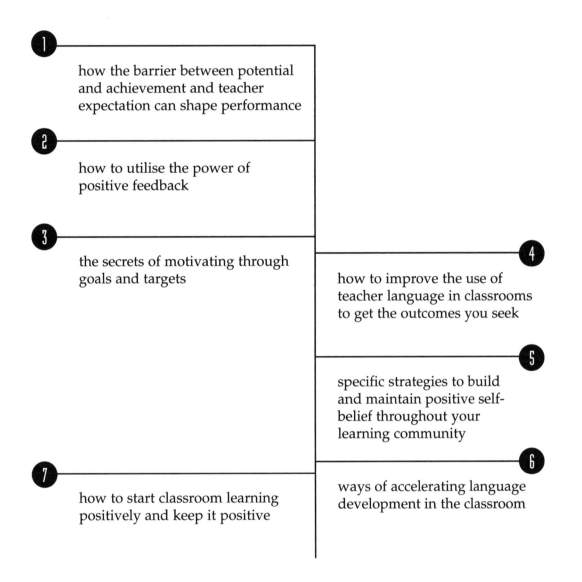

1 how the barrier between potential and achievement and teacher expectation can shape performance

2 how to utilise the power of positive feedback

3 the secrets of motivating through goals and targets

4 how to improve the use of teacher language in classrooms to get the outcomes you seek

5 specific strategies to build and maintain positive self-belief throughout your learning community

6 ways of accelerating language development in the classroom

7 how to start classroom learning positively and keep it positive

Section Two:
Creating a positive learning attitude and an achievement culture

① THE BARRIER BETWEEN POTENTIAL AND ACHIEVEMENT

> *If teachers believe that pupils can change and that learning can become easier in the right climate, then they will transmit that positive view to pupils.*

PETER MORTIMORE, *School Matters*

> *Our evidence suggests that many children who behave badly in school are those for whom self-esteem is threatened by failure. They see academic work as 'unwinnable'. They soon realise that the best way to avoid losing in such a competition is not to enter it.*

ELTON REPORT, 1989

ONE OF THE MOST PROFOUNDLY DEPRESSING MOMENTS I have experienced in this context occurred one summer day in recent years as I sat on a beach in Brighton. Nearby, a group of children of about five years of age were playing and I overheard their conversation. As one boy sat and listened to what some of the others were doing at school I heard him briefly say, *'I'm no good at school because I'm not clever enough'* before he went off and distracted himself by doing something else.

At the age of five how had he begun to make the connection between his current unhappiness in school and his intellectual abilities – *'I'm no good at school because I'm not clever enough'*? Presumably he was making sense of the presenting experience by choosing from his current and limited models of understanding the one that would seem to fit. The consequences of this, one can readily predict; a cycle of limiting beliefs which, if they continued to go unchallenged, would readily harden into learned responses which would begin to shape his everyday experiences. This would result in a low level of self-belief and poor self-concept which would inevitably sink him into a self-fulfilling prophecy.

Teachers encounter this on a daily basis. It may be that they or their colleagues have limiting beliefs about their own professional abilities or their ability to 'handle' a class perceived as difficult. They may believe some groups or individuals to be 'unteachable'. They may encounter students who genuinely believe at that point in time that they are incapable of certain levels of performance. Occasionally they will hear parents comment

– when advised that their child is experiencing difficulty – the immortal words: 'Oh . . . I was no good at this when I was at school either.'

The model below represents a version of the barrier between potential and achievement. It is a model – my own – and hence subject to all the limitations of a modelling approach.

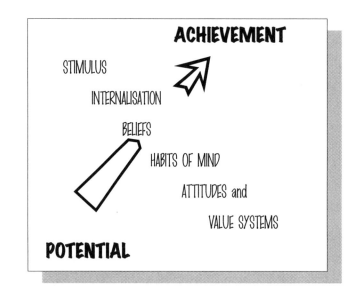

An experience is internalised and made sense of according to the paradigms of understanding available to us at that point in time. This interplay between experience and internalisation generates embryonic beliefs around the experience and can lead to habits of mind where the beliefs harden and begin to alter our subsequent interpretations of similar experience.

Such beliefs may then begin to shape our receptivity to new information. Information which challenges the prevailing belief system may be discounted, ignored or diverted from conscious attention. Information which accords with the prevailing beliefs is affirmed and at an unconscious level we may even begin to notice data which fall within this category. Eventually the dynamic between stimulus and belief system contributes to attitude and value systems.

An example might be an early and frightening experience with swimming (stimulus). Water is equated with fear and hence danger (internalisation) – at some stages in development some limiting beliefs are useful nevertheless! 'Swimming is an experience I should avoid' (belief). 'Seaside holidays are not for me' (habit of mind). 'Our family have never been great ones for swimming' (attitude). 'Swimming is for some and not for others and with our lifestyle we don't need to learn' (value system).

It is insufficient to challenge limiting beliefs without helping towards the motivation to change with strategies to effect the change. A friend who is fearful of heights chose to confront her fear by going on a walking holiday in the Swiss Alps with her children. It took a white knuckle experience on a chairlift to persuade her that motivation was not enough. What she needed was the motivation plus alternative strategies to help replace those which were disabling her and a sense of what success might be like.

In his 1991 book, *Learned Optimism,* Martin Seligman describes how we can work with individuals who are disposed to a pessimistic view about their own abilities and choices in life. Individuals who appear predisposed to limiting beliefs. In his ABCDE approach the AB and C sections refer to how we manage challenge, whilst D and E demonstrates ways of re-framing a pessimistic response into an optimistic response. In other words we can 'learn' optimism from adversity.

A is for Adversity: we encounter a difficult challenge

B is for Beliefs: we untangle our beliefs about the adversity

C is for Consequences: we are aware of the consequences of maintaining those beliefs about the adversity

D is for Disputation: we are encouraged to question those beliefs and seek alternatives

E is for Energisation: we become aware of the positive developments which may arise as a result of a more positive and liberating set of alternative beliefs

Limiting beliefs if unchallenged will:
- impact on performance in the specific area of human activity
- remain in place throughout life
- affect how one interprets everyday experiences
- shape responses to everyday experiences
- lead to 'scotomas' or blind-spots wherein some external stimuli are overlooked, discounted or dismissed
- define the range of new experiences with which one is willing to engage
- be transmitted to others with whom we have influence

For students of any age, limiting beliefs will:
- instil a feeling of learner helplessness
- channel energies into avoidance behaviours
- impact on all-round performance
- lead into a cycle of low motivation and underachievement

To challenge limiting beliefs in students:

◆ recognise that no amount of 'telling' or 'correcting' will work in changing the belief unless the student begins to wish to change

◆ be curious about what the maintenance of that 'limiting belief' does for the student – might its displacement necessitate a compensatory belief? A belief which results in a statement like *'none of the teachers like me'* might allow the owner to justify anti-social behaviour to 'protect' themselves from having to confront the possibility that the teachers may indeed *'like you'* and therefore want to know more about *you* in order to help you

◆ encourage the student to begin with simple re-framing exercises; for example, 'I'm no good at . . .' is challenged with 'What would it be like if you were good at . . .?'

◆ use the ABCDE method described above and,

◆ encourage outcomes thinking: 'if you were to be successful in what, for the moment, you are not yet good at, what would it be like? What do you see yourself doing? What would others see you doing? What would others be saying to you? How would you feel about it?'

◆ encourage distancing from the belief – 'How would you coach others to be good at . . .?' 'What three tips would you give someone who wanted to be good at . . .?'

◆ take the work on distancing further by practising the 'B' movie technique. The student imagines themselves watching a giant screen upon which their previous experience of 'failure' is acted out, then they imagine themselves stepping out from that experience and observing themselves continuing to watch that screen but from a position apart and behind. Now encourage the student to continue to observe themselves watching the screen as this alter-ego is allowed to manipulate the images and change the events which continue to be watched. Images of failure are made grey, dull and small and are replaced by more vibrant, fast-moving and colourful images of success. Encourage the student to 'run' these dramatisations of success again and again whenever the limiting belief begins to make itself felt again.

◆ catch them being successful and let them know it; encourage the student to do the same

◆ change negative self-talk to positive self-talk; change 'I can't' messages to 'I can' messages; 'minus (-) can be changed to plus (+) at a stroke'.

Remember, limiting beliefs are not confined to the students we teach. Examine your own. Are there areas of professional experience where you have limiting beliefs? Are there classes you just cannot teach? Individual students you just cannot get on with? Practical classroom strategies that you know would not work for you? If the answer to any of these is yes, then go back up the checklist and try it out! Once you've done so, consider the experience of one teacher and how her beliefs affected the outcomes of her students directly.

This teacher gave an account of her experience to a 1996 UK Headteacher's Conference, describing in great detail the moment when the direct link between teacher expectation and student performance was made explicit for her.

The teacher, now a Headteacher of a mixed 11–18 comprehensive school in Surrey, England, told of how she had been appointed Deputy Principal of a large community college some five years previously. On appointment she took up duties in the first week of September 1991 and was given a Yr 10 maths set for GCSE examination work. The children in the school were unfamiliar to the new appointee but she was, nevertheless, a little disappointed with the standard of their efforts. She had the second set of five with the setting according to ability. Being a good maths teacher as well as a good role model for other staff, she had high expectations of this set. In her words, they *'seemed to be performing at a lower level'*. She pointed out how they *'complained about the amount of effort she was requiring of them.'* Her teaching was characterised by *'a mixture of the traditional, the innovative and the idiosyncratic.'* She established firm, clearly understood protocols for classroom behaviour, punctuality, attendance and homework. Guidelines were given as to what work was to be done, by when and in what way. Everyone *was* going to pass the final examination and pass well. Good work and individual contributions were constantly praised and celebrated. She even took the eccentric step of betting each and every student a £1 coin that they would pass the term test.

When the department analysed the autumn term test results in December 1991, she was quietly disappointed that her set – set two – were no better than the norm. In the copy of the original graph shown next page you can clearly see the individual grouped scores for each of the five ability sets. Set two is no better and no worse than the pattern formed by the others. Except that. . .

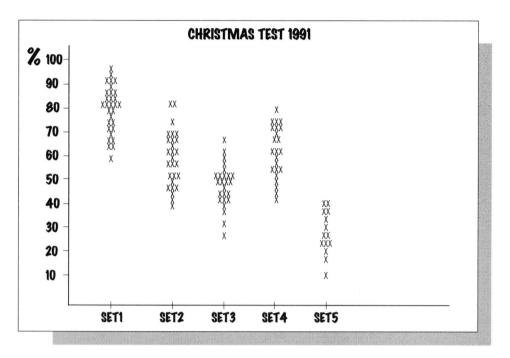

Set 4 performing at same level as Set 2 with high teacher expectation.

. . . in the Autumn term 1991 our newly appointed Deputy Principal did not have set two as she thought. She had set four. This had occurred as a result of some last minute staffing changes over the summer holidays. As a new appointee and part-time member of the maths department, she did not know the students well enough yet to recognise immediately that they were of 'lower ability'! Her expectations were that they were a second set and that they ought to perform as a 'second' set should. If you look at the original graph you can see that they duly obliged. The fact of the setting arrangement was only uncovered when the department sat down to review the results. It was at this point that she was confronted by a dilemma.

Should she adjust her expectations of the group? She had worked them very hard and had put in many, many hours on individual tutoring and support. Perhaps it would be having an adverse effect on their work generally? She resolved not to change her expectations at all. Taking the view that they deserved the best she could provide for them, she resolved to continue the cycle of high expectation and high performance. So the pattern continued: clearly communicated, widely understood protocols about work, responsibility and behaviour; structured, differentiated lessons; regular review; educative feedback; a positive, if relaxed atmosphere. What happened?

As I have said elsewhere, communication is only partly what is said. Much of what is communicated in classrooms is not in the explicit and obvious. Consistency and congruence of response is important. We communicate expectations constantly and we do so with deliberate and conscious intent but also unconsciously and out of our awareness. Despite her best efforts the group performance did slip – a little. According to her own analysis this teacher had 'probably shifted her boundaries back towards a more comfortable place.' The students had duly followed.

The 'Pygmalion principle' is widely known as a theory. Seneca gave us an aphorism which explains it. *'It is part of the cure to be wished to be cured.'* Robert Rosenthal built on the myth of Pygmalion – a man who, according to the myth, so loved a statue he had created that it came to life and responded to him. His 1968 work, *Pygmalion in the Classroom*, demonstrated that in cases where teachers had been advised that control groups were either high performers or of limited ability, they responded differently.

In one research study students who were deemed to be of 'high' potential significantly outscored another group deemed to be of 'low' potential. In actual fact both groups were chosen at random. It was the teachers and their differing expectations which were influencing the final scores.

Rosenthal identified six methods in which we communicate expectations.

    1. The teacher expresses confidence in her ability to help the student
    2. The teacher expresses confidence in the student's ability
    3. Non-verbals are congruent: e.g., tone of voice, eye contact, energy level
    4. Teacher feedback is specific and ample and mentions good and bad
    5. The teacher gives detailed input to the student
    6. The teacher encourages improvement through challenge

Outlined below are five tools for framing positive expectations as a teacher or influencer. Use them for your own professional practice and adapt them for your students to use.

To frame positive expectations teachers should:

◆ Test your assumptions and those of others who are influential in your learning community. For example:

'We will never be able to do anything with . . .' Test the assumption, 'never' by thinking of an instance or circumstance when this was or could be disproved. Ask yourself what would it take to begin to create such conditions. 'Student X always misbehaves in . . .' Test the assumption, 'always' by thinking of an instance or circumstance when this was or could be disproved. What conditions prevail in those circumstances?

Ask yourself what you need to do to begin to create such conditions.

Place a health warning around words like 'never', 'always', 'inevitably', 'constantly', 'without exception', 'bound to', 'hopeless', 'no chance' . . .

◆ Enter into the map of the student or colleague with whom you are working. Do this by re-constructing the experience from their point of view. Ask yourself, in what ways might their perception of the situation differ? How might they be making different sense of the same situation? What choices are available to them given their 'different' map? What priorities emerge as important from their different map? What cultural assumptions are in your map that are not in their theirs?

◆ Use data to set baselines not ceilings. For example, in using test score data to evaluate likely performance in examinations.

◆ Act as if. Some pundits will say, 'fake it till you make it'. Assume that behind every behaviour is some positive intent. To believe otherwise is to make it so.

◆ Make change safe. If you operate on the principle that there is 'no failure only

84

feedback', then it is easier to assume that if a learning experience or a teaching experience goes 'badly' then you can always find ways of improving and extract something positive in the process.

2 HOW FEEDBACK SHAPES PERFORMANCE

“ The English teacher writes down how you could improve it. It gives you an incentive. You want to go home and re-write it so you can upgrade it. ”

YR 11 GIRL, **reported in London Borough of Croydon,**
Pupil Motivation Research, **1996**

IMMEDIATE FEEDBACK IS PART OF ALL LEARNING SITUATIONS except perhaps in school. When children learn to speak they are corrected immediately they make a mistake, they are given the correct alternative and an opportunity to try it out. It is unlikely a parent will wait until the end of the week or the developmental stage to sit the child down and go through the corrections! Yet this often happens in formal education. Educative feedback in the classroom shapes performance. Feedback, in this case, is more than the spoken or written words chosen by the teacher to evaluate a student. To be effective it needs to be immediate.

Both Michel Thomas and Lynn Dhority are world leaders in language teaching. Their methods differ greatly but their attitude to feedback is strikingly similar. Thomas describes teaching almost exclusively in the foreign language as being like *'teaching the unknown in the unknown'* (*The Guardian*, April 29th, 1997). Dhority teaches almost exclusively through the foreign language!

Thomas says, *'What you understand you don't forget'* and for this reason he is hostile to homework, which he associates with boning up phrases for test without understanding them. If a student does not understand what he is trying to teach them at any stage, he takes them back to a point which they do understand and rebuilds the structure from there. According to *The Guardian* newspaper interview he does not *'correct a student's mistake, but brings him back in a way that lets him correct it for himself . . . the student must always be conscious of his own progression.'*

Thomas teaches in large blocks of time. The national curriculum provides 63 hours per year for a foreign language, spread over a year. Thomas works in six week blocks. This, he believes, is *'better for retaining what has been learned from one lesson to the next with no time to forget.'* Dhority teaches languages through an immersion learning environment where the whole experience is orchestrated. He describes his approach to error correction, *'the approach, like other acquisition focused approaches minimises direct correction of student errors in speaking . . . when mistakes occur I may sometimes respond softly, using a positive but correct 'echo' of what the student attempted so that the student is left with an affirmation and a correct model*

85

quietly ringing in his/her ears.' The purpose is not so much error correction but a confidence check and an affirmation. Meaningful dialogue serves the flow of conversation.

The best feedback is immediate, educative, specific and reflective. Immediate, in that it is provided soon enough for the student to act on it whilst still engaged with, or able to engage with, the original learning experience. Educative, in that it points out how to improve and gives the strategies to do so. Specific, in that it relates to that individual and is not a 'smiley face' or a truism or some other such blandishment. Reflective, in that it encourages the student to evaluate the work, consider your suggested improvements and the improved outcome they may lead to and also provides something meaningful for the two of you (or other students) to talk through.

In February 1998 Kings College London published a paper entitled 'Inside the Black Box' which showed evidence from international research of the power of educative feedback or 'formative assessment'. In some cases gains equivalent to two GCSE Grades were cited, dependent on the frequency and nature of feedback given. One piece of research from Israel showed the differing impact of three types measured by learning gain and student interest. With raw scores (for example; 7/10) there was little or no learning gain 'accompanied by positive interest in the scores from high ability students and low or no interest in the scores from low ability students. With raw scores and accompanying comments, again there was little or no learning gain accompanied by positive interest in both the scores and comments from high ability students and low or no interest in the scores and comments from low ability students. With comments alone there was a 30% learning gain accompanied by positive interest in the comments from both high and low ability students.

In many classrooms feedback systems which involve novelty, a physical movement or a gesture provide both light relief and a chance to evaluate your progress and that of the learners. Use creative response systems which are immediate and fun. Examples for students include:

◆ Traffic lights. Have a large poster representing traffic lights visible within the room. Red means not yet understood; amber is some uncertainty or doubt and green fully understood. From time to time check out which colour students are on. Often students — young and old — will sit quietly after being given an explanation or instruction rather than admit they don't understand. Make it safe to admit by making it fun!

◆ Show of hands, with fingers indicating scores. With no fingers meaning 'I don't understand at all' and five meaning 'fully understood', check out how well students have understood by getting them to hold up their scores. Have them explain their score to their neighbour. What would they need to know more about to get a score of five?

◆ Drum rolls. Some new information is more significant than others. For 'absolutely essential, must know and remember', precede your input with a drum roll and a cymbal clash. On their knees, or on the desks if you can suffer the noise, students beat out a drum roll then, together, a clap of hands for a cymbal clash. Do it twice, then in the silence that immediately follows give the key information.

◆ Australian sign language! Glenn Cappelli, an Australian accelerated learning trainer, focuses and directs the attention and interest of his training groups by using methods which include what he calls 'Australian sign language'. 'Thank you' is a touching of the bottom of the chin with the upturned flat of the hand which is then directed at the person who is being thanked. 'That's great' involves standing, moving the arms up and down in turn with index finger pointing skyward whilst wiggling your bum from side to side like Baloo the bear. Daft and slightly surreal, it's also fun and involves everyone.

◆ Devise 5. Work out five possible test questions for this last topic. What is essential to know? Write them down before testing your neighbour on your chosen five questions.

◆ Continuity lines. Stand and position yourself on the continuity line. This end is a maximum rating of ten. The far end is a minimum rating of nought. Position yourself according to how good a speller you think you are, now how good at maths you are, now how good at memorising things you are, now how good at sports you are. Everyone shuffles about realising that we all see ourselves as being good at different things. Try it with specific questions: how confident are you about getting a pass in the mock exam? Now find someone at the other end of the line and ask them what makes them feel confident/unconfident.

Both Thomas' and Dhority's feedback is positive, educative and immediate. Dhority is of the view that homework can too often be conducted in an environment which is antagonistic to 'relaxed alertness'. Often homework is associated with exercises, drill or 'finishing off'. This is confirmed when we read the words of two students whom I interviewed prior to writing this book

> **I was just colouring in things last night for my German homework and it took hours and I thought, I just don't see the point in doing this. We want homework that will help us in the next lesson, not just ticking off units that have to be completed.**

TAMAL, YR 11

> **We want homework that will help us in the next lesson. It should be relevant to the next lesson, not just ticking off units that have to be completed.**

SASHA, Yr 11

Dhority suggests other types of activity as being more useful to reinforce his language learning classes. These include listening activities using taped active and passive concert presentations, some writing activities including transcription, cloze, and also dramatised readings of texts, individually or in pairs. The important pointers emerging here are that homework should be an opportunity to reinforce understanding, perhaps by approaching a known or new problem from a different perspective or using a different problem-solving tool. Homework can also encourage the development of research skills or interviewing skills or inventory skills. It can be posed in terms of a personal challenge or test. When writing schemes of work, ensure that appropriate homework, which balances out over a period of time to help meet all your process and content learning objectives, is at least discussed with colleagues if not specified in the schemes of work themselves.

Other feedback strategies will help take you out of the dependency loop from time to time. Teach students to evaluate themselves and provide the tools for doing so. Ways of doing this include: the use of structured self-assessment templates so that students can evaluate their own work and providing observation checklists for use with oral

work, including homework which has been set as a 'reporting back' project. These work well in hot-seat activities where the observer is actually looking for evidence of different types of verbal and non-verbal communication skills. Other useful strategies are: proforma contracts between student and teacher which can be progressively updated and reviewed and increasing the number of 'teachers' by using older students to mentor younger ones.

Change the ratio of talking to doing from 80% teacher talk and 20% students doing, to 20% teacher talk and 80% of students doing. Adopt a policy of no more than 16 minutes an hour direct instruction supported by:

◆ clarity about the learning outcomes you seek

◆ communicating this to the students

◆ explaining the processes you are going to use and why you are using them

◆ building-in structured review opportunities

◆ maximising purposeful language exchange through structured interaction

◆ freeing yourself to act as coach, mentor and provider of immediate educative feedback

◆ utilising self-review and self-assessment techniques for students

◆ structuring regular opportunities for peer coaching and peer feedback

It's praise that really makes you work.

YR 8 GIRL, REPORTED IN LONDON BOROUGH OF CROYDON, PUPIL MOTIVATION RESEARCH, 1996

Evidence of the power of different types of 'strokes' in influencing behaviour and building self-belief comes from the discipline of Transactional Analysis. The psychologist Eric Berne, known for his work on human interactions and Transactional Analysis, concluded from his own observation of adults in psychological difficulties that stroking is essential for survival. For Berne, a stroke was a 'unit of attention'.

He categorised three different kinds:

1 Verbal or non-verbal. We may speak to someone, shout, cajole, plead with, extol, flatter, clamour. Many of our strokes are non-verbal; for example, nods, smiles and scowls, pats, hugs, smacks.

2 Positive or negative. A positive stroke is one which the receiver experiences as pleasant – normally, also intended as pleasant – examples being: smiles, greetings, verbal approval, praise, appreciation. A negative stroke is one experienced as painful: criticism, blows, refusals, scowls.

Because we need strokes to survive, although we grow more healthily with positive stroking, we will also accept negative stokes on the principle that any stroking is better than none. Some argue, this is one contributory reason as to why children who survive abusive childhoods often in adulthood enter further abusive relationships. This is because painful strokes are familiar and experienced as life-supporting.

3 Conditional or unconditional. A conditional stroke relates to what you do. An unconditional stroke relates to who you are. They may be positive or negative.

Example:

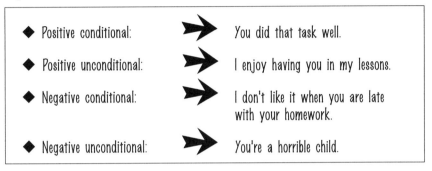

- ◆ Positive conditional: ➡ You did that task well.
- ◆ Positive unconditional: ➡ I enjoy having you in my lessons.
- ◆ Negative conditional: ➡ I don't like it when you are late with your homework.
- ◆ Negative unconditional: ➡ You're a horrible child.

Unconditional stroking is experienced more powerfully than conditional. If we are fortunate, as babies we receive unconditional positive strokes, which become more conditional and mixed with negative as we grow older and need to learn adaptations to our society. Conditional strokes are essential to our learning and growth. As indicated above, we also learn to prefer stokes which are familiar because they are predictable and we know how to respond. Hence we learn what are called 'stroking patterns'.

Plastic strokes. Often we give or receive strokes that look positive but feel negative. These may be lies that we know to be lies; for example, 'if you work hard you've every chance of getting a C grade', said insincerely. At other times, these apparently positive strokes may have a sting in their tail: 'That was a good piece of work but there were three spelling mistakes'. Strokes that are insincere or which contain an implied criticism are called 'plastic' strokes; they look like the real thing, but aren't. However, if we can't get anything better, we will try to exist on such plastic strokes.

Generally, many of us actually receive fewer strokes than we really need, because we have learnt to do without.

Stroke filter. This is a concept devised by Claude Steiner to indicate how, if a stroke doesn't fit in with our preferred 'diet' or is surplus to our mental 'quotient' of strokes, we are likely to ignore or belittle it. We generally 'allow in' and really hear the strokes we expect, or that we believe we deserve. Many people hear all the criticism levelled at them and ignore positive feedback. Others select out only the positive strokes they are willing to accept and reject the rest. We also constantly give ourselves strokes. If we pay attention to the dialogues we carry on internally, we can quickly see whether these are positive or negative. Do you praise and encourage yourself? Or do you criticise everything you do? Generally, we give ourselves the strokes we think we deserve. Many people find that changing their self stroking from negative to positive allows them to change many other things in their lives. This is the accelerated learning strategy of positive affirmation.

Combine positive strokes and directed praise for the best possible feedback. Stroking and praise can differ in intent and in effect. In the accelerated classroom they will complement and build upon each other.

Effective praise

- ◆ is delivered upon recognition of an accomplishment

- ◆ specifies the particulars of the accomplishment

- ◆ shows spontaneity, variety and other signs of credibility; suggests clear attention to the student's accomplishment

- ◆ provides information to students about their competence or the value of their accomplishments

- ◆ rewards attainment of specified performance criteria (which can include effort criteria)

- ◆ orients students towards better appreciation of their own task-related behaviour and thinking about problem-solving

- ◆ uses students' own prior accomplishments as the context for describing present accomplishments

- ◆ is given for noteworthy effort or success at difficult (for this student) tasks

- ◆ attributes success to effort and ability (for this student) implying that similar successes can be expected in the future

- ◆ fosters endogenous attributes (students believe that they expend effort on the task because they enjoy the task and/or want to develop task-relevant skills)

- ◆ focuses students' attention on their own task-relevant behaviour

- ◆ fosters appreciation of, and desirable attributions about, task-relevant behaviour after the process is completed

after Brophy, J., *Teacher Praise: a Functional Analysis*

In classrooms create opportunities for positive, purposeful and educative feedback. Be aware of your own 'stroke' regimes and the filters students use to attract and deflect praise. Use feedback as a tool to encourage students to reflect on their own performance, evaluate it and then speculate on possible improvement.

3 THE SECRETS OF MOTIVATING THROUGH GOALS AND TARGETS

> *Targets need to generate the commitment of those whose job it is to attempt to meet them, be they schools, teachers or pupils.*

MICHAEL BARBER, *The Learning Game - Arguments for an Education Revolution,* **Victor Gollanz**

> *People's beliefs about their abilities have a profound effect on their abilities. Ability is not a fixed property; there is a huge variability in how you perform. People who have a sense of self-efficacy bounce back from failures; they approach things in terms of how to handle them rather than worrying about what can go wrong.*

ALBERT BANDURA, *New York Times,* **May 8th, 1988**

THE SIGNIFICANCE OF EFFECTIVE PERSONAL GOAL SETTING in raising motivation and achievement is regularly underestimated, largely because we don't do it very well.

For a goal to mean anything to a learner – of any age – it must be owned. Some goal-setting activities in schools and colleges are flawed because the goals are not owned. In the worst cases they are institutionalised. Most often they are ritualised rehearsals of what the subordinate party – the student – believes the instigator wants to hear. Dialogue around action planning, target setting and recording of achievement is often arid because the student has not developed an understanding or a belief that changes in behaviour can impact on the outcome they want. Or, if the student does have this faith, then often he or she is unable to articulate it meaningfully because the timescales are too distant or the goal is not specific or he or she does not have a vocabulary to describe it in its fuller implications.

The significance of meaningful goal setting in accelerating learning and thus raising motivation and achievement cannot be emphasised enough. Schools should heed some of the lessons learned through the Stamford marshmallow experiment.

The Stamford marshmallow experiment took place in Stanford University in the 1960s. Psychologist Walter Mischel and his staff were working with four year-olds to establish the extent to which the capacity to defer immediate gratification might influence subsequent educational (and life) successes. To what degree was self-restraint – the deferment of immediate gratification in pursuit of a personal goal – evident at such a tender age? Of the many experiments conducted in a longitudinal survey the simplest and most famous involved 400 four year olds and a large quantity of marshmallows!

> **You can have this marshmallow now, if you wish. Just ring this bell to let me know you've eaten it because I've got to leave for about ten minutes. Or, if you want to have two marshmallows you can. But not until I come back.**

On the filmed footage that follows we can see the torment of the Faustian challenge. One girl immediately sinks the marshmallow left with her, rings the bell and chews with a self-satisfied grin. Others look at the door handle, the window, the wallpaper . . . anything <u>but</u> the marshmallow. Others distract themselves by pulling faces, closing their eyes, talking to themselves. Another, a boy, spends the time, ignoring the marshmallow but staring at his reflection in the bell siting nearby. One boy licks the table all around the marshmallow but resiliently avoids touching the marshmallow itself!

The researchers at Stamford tracked these children throughout their school careers and into early adult life. The results were dramatic. This is how Goleman describes it:

> **The diagnostic power of how this moment of impulse was handled became clear some twelve to fourteen years later, when these same children were tracked down as adolescents. The emotional and social difference between the grab-the marshmallow pre-schoolers and their gratification-delaying peers was dramatic. Those who had resisted temptation at four were now, as adolescents, more socially competent, personally effective, self-assertive, and better able to cope with the frustrations of life. They were less likely to go to pieces, freeze, or regress under stress, or become rattled and disorganised when pressurised; they embraced challenges and pursued them instead of giving up even in the face of difficulties; they were self-reliant and confident, trustworthy and dependable; and they took initiative and plunged into projects. And, more than a decade later, they were still able to delay gratification in pursuit of their goals.**

The true significance of this for students in our schools and colleges is this: the ability to conceptualise an outcome shapes behaviour and thus alters performance. Without the ability to envisage an outcome, students – of any age – become disenfranchised. Clearly not all students have that ability from the earliest years and many live in circumstances where immediacy of gratification is reinforced daily.

Goal setting – outcomes thinking – can, should, <u>must</u>, be taught. From the earliest, schools, working with parents and other influencers, should be explicit in teaching the skills of goal and target setting. The consequences of failing to do so are, again, dramatic:

> **. . . when the children were evaluated again as they were finishing high school, those who had waited patiently at four were far superior as students to those who had acted upon whim. According to their parents' evaluations, they were more academically competent; better able to put their ideas into words, to use and respond to reason, to concentrate, to make plans and follow through on them and more eager to learn . . . At age four, how children do on this test of delay of gratification is twice as powerful a predictor of what their SAT scores will be as is IQ at age four; IQ becomes a stronger predictor of SAT only after children learn to read. This suggests that the ability to delay gratification contributes powerfully to intellectual potential quite apart from IQ itself.**

From the earliest, classroom teachers should encourage their students to set themselves personal performance targets. The purpose of these targets is not to compare with the performance of others but to develop the mind-set of recognising that when we have an outcome in mind, we can act in ways which will impact on the realisation of that outcome. Personal performance targets should be informal first and formal later. They can range across any area of activity where it is agreed that an improvement in performance is desirable. They should be articulated or described in some way beforehand and de-briefed afterwards. They should provide an opportunity for the owner to move out of his or her 'comfort zone' and be recognisable as complete or incomplete within a preconceived time frame.

The activity of setting personal performance targets, whether formal or informal, should be designated as significant by all concerned. The skills of target setting must be transferable beyond the educational context, otherwise what is the point? The skills of target setting and operating towards them should not be assumed.

The five principles of successful target setting summarised and then explained below are as follows:

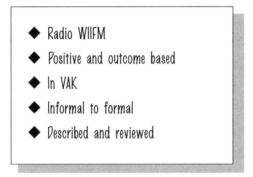

- ◆ Radio WIIFM
- ◆ Positive and outcome based
- ◆ In VAK
- ◆ Informal to formal
- ◆ Described and reviewed

Radio WIIFM is the only frequency on which target setting works. Radio WIIFM stands for Radio 'What's In It For Me?' This is best understood in terms of the brain and its survival and pattern recognition imperatives. It is not meant in a materialistic way. Unless you can connect with an outcome, unless it is something which relates to your current belief system and you can perceive worth in moving towards it, the motivation to behave differently in order to achieve it will be minimal. The challenge for the teacher or the influential 'other' here is to provide an environment and experiences within that environment that allow the individual setting the outcome to see that there are personal benefits in moving out of the comfort zone and into areas of higher challenge and risk.

In order to encourage WIIFM, goal- and target-setting activities should not occur as one-off events, nor should they be exclusively to do with academic performance, be in timescales which are too long, or be separated from other experiences which impact on their likely achievement.

Teachers should model the practices they preach. At the beginning of lessons share your specific positive outcome with your students. Affirm the positive – no more of, 'I hope we're going to behave ourselves today!'

Encourage your students to set themselves informal personal targets at the beginning of the lesson. Have them specify the achievement and visualise the realisation of a successful outcome as they say it. 'By the end of this lesson I will have . . .' There is no need to write these immediate targets down but do give some space for personal review. Personal performance targets can be used in any of the following areas:

> contributions, behaviour, attendance, time on task,
>
> punctuality, academic work, remaining in place when asked,
>
> bringing materials, homework, a specified quantity of work,
>
> specified quality of work, number of new words learned

To extend the activity ask students to work in pairs. Each explains their outcome to the other at the beginning and reviews their achievements at the end. Using the templates at the end of this book and in Section Three we can set performance targets at the beginning of units of work. These can be very specific, related to academic outcomes and written. Similarly we can do the same for academic terms utilising personal performance goal-setting templates.

Outcome-based goals and targets. Insist that the target is outcome based and is positive. Teach the learners that a positive goal or target is more compelling than a negative or avoidance one. Negative goals will not work until they are re-framed into positive. 'I don't want to be so disorganised in maths' is not as powerful as 'I will arrive on time with all I need for the maths lesson'. The former provokes negative images and concomitant feelings of anxiety and helplessness, the latter a positive image of autonomy and success. The former will take the learner nowhere.

VAK. Encourage the student to visualise a successful outcome, hear what is being said as the outcome is successfully achieved and locate the feelings that come with that success.

Visualisation is an important skill in performance improvement at all levels of human endeavour. In goal and target setting encourage and develop visualisation in your students. At the same time exploit the new knowledge from NLP (Neuro Linguistic Programming) and from Wenger's and other research on 'pole-bridging'. Have the students simultaneously affirm their desired outcome visually, auditorally and kinesthetically:

When you have successfully achieved your positive outcome what do you:

◆ see yourself doing? where? when? with whom?
◆ hear yourself saying? what are others saying to you?
◆ feel about your success? how do you feel when you tell others?

Think each response through, describe it to someone else — either imagined or real, your neighbour perhaps. Write down your responses in sequence

This combination of positive affirmation in all three modes works dramatically.

Informal to formal. Move from the informal to the formal and write it down. If we can encourage students and others to utilise goal- and target-setting techniques in everyday, life then we have succeeded in transferring a valuable lifelong skill. Evidence abounds about individuals who set themselves goals and targets along the way to those goals being more successful in 'life' than those who do not or cannot. Evidence cited in Goleman, Harris and others shows that those who consistently write their goals have an even greater performance record of success.

Goleman describes the combination of positive thinking with the ability to conceptualise a positive and personal outcome as 'the master attitude'. He talks about the work of Gary Snyder who, in 1991, worked with students in the US comparing the actual academic achievement of groups who appeared to offer different ways of coping with adversity. The groups he characterised as having 'hope' were those who believed they had both the will and the way to accomplish their goals, whatever those goals happened to be. They invariably out-performed others with equivalent and higher IQ scores and SAT scores.

In order to encourage the use of formal target-setting regimes we need to convince students of its efficacy, develop the skills, operate in realisable timescales, model the practices we espouse and provide the vocabulary for it to work.

We can utilise the types of templates provided for your use in Section Four to formalise the activity. We can also utilise the student action-planner and site target-setting within the reporting and assessment procedures. We also need to provide a meaningful vocabulary to help in the process. Here is a sample target-setting word list. Put it in the back of the school planner.

WORD LIST					
A achievement, action, ambition, application, aspiration,	**D** desire, destination, determination, development, dream, drive,	**G** growth,	**L** lead, learning, long-term, loyalty,	**P** patience, persuade, positive, progress,	**T** time-scale, time-management, trust,
	E encouragement, effort, energy, enthusiasm,	**H** honesty, hope,	**M** measures, motivation,	**R** reliability, responsibility, reward, risk,	**V** vision,
C choice, control, contentment, contribution, consistency, courage, creativity,	**F** faith, feedback,	**I** incentive, independence, inspiration, intention, interest,	**O** outcome,	**S** safety, security, self-discipline, self-knowledge, set-back, short-term, success, support,	**W** want, work,

Described and reviewed. Establish a target-setting regime which allows students to describe the target beforehand, review progress towards it and review its completion afterwards. Help them in understanding the difference between goals, targets and tasks. Essentially, goals are simply expressed, aspirational and longer-term; targets are identifiable and measurable points en route to the goal; tasks are what you have to do to meet these targets. Tasks generated by targets are what are discussed by teacher and student. The goal remains in place and gives a purpose for all other activities. Conversations about targets and tasks are often more purposeful. Issues such as motivation, procrastination, workload, prioritisation and methods of learning are areas where the teacher can give helpful coping strategies.

> At Bracken Hill Primary School, Sheffield every Key Stage 2 student receives their own personal behaviour record book. Children enter merit points given them by their teachers. Points are earned for good effort, kindness, helpfulness, being polite, bringing their PE kit or just coming on time. At the end of each week trophies are awarded for leading class points scorers, but even if a child does not win a trophy, the Headteacher writes to the parents of the top ten scorers in each class. Further to this there is something for everyone, because children who have no 'red writing', are given a bonus playtime. In some weeks they are invited to enter competitions or each is given a small prize. The pupils in Key Stage 1 have class books or individual books using stamps instead of points.

School Improvement Yearbook 1997, **Sheffield City Council**

At Wilberfoss, CE Primary School, York the Yr 5 teacher uses learning logs to reflect on what has been learned, how it was learned and feelings about the learning. Each child keeps a diary of what they have been doing, how they have been doing it and their feelings about perceived progress or lack of progress. The contents provide a point of discussion between students, between students and parents, and with the class teacher.

④ THE INFLUENCE OF TEACHER TALK

It is a two way thing, but we are used all our lives, from junior school on, to it being about us — how we should be; be like this, be like that. Why can't you be more like Gloria? But I am Andrea not Gloria.

Student quoted in *Schools Speak for Themselves*, 1996

Question in KS2 SAT Test. *'Describe how you would separate salt and water.'* **Student's answer.** *'Well first I would sit everyone down and have a nice cup of tea . . .'*

IN HUMAN COMMUNICATION the poet W.B. Yeats' assertion that 'words alone are certain good' needs to be questioned. A teacher's ability to communicate effectively depends on more than careful choice of words. Students in classrooms know what sort of mood their teacher is in as soon as he or she walks in the door! On the basis of an immediate judgement they will evaluate their teacher's state of mind and hence their likely experience over the coming lesson without a word being said. Similarly, the carefully chosen words of novice teachers or teachers who lack experience or who lack self-confidence can be betrayed by tone of voice and body language.

As teachers we influence not only by what we say but also by how we say it and what we do as we say it. It is possible that our positive and supportive words which confidently predict success for a student are contradicted by the conflicting cues which accompany it. It may be that our expectations are being communicated outside our conscious awareness.

Classic research by Professor Albert Mehrabian – a man who never heard of the Spice Girls – at the UCLA in 1971 pointed out that the words chosen and used constituted only 7% of any communication.

What do you really want?
What **do** you really want?
What do **you** really want?
What do you **really** want?
What do you really **want?**

The tone of voice accounted for 38% and the non-verbal accompaniment 55%. Based on these figures, 93% of the communication taking place between teacher and student in classrooms is independent of what is being said! This would suggest that not only do those words which provide 7% of the overall communication need to be chosen carefully but they also need to be accompanied by consistent and congruent tonal and non-verbal cues.

Years after the event you may remember a teacher who taught you, not so much for what they said, but for how they said it and what they often did as they said it. I can see and hear the Physics teacher who, on Tuesdays and Thursdays, led the Army Cadets after school. On those days he, and those others in the cadets, would appear in full uniform. In his case, it meant a Black Watch tartan kilt with a sporran and full regalia. As he conducted his lesson on the laws of thermodynamics or the Brownian motion, he would sway backwards and forwards with his sporran, partly hidden by lab coat, lapping between his legs. At the same time his high pitched Highland voice would modulate between a squeak and a squeal as he tried to win the attention of the students at the back of the room. I cannot remember anything he said in those two years I spent with him but I can see him standing with thumbs in lapels and hear the rise and fall of his voice.

When words and non-verbals reinforce each other, there is congruence and attention is directed to a congruent message. Where there is a perceived discrepancy, then attention will focus on the source of the discrepancy: often the non-verbal cues. What can be done? What ought to be done? This is, after all, part of the natural richness of human interaction.

A positive personal state of mind is reflected in our non-verbal communication, particularly voice tone and body posture. Try visualising a positive, happy personal experience whilst simultaneously adopting a hunched body posture and a frowning expression and you will see what I mean. To adopt a positive state of mind, adopt the re-framing, anchoring and affirmation techniques described elsewhere in this book. If you are about to confront your most challenging class and your most challenging student, use these techniques: anchor a positive teaching experience beforehand and, if all else fails, visualise the most difficult student standing in front of you dressed only in a tutu. This usually has some effect!

In using language be flexible and aware of the impact from the recipient's point of view. Adjust the register of the vocabulary one uses for groups of different ages.

Limit the number of subordinate clauses. Limit the length of sentences. Most adults have difficulty following sentences of twenty words or more, particularly with subordinate clauses, and other, similarly complex, structures. The last sentence, for example, has twenty words and would be difficult for a younger learner to listen to and make sense of immediately, whereas this sentence has only thirty-one words.

Avoid turning instructions into questions: example, 'Are we going to get started then?' Do not give a subsequent instruction until the first has been understood and is capable of being acted on.

Wherever possible acquaint yourself with the sorts of terms that are used in examination questions and build them into your everyday classroom dialogue. Explain them as you use them and use them in different contexts. Encourage the students to do the same and encourage them to spot these words being used. Put these words listed alphabetically in the back of your Yr 10 and Yr 11 planners. Typical words which might confuse include:

account for analyse appropriate assess	define, delimit demonstrate determine describe, discuss distinguish	give an account of guidelines	justify	outline	relate review show how
	establish evaluate explain				synthesise state summarise
calculate clarify combine, criticise comment on compare and contrast compose, compute	formulate	illustrate illustrate by example interpret	list		trace translate

In some cases students who know the answer to the problem are confused by the language of the question, particularly if it is hidden within an unfamiliar case study or scenario.

Be aware of the benefit of utilising language across the three sensory modalities – visual, auditory and kinesthetic – in order to enrich your input and improve the opportunities for all learners to access the information readily. Ensure that the key learning points are repeated at least three times and signify their importance by the 'feedback and feed-to' methods described earlier.

Our use of language carries explicit and implicit meaning. When we listen we actively select what we want to hear and sometimes this operates at a deeper level.

In a meeting the colleague who starts a sentence 'I don't want this to sound like a criticism but . . .' primes us for the criticism which inevitably follows. An awareness of the embedded commands which lie within the language we use helps in a professional role as a teacher to influence the behaviours of those learners with whom we seek to communicate.

Many years ago a friend began his teaching career at a well known public school in the south-west of England. At the time the school, which had been in existence for over two hundred years, was adding new buildings and extending the grounds. An annexe with a flat roof was constructed and was about to be used for the first time the following term. The managers of the school decided that some new rules about movement around the school were needed. One such rule, 'no student is allowed on the annexe roof' was added to others on the growing list. In over two hundred years the school had never had any student on any roof. Within a fortnight of the new term beginning, and the new rules being introduced, two pupils were caught on the roof! The embedded command within the guidance 'don't go on the roof' is 'go on the roof'!

Schools are abundant in embedded commands: 'No running in the science corridor', 'no eating in the arts block', 'no talking in assembly'. With large numbers of students moving around confined spaces, such rules are designed to provide safe and fair conditions for working in but they also go some way to undermining the very behaviours they seek.

The principle here is describe the outcomes you want and not the outcomes you don't want. In classes describe the learning and behaviour outcomes you expect. Be specific and reinforce with praise when you get the outcomes. Encourage learners to do the same. When two students are sitting next to each other and one is openly disruptive it is usually that behaviour which gets the teacher's attention.

> **Teachers never pay attention to those who are doing well, only those who are making a noise.**

Yr 11 student, Bristol School

Reinforce the positive by acknowledging the good efforts of the other student in maintaining self-discipline despite the disruption.

Separate the person from the behaviour by describing it and its effects directly to the disruptive student, stating how you feel about it and then requesting a specific change before asking the student how he or she feels about your request.

A five stage 'I' message for dealing with problem behaviour starts with a positive recognition, then:

stage one: describe the problematic behaviour, 'when you . . .'

stage two: describe the effects of the behaviour

stage three: state how it makes you 'feel'

stage four: describe the behaviour you want

stage five: ask the person how they feel about your request

The person is not the problem. It is the behaviour which is the problem. The same person will behave differently in different contexts and may behave differently at different times with the same teacher. Remind them of this when you deal with the behaviour.

Again, the choice of language can help calm such potentially volatile situations. 'When you begin to behave properly then . . .' The underlying presuppositions are that the individual is capable of behaving properly, can choose to behave properly and will do so when the correct conditions prevail. In charged situations it is important not to mix messages: telling and discussing are different – so do one or other but not both together! School and class rules should be few in number, specific, agreed with all concerned, widely understood and provide opportunities for finding, recognising and promoting positive behaviour.

Teachers should use strategies to influence and to involve the learners in managing their own involvement. The more choice an instruction implies, the more involved the learner becomes in following the instruction. Here a continuum operates:

◆ **Hope:** Assumes that the learner will work out what you want and comply. The request is never made, nor is it talked around. Since the learner doesn't know about it, there is no perceived choice with this strategy. Sometimes low self-confidence, limiting beliefs about oneself or about the learners leads us into this cul-de-sac.

◆ **Imply:** The literal request is never made, it is talked around. Minimal perceived choice. 'Memory maps are good for revision.'

◆ **Suggest:** The request is made in a way which emphasises preferred options. Here there is strong perceived choice. 'You might like to use memory mapping for your revision.' 'Are you considering an alternative note-taking method?'

◆ **Ask:** Here the request is made in a polite way that encourages one to follow. There is moderate perceived choice in this method. 'Would you please use memory mapping for your revision?'

◆ **Tell:** To simply give them a directed statement in an expectant tone, they have minimal perceived choice, they are strongly encouraged to do it. 'Using memory mapping, revise the following topics.'

◆ **Demand/Threaten:** Minimal or no perceived choice. 'Do this revision work now or you are not allowed back in my lessons!'

◆ **Force:** The strongest way of asserting changes in behaviour is physical authority, physical presence or extreme coercion. No perceived choice. Unacceptable unless there is an emergency.

> **Q.** *What is the finest weight-loss programme currently in use?*
> **A.** *The school reunion.*

IF YOU HAVE EVER BEEN TO A SCHOOL OR COLLEGE REUNION you may have overheard the sort of conversation where a favourite teacher's attributes were described in elaborate detail. Sometimes a large group will argue over who was the teacher's 'pet', with everyone in that group convinced it was them. Each arguing their own case, some openly, all secretly. It is frightening to think of the lifelong influence teachers have. What power! Twenty years after the event a dozen sophisticated adults all believing that they were the teacher's favourite. All benefiting from the positive self-belief that one individual teacher was able to build and sustain all those years ago.

When one asks teachers to describe a teacher who positively influenced them, the results show startling conformity. It is the teacher who shared her enthusiasms and let you into her life a little. The teacher who, despite what others said, believed in you and let you know it. The teacher who made it safe for you to try it out. The teacher whose eccentricity was compensated for by his passion for the subject. In every case you believe that the teacher knew who you were and took an interest in you. In every case the teacher's classroom was safe and fair.

Stanley Coopersmith's book, *The Antecedents of Self-Esteem,* attempts to distil his lifetime's work on the subject into characterising the essentials of positive self-esteem. The results of his work provide pointers to what we should do in classrooms in order to accelerate performance.

Coopersmith studied 1,700 children and their families in an attempt to discern what family conditions promoted positive self-image. He found that there were three critical elements:

 They came from backgrounds where they experienced the kind of love that expresses concern, respect and acceptance.

 In the domestic home parenting was characterised by clearly defined limits, standards and expectations and, as a result, children felt secure.

 There was a high degree of involvement in decision-making and discussion. Children were encouraged to articulate their own ideas and opinions without fear of outright rejection or dismissal.

In a learning environment the following factors which correspond to Coopersmith's findings are essential for positive self-esteem and accelerating learning.

◆ an overriding sense that the student is part of the group and their contribution, whatever its nature, is valued – they feel **belonging**

◆ students are encouraged to set and work towards their own achievable goals and reflect on their progress as they do so – they are working to their **aspirations**

◆ the classroom and the learning environment are safe havens for learning where there is consistency in expectations and standards – they experience **safety**

◆ a realistic level of self-knowledge is supported by the belief that individuality is not threatened by undue pressure to conform – their **identity** and individuality are recognised

◆ mistakes are valuable learning tools in an environment where one can take risks and achievement is valued – the learner achieves **success**

> I liked the BASIS approach and I remember the comments on safety – hence writing frames, which I use a lot, are being disseminated across the curriculum and are already being used in Science and English.

MANDY REDDICK, ENGLISH TEACHER

At a practical level, little or no lasting learning will take place unless there is a positive and purposeful learning environment where both teacher and student believe in what they are doing and what they are capable of achieving.

BELONGING

> The process of being consulted, having one's opinions seriously considered, feeling that one's contributions are valued and that they may well result in change for the better are all powerful builders of morale, confidence and commitment.

HMI, *EFFECTIVE PRIMARY SCHOOLS*, 1989

To feel approved of and respected by others, particularly in relationships which are regarded as significant, is what is understood by belonging. Students with a sense of belonging feel as though they are part of a group which is of importance to them. They feel recognised and acknowledged. In such groupings they can experience the importance of trust, loyalty and consistency.

Richard Whitfield, in a paper entitled 'Human Attachment as the Bedrock of Mentalising and Civility', speculated that 50% of school-age children in the UK do not know they are unconditionally loved. If they do not get a sense of being loved – of belonging in the home – and they do not get it in school, then it will be sought out on the streets. If one looks at the psychological profile of gangs – how they are formed, recruit members and maintain themselves – then we can see the significance of the need to 'belong'.

The need to belong and its effect on performance has long been recognised by marketing strategists. During the last war, mothers were lectured about the need to feed their babies on orange juice. The combination of radio lectures and pamphleteering yielded poor results. Very few were using the orange juice. When groups of young mothers were brought together to discuss the problem with a doctor present on some occasions as a source of information, the group very quickly took up and continued to use the product. The facts had become their facts and the decision their decision, not someone else's. The sense of belonging had changed their level of performance.

Students with limited skills in this area experience difficulty in making and keeping friends, are often shy, attach their affections inappropriately, seem isolated and can be insensitive to the emotions and needs of others. Such students are seldom comfortable in groups. They may be very reticent to contribute to group discussion. They may seem to be on the periphery of class activity. Often they will make highly dependent and inappropriate emotional attachments. Their reticence can lead to underachievement where they exclude themselves from taking risks for fear of rejection.

Build a sense of belonging at school level by:

◆ interviewing all new students on arrival (say Yr 7) as part of a personal and social education programme and record the outcomes on video. This method is used by Mallet Lambert School, Hull. The school visits local partner primary schools and conducts interviews with the Yr 6 pupils. The video outcomes are then used for subsequent review and action planning

◆ encouraging a variety of inclusive group activities, some of which are non-competitive – e.g., field trips, form assemblies, form groups responsible for an area of the school or a visual display in a public space on a given theme

◆ monitoring instances of authorised and unauthorised absence and follow-up by interviewing individuals with recurrent patterns of absences

◆ using mentoring schemes with senior students or outside organisations such as Education Business Partnerships or Compact

◆ constructing student satisfaction surveys and involving students in the design, collection and analysis of questionnaires and completion of interviews

◆ providing a separate induction day for new students on day one of the new term

◆ mounting photographs in 'communal' spaces with a biographical pen portrait; every student in the school to have their photograph up by the end of the first term

Build a sense of belonging with parents by:

◆ using parents' newsletters termly to report activities in school; use the newsletter to explain the positive behaviour strategies used by the school with considered, practical suggestions as to how the same principles could be modelled at home

◆ encouraging parent volunteers in the classroom

◆ encouraging parents and children to read together; schools can support parents by providing some guidelines for helping with reading

◆ establishing a homework hotline – St George School, Bristol, has devised a telephone hotline to help parents find out what homework has been set for their child. The project, part funded by the DFE, allows the school to collect the homework set by each teacher each day and record it onto a telephone answering service. Parents can phone through and, by using their own telephone keypad, find out the specific homework set for their child

Don't worry about homework, the teacher will help and explain what you have to do. Homework is fun, the only bad thing about homework is that your mum and dad and even gran can ring the homework hotline to check what you have to do.

AMY HANSON, YR 7, ST GEORGE SCHOOL

◆ setting up a parents' library – a resource base of materials which could include books to read with children, ideas for building and maintaining positive self-esteem in children

◆ seeking parents' opinions – classroom teachers or form tutors can help with a parental satisfaction telephone survey by using a standard proforma and an agreed method of randomly selecting parents to call to discuss what the school can do better

◆ organising parental visits. These may be difficult for some parents without access to creche or baby-sitting facilities. Older secondary students, working under supervision with qualified adults may overcome this barrier for those key parents' evenings during the year

◆ offering parent guidelines in ways to promote positive self-esteem in their children

Build a sense of belonging at classroom level by:

◆ using a variety of individual, pair and group activities

◆ ensuring that every student has the opportunity to work with every other student by the end of the first term

◆ using circle time which allows learners to talk safely and candidly about things which help or hinder their learning (see p.159) and applying the principles which it promotes

◆ monitoring your distribution of attention – who gets it and for what? Be aware that boys put up their hands an average of four times more than girls, in science lessons it is twelve times and in languages three times!

◆ structuring positive feedback opportunities between students into your lessons; use, for example, strategies such as 'Australian sign language' and 'each one teach one'

◆ providing opportunities to increase awareness of classmates' families, background and interests; in primary schools use, for example, 'the getting to know you wheel' and the 'class discovery book'

As a parent you can build your child's sense of belonging by:

◆ for parents of younger children – shadowing your child – an opportunity to follow a son or daughter over the course of the day

◆ making a strength collage which reminds your child of all his or her strengths

◆ using the examples of positive behaviour management templates provided in this book

◆ creating 'together time' with your child as an opportunity to spend time doing things of joint interest and sticking to it!

◆ teaching your child that who we are and what we do are different things and that we can choose our behaviours at any time

◆ encouraging the writing down and discussion of goals; what would their successful achievement involve?

◆ reviewing the home rules from time to time; in what way are they similar or dissimilar to school rules?

ASPIRATIONS

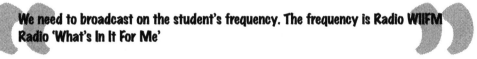

We need to broadcast on the student's frequency. The frequency is Radio WIIFM Radio 'What's In It For Me'

B. DE PORTER, *Quantum Learning*, Piaktus Press

Many students in schools and colleges will come from homes and communities where there may be a lack of positive role models. It may be that no one they know has ever gone into further or higher education. There may be three generations within the immediate and extended family who have never experienced full-time employment. Family circumstances may have made it difficult to think beyond the immediate needs of survival. Day-to-day existence in the home may be characterised by uncertainty in relations, lack of clarity about protocols such as meal- and bed-times and who takes responsibility for what. There may also be an unresolved atmosphere of tension and stress which flares up when difficulties arise.

In these circumstances immediate gratification may be the norm. The capacity to defer immediate gratification by working towards an outcome may be a skill which, never having been nurtured, has never been learned. In some circumstances, deferred gratification may constitute a risk strategy which the limited means of the household doesn't permit. The consequence, for some learners, is that they will never have observed it in their immediate environment.

The Coleman Report was a comprehensive investigation into education in the US. It concluded that student attitudes regarding their effectiveness were the most significant determinant of whether they failed or succeeded in the classroom – more significant than academic performance, class size, yearly expenditure per student or level of teacher preparation.

If, as Robert Reasoner observes, *'the key to self-motivation and purposeful behaviour is to help children internalise goals for themselves and to work towards their attainment'*, then this is a set of skills which will have to be modelled within the school in addition to being explicitly taught and formally and informally reinforced.

A learner needs to believe that learning has some purpose. A lack of aspiration leads into a downward spiral of negativity. Aspirations provide motivation and a feeling of purpose about life. Learners with aspirations can set realistic and achievable goals and take responsibility for the consequences of decisions relating to those aspirations. They are more independent and, in Maslow's term, *'self-actualising'*.

Learners who are unable to work towards meaningful goals often lack self-empowerment and appear aimless. Unable to see alternatives or constructive solutions they will often be over-dependent on others, be attention-seeking or manipulative. They may be unwilling or even unable, to acknowledge the consequences of their own actions.

Build aspirations at school level by:

◆ constantly affirming the positive!

◆ using role-models from the school and local community to promote positive views about what can be achieved – link up with local sports teams to help with speakers

◆ 50% of respondents in the Keele University 'Attitudes to School' survey said in their school, students made fun of the hard workers: work hard to create an 'it's cool to be keener' culture

◆ giving regular information on progression routes in a planned, systematic way

◆ building-in the use of personal performance targets as part of lessons from the earliest

◆ utilising the school planner to provide space for recording personal goals and targets, making sure that it has a reading age within the capability of the students who use it

◆ formalising target setting to build upon the personal performance work done in classes and teaching the skills and lifelong benefits of target setting

◆ using daily spaces in the school planner for positive affirmations

◆ setting up further and higher education visits in Yr 10

◆ equipping students with the vocabulary to articulate feelings about motivation, performance, behaviour: put the goal-setter's vocabulary list in the school planner

106

◆ involving parents and/or other adults in goal setting

Build aspirations with parents by:

◆ writing to them early and in a lively and engaging way to emphasise the crucial role their expectations and support will have in their child's success

◆ specifying targets for parental involvement in the school development plan

◆ on parents' evenings, providing a small feedback card on which they can confidentially write a concern for their child on one side and a hope on the other. Collect the cards from parents as they leave and you have some customer feedback

◆ providing an outline of school work experience activities and invitations to careers events

◆ communicating school activities and school successes via a regular newsletter

◆ including details of the successes of former students in the newsletter

◆ encouraging active support for school industry days and similar events

◆ ensuring senior staff are always represented at parents' meetings

◆ providing feedback and comments on work via the student planner

Build aspirations at classroom level by:

◆ utilising formal and informal goal- and target-setting strategies

◆ providing the BIG picture not only about the subject and your teaching but also about progression routes and career opportunities

◆ connecting the learning and showing relevance by using contemporary examples, metaphors and case-studies that relate to the student's world

In business studies GCSE I always use case studies that are age-appropriate so rather than Marks and Spencer and Woolies, which everyone writes about, I use Virgin, Our Price and HMV. They're in there every Saturday so it means something.

GED CASEY, BUSINESS STUDIES TEACHER

◆ reinforcing the positive by catching limiting self-talk and helping re-frame it – turn 'I cant's' into 'I cans'

◆ modelling positive behaviours yourself! Have high expectations of what you will do for those students at all times: stop yourself now and again and ask yourself are they high enough?

◆ involving former students in informal inputs on what they have done and are doing now

◆ posting positive affirmations by role models around the room

107

As a parent you can build your child's aspirations by:

- ◆ having high expectations yourself

- ◆ talking over possibilities and choices regarding school options and links to careers or further qualifications

- ◆ sitting down with your child now and again and reminding yourself of all the things that he or she is good at, no matter how modest, and then listing as many jobs that need people with those qualities

- ◆ encourage your child to set targets which are readily achievable – school or home – and celebrating their achievement to show that attitude can help success

- ◆ encouraging thinking about longer term goals and encouraging your child to describe what successfully achieving them would be like

- ◆ assigning meaningful duties to each family member to encourage a sense of responsibility

- ◆ helping your child with a daily schedule and helping him or her create 'A' time – which is their priority time – for significant obligations including homework

- ◆ giving your child practice in making decisions with implications

SAFETY

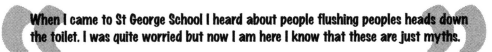

When I came to St George School I heard about people flushing peoples heads down the toilet. I was quite worried but now I am here I know that these are just myths.

TANYA LACEY, Yr 7

According to research with adolescents in England and Wales conducted by the Equal Opportunities Commission and MORI, 64% of respondents indicated that verbal bullying – the psychological intimidation of being made to feel different or excluded or solitary – was feared more than physical bullying.

A feeling of safety or security involves a strong sense of certainty. It can be defined as 'feeling comfortable and safe within the group, where the expectations and ground rules are known and accepted.' Students who feel safe can take risks. Safe environments have clear practices and generally understood roles and responsibilities. Safety also includes the assurance that basic comfort needs will be met.

Evidence of learner insecurity can be seen when students avoid lessons, situations within lessons or show disproportionate discomfort with new experiences. Distrust, challenges to authority, insecurity around friendships and over-reliance on particular classmates are also indicative of excessive personal anxiety.

Build safety at school level by:

◆ soliciting and listening to the views of students instigating a positive behaviour programme and a systematic scheme of rewards and applying them consistently

◆ establishing a 'buddy' system where older students mentor younger students such as that at The Castle School, Taunton, where Yr 10 mentor Yr 7

◆ monitoring instances of bullying and taking affirmative action to prevent them

◆ actively involving students in school council activities and acting on their contributions

> We have a school council twice a term. I am a rep, but no one ever tells us any problems and they never listen anyway ... being heard would make a difference.

YR 11 STUDENT, BRISTOL SCHOOL

> Yeah, they only do things when the Governors come around, or if they recommend something, not if we the pupils recommend it.

YR 8 STUDENT, BRISTOL SCHOOL

◆ ensuring that all students experience trust-building activities and similar work as part of PSHE

◆ publishing a primary liaison newsletter like the one written by Yr 7 students at St George School. It is sent to Yr 5 and 6 students in partner primary schools. It seeks to reassure the students that life in secondary school is safe and uncomplicated. It disabuses the younger students of some of the myths about the larger school which may have been causing them stress and anxiety

◆ paying attention to basic hygiene needs

> The toilet doors are very low so that people can see you ... Please make the toilets higher. It would make you in a better mood and not so angry about doing your work.

YR 5 GIRL, REPORTED IN LONDON BOROUGH OF CROYDON, PUPIL MOTIVATION RESEARCH, 1996

◆ declaring the school a 'No Put Down Zone' and posting reminders in every classroom

◆ installing a behaviour and rewards policy which is consistently applied and on which students have been consulted

◆ creating a positive ethos. Byron Wood Primary School, Sheffield made the creation of a positive ethos their priority for 1994/96 –

> a great deal of time and effort was put into developing a whole school Behaviour Policy. It was implemented in the September and has become a key factor in encouraging the positive and stable ethos of the school. Now that this is well established and the

majority of the children's self-esteem has been raised, it is possible to concentrate more on the National Curriculum and the raising of academic standards.

BYRON WOOD PRIMARY SCHOOL, SHEFFIELD

◆ developing staff awareness of positive reinforcement techniques

Build a sense of safety with parents by:

◆ communicating school policy on behaviour and attendance issues clearly and early

◆ establishing a school–home 'contract' where the school describes what it sees as its role and its responsibilities and describes what is expected of students and what would help from parents

◆ building-in a structured programme of assertiveness training as part of the Personal and Social Education programme, describing in detail how it works, what it contains and how it can be practised at home

◆ using circle time, peer mediation or 'no blame strategies' to reduce incidents of bullying and create a more supportive and open ethos

◆ building-in a structured programme of collaborative and team problem-solving as part of the Personal and Social Education programme

◆ encouraging positive non-judgemental attitudes to counselling amongst staff

Build a sense of safety at classroom level by:

◆ using trust building activities

◆ actively seeking an environment of trust, openness and honesty where interpersonal issues which may impair learning can be addressed directly by all concerned

◆ making it safe to get something wrong by emphasising that learning is often messy, creating frequent feedback loops, showing how we need feedback otherwise we don't progress

◆ marking work educatively

◆ applying class and school rules fairly and consistently

◆ seeing your students and getting to know them in different contexts

◆ avoiding put-downs, sarcasm, name-calling

◆ reinforcing positive behaviours by deliberately praising them

◆ anticipating disruption, deal with it immediately or signalling when and how it will be dealt with, calming by separating the problem behaviour from the person

As a parent you can build your child's sense of safety by:

◆ positive reinforcement about what the school and you will do together to help your child progress

◆ being open about success and failure and evaluating both non-judgementally

◆ participating in school open and consultation evenings

◆ reminding yourself that your child is more than his or her academic achievements and that we provide support at home to help him or her realise that potential in life and academic success is only a part of that process

IDENTITY

> The reality is that the quality of life does not depend on what others think of us and what we own. The bottom line is, rather, how we feel about ourselves and what happens to us. To improve life we must improve the quality of experience.

MIHALY CSIKSZENTMILHALYI, *Flow: The Psychology of Optimal Experience*, Harper Collins Publishers

In May of 1996 *The Guardian* newspaper carried an article written by a middle-aged Headteacher of an English primary school. In the article she described how she and her twin-sister had both sat the 11-plus exam for entrance to grammar school. She passed, her sister failed and from that point their lives adopted separate directions. She became the 'clever one' and her sister the 'pretty one'. She went on to a higher education course, whilst her sister left school at 16. She entered a profession, her sister married early and had children. Her children went on to higher education, her sister's children entered trade apprenticeships. The author made no judgement about what was better but there was a strong sense of bitterness that this 'rite of passage' should have, in her words, caused their 'lives to separate forever'. The impact of how we feel and how we are made to feel about ourselves shapes experience and becomes our sense of identity.

Identity includes the acquisition of accurate self-knowledge in terms of roles, relationships and attributes to foster a feeling of uniqueness.

'A well defined sense of self and identity provides us with effective strategies for managing psychological stress – the major stress in our society' (David Elkind). Evidence of weak identity can be seen when the learner is unduly sensitive to criticism, resists participating in any activity in which they risk failure and is unduly anxious to please. Often they will be awkward with praise, either refuting it when offered or becoming embarrassed or being unable to see it in themselves.

Learners with a strong sense of identity are less likely to experience the counter-productive consequences of negative stress. A strong sense of identity means that the learner has knowledge of their own strengths and weaknesses, values and beliefs. They have an 'inner-resilience' which makes them less susceptible to becoming disillusioned and self-doubting. They achieve more.

Build a sense of identity at school level by:

◆ promoting and acclaiming individual and team successes across a wide range of academic and non-academic achievements

111

◆ developing regular one-to-one reviews and individual action planning

◆ using non-uniform, fancy dress days, sponsored activities and similar events with a social dimension to allow students and staff to participate together

◆ in art, using a montage about 'me', frame and display the outcomes (STEWARDS SCHOOL, HARLOW)

◆ encouraging individuals to take on responsibilities within the school

◆ enthusing staff to model the sorts of positive attitudes and behaviours you seek to support

Build a sense of identity with parents by:

◆ ensuring that staff know who the student is on consultation evenings! Provide sets of photographs if necessary and brief staff beforehand

◆ giving enough time during consultation evenings for parents to share concerns and anxieties and also some of their positive feelings about their child; encourage this amongst staff

◆ turning consultation evenings from exclusively retrospective events to prospective by involving them in target-setting activities

Build a sense of identity at a classroom level by:

◆ knowing the names of all the students you teach

◆ using the names as you ask questions or invite contributions

◆ finding something unique and positive about every student and letting them know it

◆ sharing your outside interests and enthusiasms and take an interest in those of your students

◆ practising changing negative messages as a class activity

◆ using positive role-model posters and discussing what it is or was about that person which makes them special

◆ developing a vocabulary and agreed principles for constructive feedback between students

◆ exploring the concepts surrounding identity using collage, time-lines, autobiography, scrap books

◆ providing opportunities – especially for boys – to express emotions and develop an affective vocabulary

As a parent you can build your child's identity by:

◆ giving your child specific and positive feedback, saying what it is he or she has done that has pleased you and what you like about him or her

◆ making sure you use at least four positive strokes for every negative you give your child

◆ ensuring that fathers find quality 'together' time with sons. Steve Biddulph, an Australian family therapist, presented a paper at a teacher's conference in

June 1997 which claimed that men who spend more than 55 hours per week at work could be contributing to their sons' behaviour problems. He said that although boys raised by single mothers were most at risk of taking on inappropriate role models, those from two parent homes also suffered where their father opted out of parenting. He said that fathers should read with their sons and engage in play fighting with them. He went on to claim that under-fathered boys could easily be recognised at school because they are not sure of their own masculinity, they have an aggressive style of relating, acting tough or swearing

◆ teaching your child to disarm negative messages by re-framing or replacing with positives: 'maybe I am short but I'm also clever', 'well if I was upset in class there's nothing wrong with having feelings'

◆ helping your child build a well-balanced self-view by listening to the way he or she responds to questions like, 'If you could change just one thing about yourself, what would it be?' Balance out the limiting self-belief with countering positive beliefs

◆ sharing family photo albums

◆ discussing family autobiographies

◆ creating 'no put-down zones'– spaces in the home where no one is allowed to talk disparagingly of any other family member; point out the put-downs

◆ employing feedback rules: earned, immediate, specific, individual, repeated

◆ learning positive self-talk to turn the negative messages that run in our heads into positive ones

◆ using this checklist with your children to help them stay cool

---

Why be angry? Ten tips for keeping cool . . .

1 remember no one can make you feel angry; you are the only person who controls your mind; you can choose to be calm

2 imagine yourself in the calmest, happiest place on earth; notice what it's like being there

3 take the inner-voice which is going over and over what is annoying you and reverse it; for example, if someone has said hurtful things to you and you are repeating them in your head try 'reversing' them so they carry the opposite meaning

4 remove yourself from whatever or whoever is making you angry

5 close your eyes and imagine the other person dressed as a clown, a frog, a muppet character or anything which makes 'them' look silly

6 take whatever the other person has said to you and repeat it in as silly a voice as you can manage; repeat it five times then ask yourself, 'is it really so important or is it silly?'

7 use an 'I' message to tell the other person how you feel and what you want them to do in future: 'when you . . ., I feel . . ., in the future I would like you to . . ., how do you feel . . ?

8 try to look at it from the other person's point of view; think of three good reasons why they might have behaved in the way they did

9 do some physical exercise

10 breath deeply and count slowly as you exhale; repeat

113

SUCCESS

" I love getting a sticker. If I get five stickers my mum gives me a treat. "

YR 5 GIRL, REPORTED IN LONDON BOROUGH OF CROYDON, PUPIL MOTIVATION RESEARCH, BRMB INTERNATIONAL, 1996

Regular and positive affirmations of success – however large or small – reinforce the belief that the learner has control over his or her own life. It helps prevent 'mental drop-out' and it attunes the positive potential of learners. The presence of 'success' in learners is characterised by a 'feeling of accomplishment in areas regarded as valuable or important.' These learners will also have an awareness of their own strengths and be able to place any limitations in context.

Students who feel good about themselves and their abilities are the ones who are most likely to succeed. Students who are convinced they are unlikely to succeed will be unlikely to take risks, contribute ideas or offer opinions. They will frequently lament their own inadequacies and preface statements with 'I'll never' or 'I can't'. They are the students who will often appear frustrated or opt-out of challenging activities.

In recent research into motivation in schools, Year 5 respondents talked about the reward system, whereas Years 8 and 11 focused more on the punishments. The report commented, 'this alone speaks volumes' concluding, that there was a general cry from both year groups for 'more encouragement and reward and much less emphasis on demands, punishments and restrictions.'

Build a sense of success at school level by:

◆ allowing the reward system within the school to mature as the students mature. For example a more attainable, well structured rewards structure where the range of prizes – if these must be used – are more attractive to older students and presented in the form of choices from a catalogue. The ultimate aim is to wean students away from the extrinsic motivation of rewards systems by improving the sophistication of personal performance setting

◆ 'talking up' achievement of different sorts in assemblies and form tutor time

" Somervale School, Midsomer Norton, has a large map of the world on the wall outside the Headteacher's office. All around the map are small photographs, and a biographical portrait, of ex-students who now work or do voluntary service or are studying in different parts of the world. There are dozens of photographs and each day there is usually a group of pupils looking at the map and talking about the people in the photographs. "

◆ sending students to the 'office' . . . when they are successful!

◆ discouraging student comparisons with other students' work: focus on personal performance improvement

114

- breaking down steps to improvement into small realisable chunks
- providing formal feedback on performance through a variety of means
- establishing 'achievement' days or weeks across the school and promoting them through assemblies and form meetings

Build a sense of success with parents by:

- celebrating a breadth of different types of success: academic, recreational, sporting, social, community activity, participation, effort
- involving as wide a cross-section of students as possible in all open evenings, awards nights, performances and arts events
- collecting a portfolio of students and former student success stories and leaving it in the school or college foyer
- appointing a staff member as media relations representative with some release time to establish and build relations with the local media
- encouraging form tutors to speak to everyone of their tutees' parents by telephone to introduce themselves and to offer a personal contact in the event of any need. Use this time to signify the value of positive home support

Build a sense of success at classroom level by:

- using strategies such as hobby days or talks for students to display their real interests
- fostering an identity within your class by emphasising collective achievements
- structuring mentoring activities where older students act as tutors or counsellors for younger students
- using co-operative learning techniques to build team skills and with younger learners using class team certificates for different types of contribution
- teaching active listening skills for giving and receiving feedback
- explaining the effects of negative self-talk and how to deal with it
- finding an area where your student is guaranteed to succeed and promote it
- avoiding grading for effort – only the student genuinely knows the correct grade for this!

As a parent you can build your child's sense of success by:

- banishing visits to the lost cause archipelago and all its forlorn isles: 'one day I'll', 'perhaps I'll', 'maybe I'll', 'you never know if I'll!'
- asking your child, 'when you make a mistake, how do you feel?' Stress that everyone makes mistakes and that you can learn from them; reinforce success by achieving a step at a time
- setting up a consistently adhered-to time for homework and creating the expectation that it will take place then. Provide a quiet atmosphere and physical space for it to take place

◆   teaching your child to affirm his or her success by positive self-talk

For all of these practical approaches to work, the teacher also needs to communicate skilfully and with consistency and self-knowledge.

6 QUESTIONING STRATEGIES FOR TEACHERS

> *Probably the single most important class management skill responsible for the development of pupils' thinking is the engineering of situations where the maximum of collaborative work and talk is taking place between pupils.*

P. Adey, M. Shayer & C. Yates, *A Teacher's Guide to Thinking Science, The Curriculum Materials of the Cognitive Acceleration through Science Education Project,* **Nelson**

EVERY TEACHER IN A SCHOOL IS A LANGUAGE TEACHER. The acquisition of language through carefully crafted opportunities for learners to utilise, practise and demonstrate skill is an essential pre-requisite for all successful classroom work. Developing and using language in a variety of contexts will empower learners in their progress through school.

Ronald Kotulak in *Inside the Brain* cites research by Jarellen Huttenlocher of the University of Chicago which challenged the old notion that some children learn words faster than others because of an inborn capacity. She showed that when socio-economic factors were equal, babies whose mothers talked to them more had a bigger vocabulary. Aged 20 months the difference between the babies of mothers described as 'talkative' and those who were less talkative was, on average, 131 words. By 24 months the difference was 295 words. Work done by Betty Hart of the University of Kansas and Todd Risley of the University of Alaska found that parents who talked more to their children improved their IQs. Kotulak summarises the work in the following way, *'parent's education, social status, race or wealth are not important to IQ levels as how much they talked to their children and interacted with them in other ways. Parents who talk to their children the most tend to praise their children's accomplishments, respond to their questions, provide guidance rather than commands, and use many different words in a variety of combinations. This type of interaction can accurately predict the vocabulary growth, vocabulary use and IQ scores of children.'* This is a mandate for language-rich classrooms.

Without the facility to express themselves and communicate clearly through language, learners are disempowered and ultimately disenfranchised.

In 1956, Benjamin Bloom published what he called a 'Taxonomy of Educational Objectives'. This hierarchy of six thinking levels provides a useful prompt for structuring language development activity. It can be used for differentiating tasks and provide question prompts for all ability levels in addition to making the assessment of work more readily understood by students.

For the purposes of this language application, I assume Bloom's model to be hierarchical, and so a student would be able to work his or her way up the strategies according to his or her own development and progress. Teachers can use the taxonomy as a structure for a more sophisticated approach to using questions.

❶ Knowledge

Knowledge is simply the ability to recall information, recite or list facts. Students can say they know something if they can recite it or write it down or recall its location.

❷ Comprehension

Comprehension means that a student can describe what they know by describing it in their own words. They are able to restate, give examples, summarise or outline basic key points.

❸ Application

Application means that the information learned can be applied in different contexts. Students are able to transfer knowledge learned in one situation to another.

❹ Analysis

Analysis is when a student can compare and contrast, categorise, recognise inferences, opinions or motives. At this level a student can characterise the attributes of something, thus allowing the constituent parts to be studied both separately and in relation to each other.

❺ Evaluation

Evaluation allows a student to make judgements about what they have analysed. Judgements are made against agreed criteria and this guides decision-making and the critique or rationale of an argument.

❻ Synthesis

Synthesis is the construction of new wholes based on an informed and detailed understanding of constituent parts. Formulating a new theory, an original argument, a summary rationale, a forecast or prediction all require complex and sophisticated thinking.

The different types of activities and questions used to elicit different outcomes are listed below. Teachers can use this planner when helping students plan their own class work or to think about their own use of questions in class.

A TEACHER'S GUIDE TO STRUCTURING ACTIVITY AND ASKING QUESTIONS

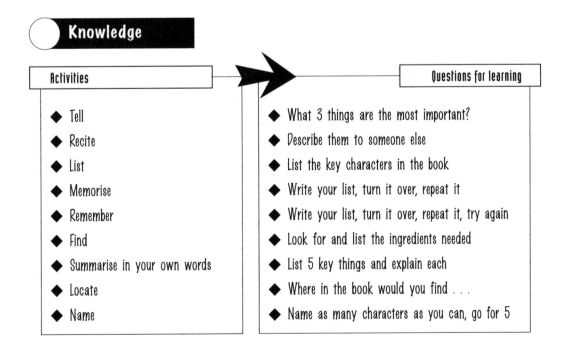

Knowledge

Activities	Questions for learning
◆ Tell	◆ What 3 things are the most important?
◆ Recite	◆ Describe them to someone else
◆ List	◆ List the key characters in the book
◆ Memorise	◆ Write your list, turn it over, repeat it
◆ Remember	◆ Write your list, turn it over, repeat it, try again
◆ Find	◆ Look for and list the ingredients needed
◆ Summarise in your own words	◆ List 5 key things and explain each
◆ Locate	◆ Where in the book would you find . . .
◆ Name	◆ Name as many characters as you can, go for 5

Comprehension

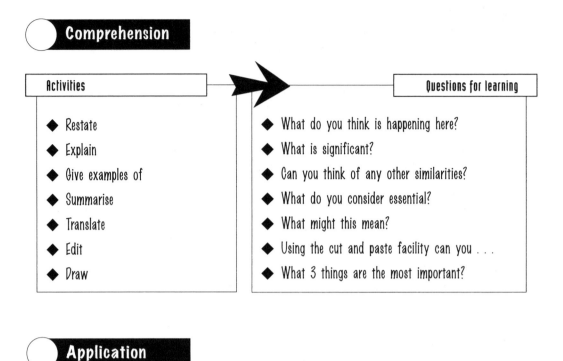

Activities	Questions for learning
◆ Restate	◆ What do you think is happening here?
◆ Explain	◆ What is significant?
◆ Give examples of	◆ Can you think of any other similarities?
◆ Summarise	◆ What do you consider essential?
◆ Translate	◆ What might this mean?
◆ Edit	◆ Using the cut and paste facility can you . . .
◆ Draw	◆ What 3 things are the most important?

Application

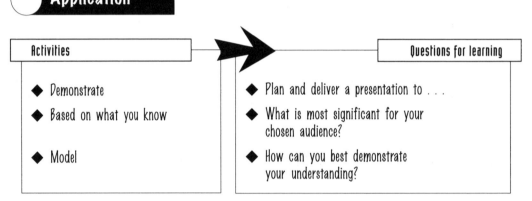

Activities	Questions for learning
◆ Demonstrate	◆ Plan and deliver a presentation to . . .
◆ Based on what you know	◆ What is most significant for your chosen audience?
◆ Model	◆ How can you best demonstrate your understanding?

Analysis

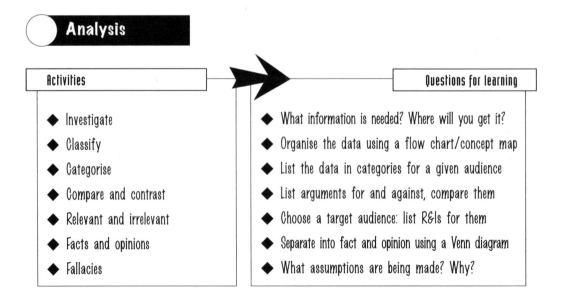

Activities	Questions for learning
◆ Investigate	◆ What information is needed? Where will you get it?
◆ Classify	◆ Organise the data using a flow chart/concept map
◆ Categorise	◆ List the data in categories for a given audience
◆ Compare and contrast	◆ List arguments for and against, compare them
◆ Relevant and irrelevant	◆ Choose a target audience: list R&Is for them
◆ Facts and opinions	◆ Separate into fact and opinion using a Venn diagram
◆ Fallacies	◆ What assumptions are being made? Why?

Evaluation

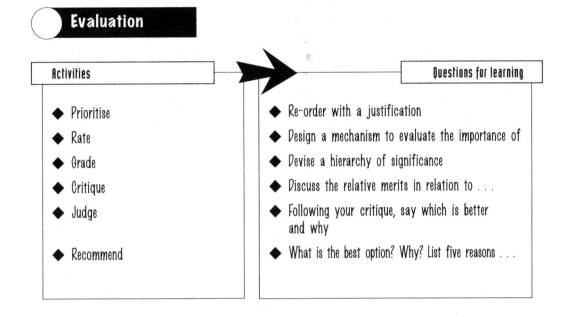

Activities

- Prioritise
- Rate
- Grade
- Critique
- Judge

- Recommend

Questions for learning

- Re-order with a justification
- Design a mechanism to evaluate the importance of
- Devise a hierarchy of significance
- Discuss the relative merits in relation to . . .
- Following your critique, say which is better and why
- What is the best option? Why? List five reasons . . .

Synthesis

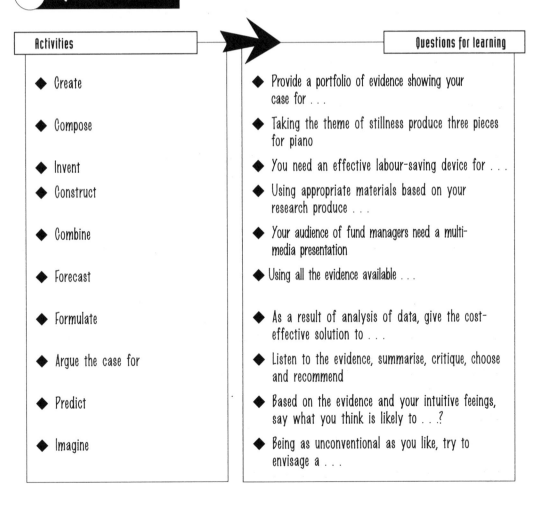

Activities

- Create
- Compose
- Invent
- Construct
- Combine
- Forecast
- Formulate
- Argue the case for
- Predict
- Imagine

Questions for learning

- Provide a portfolio of evidence showing your case for . . .
- Taking the theme of stillness produce three pieces for piano
- You need an effective labour-saving device for . . .
- Using appropriate materials based on your research produce . . .
- Your audience of fund managers need a multi-media presentation
- Using all the evidence available . . .

- As a result of analysis of data, give the cost-effective solution to . . .
- Listen to the evidence, summarise, critique, choose and recommend
- Based on the evidence and your intuitive feeings, say what you think is likely to . . .?
- Being as unconventional as you like, try to envisage a . . .

119

Add language to 'doing' wherever possible. Aside from the intellectual benefits associated with pole-bridging, this enhances language acquisition and encourages different types of thinking. Boys particularly will benefit from activities which encourage them to organise, reflect on and speculate with information. Nationally there remains an 8–10% differential at GCSE with girls outscoring boys. Some put this down to the different ways boys and girls acquire and use language in the home, through play, through socialisation with peers and in the ways they are talked to at home and, often, in school. Girls read as much as six times more than boys. Their play is likely to be characterised by a greater degree of collaboration and interaction reinforced by language exchange.

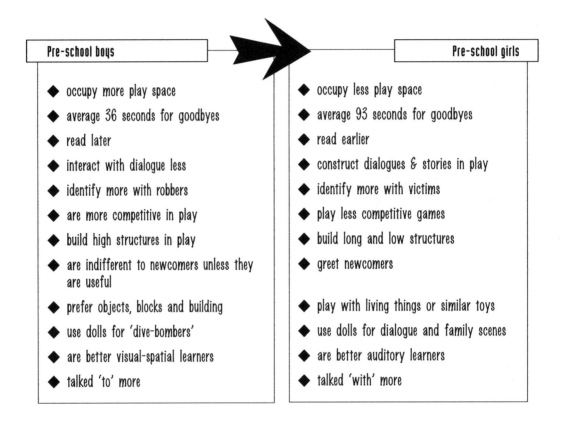

Pre-school boys	Pre-school girls
◆ occupy more play space	◆ occupy less play space
◆ average 36 seconds for goodbyes	◆ average 93 seconds for goodbyes
◆ read later	◆ read earlier
◆ interact with dialogue less	◆ construct dialogues & stories in play
◆ identify more with robbers	◆ identify more with victims
◆ are more competitive in play	◆ play less competitive games
◆ build high structures in play	◆ build long and low structures
◆ are indifferent to newcomers unless they are useful	◆ greet newcomers
◆ prefer objects, blocks and building	◆ play with living things or similar toys
◆ use dolls for 'dive-bombers'	◆ use dolls for dialogue and family scenes
◆ are better visual-spatial learners	◆ are better auditory learners
◆ talked 'to' more	◆ talked 'with' more

Based on Moir A., Jessell, D., *Brain Sex: The Real Difference Between Men and Women*, Michael Joseph

Observers note that in play girls are less object focused than boys and will construct commentaries and dialogues with the objects of play. Boys are more often object focused, collectors, hierarchical, risk-takers and doers. They are less likely to develop an affective vocabulary. In his book *Britain on the Couch – Treating a Low Serotonin Society*, Oliver James summarises some of the significant findings of research into social conditioning in the home and in play:

 At all ages in childhood, parents react differently to different-sexed offspring, encouraging sex-typical behaviour expected of the opposite sex.

 From infancy, boys get more reactions from both parents, both positive and negative.

120

Boys are given toys that require active problem-solving and parental involvement. Girls' toys give less opportunity for innovation, adult-involvement and initiative.

4 Boys are encouraged to explore and play more and to do so alone. Girls are kept within mothers' eyesight, making them more used to having to conform to adult expectations.

5 Fathers play rougher with boy infants than girl infants and insist on higher, achievement-oriented standards from their sons. They encourage dependent, passive behaviour in daughters by comparison.

6 Mothers respond to their sons' requests for help with problems but they respond with criticism if daughters make the same requests.

7 Fathers encourage assertiveness and directness in sons and react, like mothers, with criticism to daughters by comparison.

8 Both parents interrupt and talk across daughters when they are talking more than sons, who get listened to.

9 Studies of teachers show they are liable to presuppose aggressiveness in boys and social co-operation in girls even if they do the opposite.

10 From as soon as they are mobile, children form groups according to gender and are encouraged to do so. This limits their experience of opposite-sexed behaviour and peer pressure to behave other than as their sex is meant to.

O. James, Britain on the Couch – Treating a Low Serotonin Society, Century

Activities in school which require language exchange, which require the development and use of an affective vocabulary in a range of collaborative settings will thus have a compensatory benefit for many boys.

Adding language to doing could mean disrupting tasks deliberately to insist on explanation, reflection and speculation: 'pause now, take a minute to explain to a neighbour what you are doing, how it connects with what went before and what you think will happen next . . . now continue'. At the computer terminal use a protocol which requires the observer to be 'coach'. The person at the keyboard only does what the coach tells him or her. Thus a language loop is created. In design activities, in planning science experiments, in constructing essays and in planning stories, templates which require structured thinking and analysis will help with progress.

Seek opportunities to develop language acquisition. For example, as you take the register . . .

> I often call the register and ask for different replies in the target language, for example a colour, a number, an animal in French and I use more action and mime to remember key words and phrases. With all classes I now use more movement. They move around to match up with a partner to do a short role-play. We work in groups on a survey and then re-group to report back findings.

ALAYNE VERRALL, YR 7 LANGUAGES TEACHER

Some further thoughts about questioning strategies are included in the following questions . . .

◆ Do you provide 'wait time' when you ask a question? The younger the learner, the longer the wait time needed from you whilst they process for answers. Make sure you pause and avoid trampling over their thinking time by providing peremptory answers to you own questions.

◆ Do you ask follow up questions? If so, do they take the thinking to a higher level?

◆ Do you mix open and closed questions? How do you cue the response to open-ended questions?

◆ How do you enhance the quality of questions in group working? Do you use the individual, pair, share, present method to its best effect? Do you provide students with the sorts of questions they might want to ask?

◆ Does your questioning motivate? Can you use the motivational numbers – 3s, 5s and 7s – to put challenge within a task? Can you preface your question with an individual's name and a motivational challenge: 'Julie, I know you can give me three examples . . .' Can you do so in ways that make it safe to get it wrong?

◆ Do you ask students to explain their thinking? How do you extend this when you ask the question, 'what makes you think that Ben?' and get the answer 'dunno sir'?   Do you provide other extending questions: 'What other alternatives did you consider? Why did you reject them? What makes this choice the best?'

◆ Do you reflect back? 'So, if I'm right what you are saying is . . .' Do you ask them to listen actively? Summarise? Speculate? Do you play devil's advocate? Can you encourage upside down thinking by asking for the opposite point of view, or an outrageous alternative?

◆ Do you encourage thinking about thinking through your use of questions? Do you provide opportunities for students to explain the processes they choose as well as describe the outcome?

 HOW TO START LEARNING POSITIVELY AND STAY POSITIVE

> *The central evidence of a schools performance, however, is what happens in classrooms. If the quality of a school is to be monitored this is where it must be done.*

MICHAEL BARBER, *The Learning Game – Arguments for an Education Revolution,* **Victor Gollanz**

> *It's all to do with respect. Some teachers' classes are silent. Others, no one respects them; you could sit in a class and watch six or seven boys taking the mickey out of them and nobody gets any work done . . . It's those who are more of a person, not a teacher — it's not only what's happening in school that counts, it's what's happening in the world; with some teachers you can have a conversation. It's not so much the teaching part, it's who the teacher is. It's not so much what he actually knows, it's the method he uses.*

Yr 11 boy, reported in London Borough of Croydon, Pupil Motivation Research, BRMB International, 1996

At a conference for Leicestershire Headteachers in September one of the participants described how on her arrival at the school as a new Head one of the first actions she took was to re-designate the title 'Pastoral Head of Year' to 'Year Achievement Co-ordinator'. She pointed out the significance of the change of emphasis she sought. Whereas before there was an emphasis on pastoral care and it was divorced from academic achievement, what she wanted was a 'pulling together' where academic achievement and pastoral support were clearly linked. Her school had, she felt, fallen into the trap described by the HMI Report 'Access and Achievement in Urban Education' of combining *'a supportive and caring attitude with low expectation'*.

At the Sacred Heart School in South London this has been taken a stage further through their Upper School reporting system. This is how the school describes the changed emphasis.

> Traditionally students at the school have been placed on report as an intermediate disciplinary measure for long-term problems with motivation or behaviour. Because it was seen as a punishment, such students frequently lost this booklet or 'forgot' to get teachers to fill it in. The system failed because the students could not see 'what's in it for me'. The booklet has now been renamed Upper School Achievement Booklet and its purpose is self-monitoring of behaviour and achievement. The inside cover contains a contract drawn up between student, Head of Upper School, parent and form teacher which identifies daily and weekly targets. Each page represents a day divided into lessons. For each lesson the student must record the following through ticking a series of boxes
>
> 1. punctuality
> 2. equipment
> 3. time on task (%)
> 4. co-operation with teacher
> 5. co-operation with peers
> 6. referred
> 7. homework
>
> The student then awards him or herself a mark out of ten for the lesson and then presents it to the classroom teacher. He or she confirms the score and writes a brief comment or alters the score explaining why and signs it. This process opens a dialogue between student and teacher. 'You can't give yourself because . . .' is much more fruitful than 'not bad today I'm giving you 8'. There is also a section for registration and the student has to record details on punctuality and co-operation. Each day the form teacher monitors the scores and at the end of the week the Head of Upper School reviews the booklet with the student in terms of agreed targets.
>
> SACRED HEART SCHOOL, LONDON

123

Commenting on the impact of the scheme, which is intended to be positive, to be motivational and to promote dialogue with two-way feedback, the school goes on to add:

> The Achievement Booklet is a powerful tool because the student gets immediate specific feedback on his or her behaviour. It is deemed by the student as a genuine attempt to improve levels of achievement and behaviour rather than simply a punishment. For the vast majority of students it works well, they don't lose this booklet or forget to fill it in. Furthermore several students who do not display major behavioural problems have volunteered to be put on report! They do this because they understand 'what's in it for me'.

CRIS EDGELL, SACRED HEART SCHOOL, LONDON

At St John the Baptist School, Woking, the Deputy Headteacher, Ann Nash, has gone through the school planner provided to all students to check that the reading age of the material in the planner allows the students to access it and each year group has a planner which is slightly more sophisticated in terms of language than the preceding year. The planner is an important learning tool which 'matures' as the students go through the school.

A classroom, without proper organisation, can serve as an active teaching tool, a textbook in three dimensions or a passive space housing a disarray of things. Physical space permitting, it helps if we can organise it in zones.

Some primary and junior schools have already begun to use the Multiple Intelligences model to designate different types of learning areas. So we have an interpersonal area where we work together and collaboratively in different groupings, a quiet space for intrapersonal work, visual area where art work can be done and where art materials are available, a mathematical and logical area perhaps housing a computer and problem-solving tools and activities, and a linguistic area where reference and story books and tapes can be found. The classroom will have a facility for listening to or making music.

Nearby there may be access to a larger space in which physical movement can take place. The class may also have its own designated garden or environmental area for which it is responsible. Learning about photosynthesis might involve acting out the process in one area, reading about it at another and at others, singing about photosynthesis, charting its processes, discussing plant and human life cycles, visiting the garden, and, finally, reflecting on events that have transformed the pupils lives just as chloroplasts transform the life cycle of plants.

Other ways of organising zones could include:

- ◆ 'Come on in' zone: a space where students can store personal belongings and which creates a positive feel – plants, student artwork, today's schedule

- ◆ 'Busy' zone: a number of spaces which adapt for whole or small group work and which may have learning 'islands' organised by the type of work which happens there

- ◆ 'What's new' zones: items of topical interest, photographs, messages, cards, today's birthdays

◆ Library zone: classroom reference materials

◆ Soft, safe and stretch zone: an area for sitting and working together free of desks for story-telling, circle time

◆ 'Moving and learning' zone: for energising activities including dance, drama and role-play

Montessori-trained teachers are trained to welcome every youngster at the door using his or her name. It makes a big impact to know that the teacher has recognised you and wants you in his or her class!

According to research reported in Jensen (1994), visual display related to the topic being taught placed above eye level and which can be read from every part of the room will reinforce recall by as much as 70%. You should certainly utilise this for keywords and, if the same keywords can appear in a pre-module briefing sheet and be referred to during the lesson, then recall will accelerate. Use a laminating machine to encapsulate the keywords and you can use them again and again. If you cannot get all of the keywords up – 8 sides of A4 in KS4 Geography! – then bid for corridor or other display spaces. Once this happens, students are learning about your subject in and out of your classroom and you can quiz them on what they have seen.

The power of the accelerated learning in the classroom model is most evident when the strategies align together. At Holy Family RC Primary School in Langley, Berkshire, some dramatic improvements have arisen as a result of a holistic approach. Here is how Year 6 teacher, Sara Caldwell, describes what she achieved:

> I was disappointed with our Year 6 SAT results of 69% achieving level 4 and above in 1996 and was determined to improve these results to match the children's potential. The new school year saw me introduce a number of Accelerated Learning techniques into my teaching. These included brain breaks, the use of 'traffic lights' to monitor my effectiveness, mind mapping and memory techniques. These were a great boost to my own delivery and children's learning so it was quite natural when planning the revision programme to base it around Accelerated Learning recommendations. The children enjoyed the processes involved and the results produced a startling improvement of 23% up to 92% of children achieving average or above. I haven't finished there for I firmly believe that as I learn more about how children learn, then I will aim for 100% success. I am beginning to believe that all children can achieve if only I can become expert in teaching them.

All the elements of success in applying this model are hidden in this short description: the positive belief about improvement and the part the teacher can play in bringing about improvement; variety in teaching strategies; frequent physical breaks; enjoyment and fun; review and recall through immediate feedback and memory tools; an attitude that sees the teacher learning alongside the students.

Research involving learning groups who are positively reinforced shows that they out-perform groups who are negatively reinforced when learning and being tested on the same material. Performance in memory tests suggests that beginnings and endings are easier to recall. Begin and end your lessons positively.

Begin lessons via the BIG picture. Specify what you are going to do and how you are going to do it. Be explicit and to reinforce use some sort of visual reference system such as a corner of the board to write what you are going to do. This way you and the class are constantly checking against progress.

Initiate and encourage participation through a participative review activity. Avoid the 'put your hand up and tell me what we did last week' approach. It is the death knell of participation. One of the best ways to paralyse a learner into speechlessness is to pounce on them with the question 'tell me what you know about', so avoid that too! A better way is to initiate a paired discussion. 'Last week we were working on . . . I'd like you to think about three things which you can remember about . . . which we did last week. Take a moment . . . now turn to your neighbour and describe what you remember.' After the discussion has gone on for two or three minutes at most, invite contributions by asking 'what have you been talking about?' rather than 'what do you know?' There is a difference of emphasis. Reinforce with praise and humour.

Motivate by giving challenges in 3s, 5s and 7s – the magic numbers! Try to use the language – often arcane – found in exam papers in classroom dialogue and when issuing your motivational challenge. 'Today we are going to compare and contrast the reasons for . . . and by the end of the lesson you will know at least three ways of . . .'

Reinforce with praise and create opportunities for everyone to encounter success. Attach positive unconditional strokes on a ratio of four to every negative stroke. Again, avoid being formulaic here: be aware of the impact made by the different sorts of feedback you give. In NLP they say 'the meaning of the communication is the response you get!'

Regular review which involves the students actively reflecting on what they have done, how it connects with what's gone before and how it may connect with what's to come. Feedback loops which are immediate and which are fun and which affirm the positive help avoid misuse of time. Finally, as far as starting positively and staying there is concerned, operate a positive behaviour management strategy characterised by openness, two-way feedback, positive reinforcement, describing the behaviours and outcomes you want and separating the problem behaviour from the person.

Here's a checklist to help

- ◆ arrive on time, welcome students and start with low-threat activities
- ◆ provide the BIG picture
- ◆ a participative review of what's gone before to maximise speculation and prediction through active discussion
- ◆ specify the outcomes for the lesson and issue a motivational challenge
- ◆ catch students being good – catch them being successful and let them know it
- ◆ attach praise on a regime of 4:1 unconditional positive strokes
- ◆ always describe the behaviours you want and not the behaviours you don't want
- ◆ separate the person from the problem behaviour
- ◆ maximise the contributions and reinforce with praise and humour

◆ encourage constant failure-free feedback and build-in regular review activities

◆ describe the processes you use and explain why you use them

◆ have students review their experience of the lesson: three things I didn't know before; three things I liked; the three most useful things; three questions I'd like answers to

◆ preview the next lesson

◆ SECTION TWO: REVIEW

 Beliefs impact on performance. Are there any examples of 'limiting' beliefs which you currently hold about an aspect of your own life? How might they impact on your everyday experience? Where do they originate? Can you envisage an outcome where such beliefs were revised? What might the consequences of this be?

 In what different formal and informal ways do students experience 'feedback' in classrooms? How much of it is educative?

How might 'outcomes' thinking impact on performance? What methods could a teacher use to develop the skill in students?

'The enemy of understanding is the talking teacher'. In your classroom, how do you maximise purposeful language exchange amongst students?

What specific interventions do you consciously make to build and maintain positive self-belief in your classroom? What types of learning experience have generated growth in self-esteem with individual students in your care?

 It is said that Einstein's mother would ask him, on his return from school, 'What questions did you ask today?' How do you encourage your students to ask useful questions?

The brain pays attention to beginnings and endings. What might you do to improve the beginnings and endings of your lessons?

Section Three:

The strategies to accelerate learning in the classroom

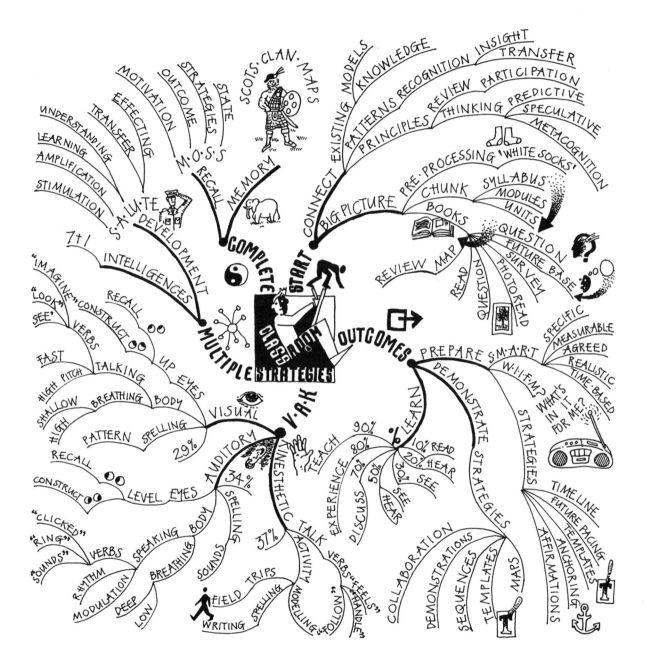

ACCELERATED LEARNING IN PRACTICE — brain-based methods for accelerating motivation and achievement

Preview of Section Three:

The strategies to accelerate learning in the classroom

IN SECTION THREE YOU WILL LEARN:

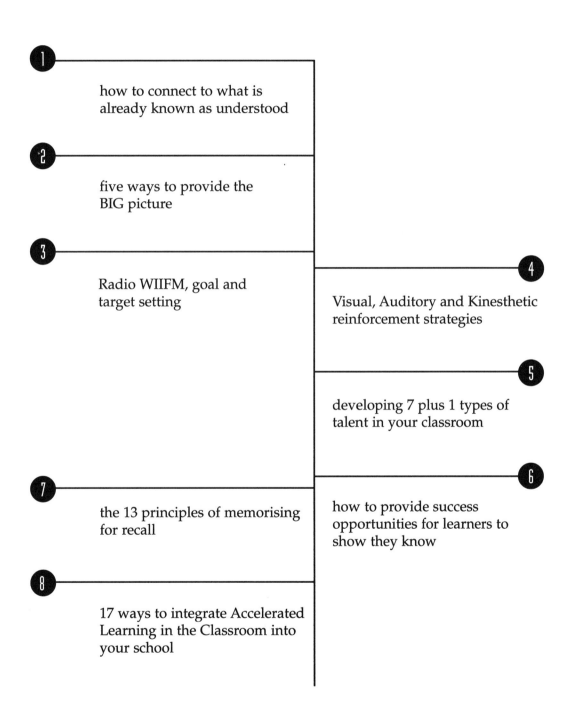

1 how to connect to what is already known as understood

2 five ways to provide the BIG picture

3 Radio WIIFM, goal and target setting

4 Visual, Auditory and Kinesthetic reinforcement strategies

5 developing 7 plus 1 types of talent in your classroom

7 the 13 principles of memorising for recall

6 how to provide success opportunities for learners to show they know

8 17 ways to integrate Accelerated Learning in the Classroom into your school

Section Three:

The strategies to accelerate learning in the classroom

① CONNECTING THE LEARNING

> ❝ We have got to do a lot fewer things in school. The greatest enemy of understanding is coverage. As long as you are determined to cover everything, you actually ensure that most kids are not going to understand. You've got to take enough time to get kids deeply involved in something so they can think about it in lots of different ways, and apply it – not just at school, but at home and on the street and so on. ❞
>
> HOWARD GARDNER, *Educational Leadership*, ASCD, 1993

CONNECTING TO WHAT THE LEARNER ALREADY KNOWS AND UNDERSTANDS is an essential prerequisite for accelerating learning. The brain constantly seeks patterns of meaning based on those patterns which are already known and understood and its capacity to recognise and learn new patterns. Leslie Hart said of this propensity, *'recognition of patterns accounts largely for what is called insight, and facilitates transfer of learning to new situations or needs, which may be called creativity.'*

Recognising and building on this innate pattern-making facility is a powerful starting point when we commence teaching or learning new material. The deliberate priming of the learners as to what is to come not only alerts the brain to search for familiar patterns and connections but also directs attention to the possibility of new ones. Apply the 'white socks principle' (see p.137). So too is the recognition that students come to us with existing knowledge and with mental models for making sense of that knowledge. We need to find out what they already know and understand and build upon it. In some cases this may involve undoing some flawed understandings and challenging their existing mental models before we can build onto more solid foundations. Teaching has never been and never will be about the transfer of information.

Take, as an example, this short excerpt from an English language comprehension text cited by Susan Kovalik in her 1994 book, *Integrated Thematic Instruction*, with the questions which follow:

> 'Cayard *forced* America *to the left, filling its sails with 'dirty' air, then tacked into a right hand shift . . . That proved to be the wrong side.* America, *flying its carbon fibre/liquid crystal main and head sails, found more pressure on the left.* Cayard *did not initiate a tacking duel until* IL Moro *got headed nearly a mile down the leg . . .* Cayard *did not initiate a jibing duel to improve his position heading downwind and instead opted for a more straight-line approach to the finish.'*

1. Who forced America to the left?

2. *What kind of air filled America's sail?*

3. *Which boat had carbon fibre liquid crystal main and head sail?*

It is correctly pointed out that 'does answering the questions successfully mean you understand what the paragraph is saying?' The example correctly suggests that the questions could be answered successfully without any understanding of the context, without a capability of generalising based on new learning and without any ability to apply new learning to a different context. In other words it is quite possible to successfully answer the questions without having a clue as to what's going on!

If we continue to transfer information without checking for understanding, without relating to the existing mental models which allow or disallow the student to integrate the new information, without relating the new information *to their world*, then we build in failure from the outset.

Basic mathematics provides a good example of how this could be done. I asked a lower school maths teacher what the very basic things *every* child, irrespective of ability, should be able to do in maths before leaving school. What should they be able to do, remember and transfer into everyday situations, without which they would be seriously disadvantaged in life? How should it be taught so it would be remembered *forever*? Here is an extract of *some* of the things which were described:

ADDITION AND SUBTRACTION – *four basic rules for working without a calculator and practised through giving and receiving change*

RECOGNISING NUMBER – *a sense of the relative size of numbers emphasised through simple games like 'What is bigger?' and 'Is it better to have? . . .'*

TABLES – *how to make sense of information presented in this format; practise on football tables*

BASIC MULTIPLICATION AND DIVISION – *exchanging money on holiday abroad; estimating what your car does to the litre or gallon*

AREA – *estimation of floor area for a new carpet for your bedroom*

INTEREST RATES AND PERCENTAGES – *borrowing money on credit for a new stereo system; calculating VAT*

METRIC AND IMPERIAL UNITS – *how to get a good 'feel' for amounts*

ROUGH CONVERSIONS – *travelling*

24 HOUR CLOCK – *what it means in real time*

INCOME AND EXPENDITURE – *working out whether the wages for a new job leave you better off or not*

HOUSEHOLD FINANCE – *where your money is going*

TAX, NATIONAL INSURANCE AND SUPERANNUATION – *what is it for and where does it go?*

134

And here are some of the ways in which these were taught, bearing in mind the need to connect to what is already known and the innate tendency to look for recognisable patterns of meaning.

Understanding the rough amounts in Metric and Imperial Units. *'It was as important that children should have a good "feel" for what each unit corresponded to so I used:*

mm – *the thickness of a 1p*

cm – *the length of your thumb nail*

metre – *a 'big' step, we'd march around saying 'big, step, metre'*

km – *we would choose somewhere near to the school and march them there singing kilometre, kilometre, kilometre as we went*

litre – *bottle of coke*

gram – *£5 note*

kilogram – *bag of sugar*

I used similar examples with Imperial units and I also made them visual. We had a teaspoon of sugar for an ounce, then two packs of butter for a pound and a cat for a stone. Then I'd get them to remember feeding the cat on 16 teaspoons of sugar and 14 pounds of butter. We'd make up songs that they had to practise like "just a teaspoon of sugar makes the ounces go down" and do "fun tests" and competitions constantly.'

Remembering the significance of Tax, National Insurance and Superannuation and understanding what it is for. *'Here I always used a story to combine the three things and what they paid for. The story was about a student who has been taken in a taxi from hospital and is going 30km to prison handcuffed to a Police Officer for fiddling the unemployment benefit. On the journey he passes Buckingham Palace and sees the Queen in an army uniform. Tax at 30p in the pound pays for education, health, police, prisons, royal family, defence and pensions but not taxis as one lad put in his exam one year! With Superannuation, I'd say it sounded like supergran and all grannies are different and some of us don't have one so there was no standard rate, it varied and you may not even pay it.'*

The five key principles for connecting the learning follow:

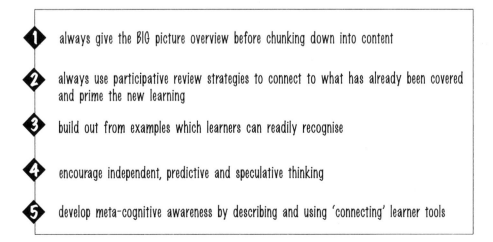

1. always give the BIG picture overview before chunking down into content

2. always use participative review strategies to connect to what has already been covered and prime the new learning

3. build out from examples which learners can readily recognise

4. encourage independent, predictive and speculative thinking

5. develop meta-cognitive awareness by describing and using 'connecting' learner tools

We will say more about the significance of the BIG picture in the next section and how it can build into and from connecting activities. Participative review activities are designed to allow every student to participate in a non-threatening way. They keep the retention of information high. They allow the possibility of the retained information being transferred to novel contexts. Most importantly they aid the learner to build new knowledge onto what they already know and understand.

Participative review strategies include:

◆ 'Three things'

'I'd like you to describe three things that you remember as significant about the last lesson. Then swap your three things in pairs. Try to get at least five significant things between you.'

After a minute on their own, allow two or three minutes in pairs then solicit contributions from the whole group. Encourage participation and prompt contributions by asking them to describe what they have been talking about not what they remember. Reinforce with praise and humour. Variations and extensions on this can include:
'three most important/three most useful/ three things to teach someone else'
'three important questions which someone should be able to answer'
'agree what the keywords were – use them in a sentence to show understanding'

◆ 'One, Two, Four, Eight'

'Think of one significant piece of information from the work we did last time. Now take your one thing and swap it with someone else so that you have two pieces of significant information. Now swap your two again so that you are left with four. Finally, go for eight or as near to eight as you can manage!'

◆ 'Interview mapping'

'Interview at least three others and from each find out what three things they considered most important about the work we did last time. Then review your findings in pairs.'

To lead out from the participative review we would encourage speculative thinking about either the content, or the nature, of the input to come, or both.

PROVIDING THE BIG PICTURE

 I begin first by becoming aware of the overall length of the work, then of how it will divide itself into sections (perhaps movements), and then of the kind of texture or instruments that will perform it. I prefer not to look for the actual notes of the composition until this process has gone as far as possible. Finally the notes appear.

Michael Tippet, 1963 [quoted in Odam]

AT ERIAS HIGH SCHOOL, NORTH WALES, Deputy Headteacher Martin McGarry has re-designed a visual version of the accelerated learning cycle. The new, improved (!) version is in colour and is a jigsaw of recommended strategies within the cycle. Framed A3 versions are in every classroom to encourage checking out as we go and an A4 version is in the staff handbook to help with structured lesson planning.

At St John the Baptist RC School, Woking, providing the BIG picture at the beginning of lessons is now part of school policy. Included in the Staff Handbook are ten recommended strategies for improving the quality of learning. Every teacher begins his or her lesson with an overview of what they are to do, how it connects with what went before and how it will connect with what is to come. Review at the end of lessons is also school policy.

Lorraine Barker, Deputy Headteacher at Mirfield Free Grammar School, helps staff and students understand the significance of providing the BIG picture through what she calls 'The White Socks Rule'. She says it directs the focus of attention without being directive, it's like *'sending students out for a break mid-morning and when they come back in twenty minutes later asking them how many others they saw wearing white socks. Or for a more useful approach, signalling **before** they go out that they might like to be aware of how many others there are wearing white socks.'* This principle is known as pre-processing and is based on the fact that the brain constantly searches out patterns of meaning and does so as part of learning.

The 'photoreading system' developed by Paul Scheele utilises the principle of pre-processing to activate the unconscious pre-processing structures of the brain. It is argued that the brain has a strong facility for processing visual information without engaging conscious attention. Typically, the method would encourage scanning pages smoothly yet very quickly without attempting to 'read' or to consciously assimilate and engage with the material. Utilising our peripheral vision we work through and get a sense of structure and glean the main points. Scheele argues that on any page, 4–11% of the words carry the meaning. Look for these 'trigger' words and we effectively cue our understanding before actively and consciously engaging with the text.

Sternberg of Bell laboratories found that even when we came up with the appropriate answer to a question, the brain continues to process alternative prospects of the question, non-consciously. It literally practises thinking while you're not even aware of it!

E. JENSEN, *Brain Based Learning and Teaching*, Turning Point

By providing the questions at the beginning of a unit that learners will be able to answer by the time they reach the end of the unit, we pre-process. By encouraging the learners to quickly scan text to familiarise themselves with its physical structure and organisation we pre-process. An extension of this is to get them to isolate 'trigger words' quickly from the text before reading for detail and with only these trigger words encourage speculation as to what the text is about: then we read for detail.

At both Lutterworth Grammar and Community School, Leicestershire, and the Sir William Nottidge School, Kent, students encounter the 'white socks principle' through different types of pre-processing activities. Teachers are encouraged to provide an overview of each syllabus and chunk it down into shorter learning units.

At Lutterworth, each subject area has been encouraged to break down its syllabus into modules which can be taught in discrete time units. For each module, students are given a pre-briefing paper which outlines exactly what they are going to do and what the learning objectives are. At Sir William Nottidge each unit of work has a summary provided to each student at the beginning. The summary specifies the unit of work, the learning objectives, the keywords used and the questions the students will be able to answer by the end of the unit. In each category there is a section for students to tick whether they know and understand before and after.

Cris Edgell is Deputy Head of Upper School and Co-ordinator of Key Stage Three Science at Sacred Heart School, South London. An understanding of the principles of good classroom practice underlies his co-ordination of the teaching of KS3 Science. This is his BIG picture of the dramatic improvement in results achieved this year.

After a year developing detailed differentiated work schemes in response to the Dearing Report we were at last in a position to concentrate our energies more fully on teaching strategies. Meetings were devoted to reviewing each unit in order to share best practice within the team. In particular we attempted to diversify our teaching methods to access the learning preferences of our students. Science lends itself very well to VAK delivery but teachers often need reminding of their own bias. Team teaching and peer observation helped to redress this. Sometimes teachers became unnerved by the sheer weight of the syllabus but I insisted that they take all the time necessary to teach concepts thoroughly – 'doing the syllabus' is not the same as teaching science!

Poor SATs results for the previous two years meant that our expectations of students had fallen too low. We agreed to teach each class to a standard about one level higher than their pedigree might suggest. The result of this simple exercise was an immediate raising in self-esteem and a revision of personal goals. Frequent and accurate feedback on tests, quizzes and assessments meant that students could plot real progress throughout the year. They were trained in the skills of drawing together apparently disparate concepts or information in order to complete the big picture. With the approach of the SATs, students were armed with checklists and revision guides and were confident enough to fill in gaps in their knowledge on their own.

The 1997 SATs results confirmed that a total frame shift in expectation had led to a comprehensive rise in achievement. There had been an increase from 35% to 56% of students attaining L5 and above and for the first time ever, the school celebrated Level 7 students (5.3%). Not a single child scored below Level 3.

TABLE 1

Year	N	2	3	4	5	6	7
1997	0	0	15	43	35	15	6
%	0	0	13.2	37.7	30.7	13.2	5.3
1996	2	3	34	37	25	10	0
%	1.8	2.7	30.6	33.3	22.5	9	0
National 1996 %	0	2	9	26	35	17	4

TABLE 2

Level (%)	1997 school	1996 school	1996 national
7 and above	5.3	0	4
6 and above	18.5	9	21
5 and above	49.2	31.5	56
4 and above	86.9	64.8	82
3 and above	100	95.4	91
2 and above	100	98.1	93

TABLE 3

Table 3	N	2	3	4	5	6	7
boys %	0	0	12.9	33.8	35.5	8.1	9.6
girls %	0	0	13.4	42.3	25	19.2	0

The tables above show the number and percentage of students reaching the various levels in this year's KS3 tests in Science. All Yr 9 students were entered for the exam (62 boys & 62 girls), of which 107 took the 3-6 paper and 7 the 5-7 paper.

CRIS EDGELL, SACRED HEART SCHOOL, SEPTEMBER 1997

Amongst the success factors which the school identified as contributing to the dramatic improvements were:

◆ improved teaching strategies

◆ effective use of comprehensive and differentiated schemes of work

◆ provision of text books for all Yr 9 classes

◆ frequent testing and immediate feedback

◆ accurately set classes

◆ high academic and behavioural expectations

◆ careful monitoring of groups and individuals

◆ development of effective SEN materials

◆ matching teachers' strengths to particular classes when timetabling

◆ plenty of exam practice

◆ revision classes

◆ provision of revision checklists and guides

A learner working on his or her own needs the BIG picture first so that all the subsequent learning experiences can be ordered and assigned a level of significance. Some of the best ways of beginning to work on a text are summarised below. Let us assume the student has to use a large and unwieldy textbook for study purposes. This method is better suited to older learners. This is how he or she might get the BIG picture and begin to extract the information they need:

Step one. Before starting, quickly note down some questions you seek answers to. Outline some of the questions on cards or post-its and have these nearby – perhaps on a wall – as you begin. Ask yourself again, to what use do you wish to put the information in the book to?

Step two. Future-base – by the end of reading this book what outcome do you wish for yourself? Envisage the successful achievement of that outcome. What do you see yourself doing, hear being said and how do you feel? Then relax, breathe deeply, make yourself comfortable and continue . . .

Step three. Survey the book first – flick through the pages to get a 'feel' for its content and layout – do this quickly and simply scan for visual information and as you do so you will begin to notice certain key words;

look at all sections including the index and appendices. Do this several times quickly. Refer back to the original questions you noted down. You will already have begun to get a sense of the book's order and layout and what can be found where.

4 **Step four**. Relax again before 'photoreading' the book. Move through a page at a time taking in the visual information from all of the page. Soften the focus of your eyes so that all of the information is available. Spend about a second or two on each page. Relax and don't linger on any page. The method is not to 'read' in the conventional sense but to absorb information to help with your next stage.

5 **Step five.** Formulate questions for those sections you wish to use. This is where you begin to search more closely for the information you need. Again, do this quickly and smoothly. Before returning to those sections and scanning down the centre of the page, dip into the text for more focused reading, finding cues which will begin to answer your questions. If it is your book, use a highlighter pen to note key paragraphs – they will often be the opening paragraphs or the first few sentences from the opening paragraphs – and alongside the highlighted marks note in pencil why it is of use or interest. Relax again. Take a break if necessary.

6 **Step six.** Rapid read those areas of the text which the cues have alerted you to. Read for meaning and comprehension at this stage and only read the sections which you have identified as of real significance, before finally going to:

7 **Step seven.** From the pencil comments you have made on the relevant pages and the detailed reading of the significant sections, go back and build up a memory map or text and context notes. Review your map or the notes as they build up by referring to your original questions.

3 SPECIFYING OUTCOMES

> A little girl came up to me one day and said, 'Mr Jensen, Mr Jensen, look at my paper.' She showed me her paper and every single word on it was mis-spelled. I looked at her and said, 'Maureen I really like your paper — the margins are nice and neat, and your printing is clear and readable.' And she said, 'Thank you, Mr. Jensen — I've really been working hard on it. Next, I'm going to work on my spelling.

E. JENSEN, *Brain-based Learning and Teaching*, **Turning Point**

> *Learning a motor skill by observing and mentally practising it through visualisation allows the brain to rehearse the neural pathways that control the muscles involved. These rehearsals involve minute muscle fluctuations that send a wave of sensory information from the muscle to the brain and strengthen the networks.*

C. HANNAFORD, *Smart Moves: Why Learning Is Not All In Your Head*, **Great Ocean Publishers**

THE LITERATURE OF MANAGEMENT DEVELOPMENT ABOUNDS WITH METAPHORS, particularly from the animal kingdom. In the last year I've read or heard about herds of buffaloes and flights of geese in the context of leadership and followership, about habituation and boiling frogs, about blind men holding on to different parts of an elephant and training dolphins by differentiation! My favourite involves whales.

Some years ago there was a Safari Park at Windsor, England. Before it closed down and became a Lego theme park it contained 'wild' animals who, for a small entrance fee, would come and defecate on your car and remove your windscreen wipers. It also had a marine pool. In this pool you could watch the antics of sea-lions, dolphins and a large killer whale. As you walked to your seat in the marine pool you passed a plated glass window below surface level. This would be your first sight of the whale. He was on one side of the plate glass with his eye up against it looking at you; you were on the other side looking at him. Later he would leap out of the water, crash back down again and you would wish you had sat further back. The question everyone asks is how do you train a ten ton killer whale to jump over a rope six feet above the water in return for a bucket of sprats?

The way it is done is to take the rope and place it well under the surface of the water. When the whale passes over the rope it is rewarded. The rope is raised six inches at a time and each time the whale passes over the rope it gets its reward. A little at a time the rope is raised out of the water. Each successful leap is rewarded with a bucket of sprats. The principle is to chunk it down into realisable units and reward success on each achievement. You motivate a whale in much the same way as you might motivate an intransigent Yr 9 student!

The story of the whale reminds us of the difference between goals, targets and tasks and the difference between short-, medium- and long-term aspirations. A goal is 'a dream with a timescale': it is aspirational and at the outer edge of performance. Targets are journey points along the route to the goal. They can be specified in terms of detailed outcome. Sometimes the acronym *SMART* is applied here: Specific, Measurable, Agreed, Realistic and Time-based. Tasks are what you do to meet targets.

It also reminds us that we may need to differentiate and certainly encourage learners to adopt personal targets. Dolphins are encouraged to perform through a slightly more sophisticated reward structure and one which is differentiated. To get a dolphin to do more than leap over a rope and eat sprats, the trainer rewards performance and then changes the pattern. Sometimes when the dolphin leaps there is no reward. Then the dolphin leaps again: no reward. After a third leap without reward the dolphin changes its strategy. It leaps but it twists or it leaps twice with spins or it leaps backwards. This time the innovation is rewarded with the sprats. The dolphin has learned to perform at a different level for a improved reward!

142

In classrooms be specific about outcomes. When setting work, be specific about what a successful piece would look like. Encourage discussion around this and have students describe in advance the sort of finished product they seek.

In working with targets, they must be differentiated. The best way to differentiate the target is to start with the learner's own aspiration – their Radio WIIFM (What's In It for Me). To get to this we have progressed through informal personal performance targets for short-term performance improvement or maintenance to formal medium-term targets which are written, negotiated and reviewed. Five ways of enhancing this process are described below. They are time-lines, future-basing, templates, anchoring and affirmations.

Time-lines and time-line therapy has a heavy industry of subscribers to the practice. Used in therapy and counselling, it works on the premise that we have a concept of time which can be delineated in space. For some it takes the form of a line angled with the future laid out in front or to the side and the past behind or to the other side. The present is where we stand in the middle. Stepping up and down is to step back and forwards on the time-line. Examples of practical applications include projecting forward to a given point and experiencing what it is like to be successful – perhaps to have achieved the personal goal – there. Or, going back and examining an experience 'as though you were there' and considering the consequences of actions taken there. In a learning situation it can be used to project forward to a point where a goal has been successfully achieved. What is it like there? What are you feeling, saying and doing? How are others responding to you? Stay there for a moment and enjoy the feeling of success, now walk back down the time-line to the present and give yourself advice about how to get to your goal successfully.

Future-basing develops time-lining into a problem-solving tool. Its origins are in NLP. It works by starting from the position of having successfully achieved an outcome rather than confronting the desired outcome as a problem or challenge. It is like being at the top of the hill looking down, rather than being at the bottom looking up, where all is effort and difficulty. In schools it is highly successful in planning and I have seen it used for three-year development plans, for departmental improvement plans, for successfully introducing schemes of work and, in one case, for introducing a new learning tutor system across year groups.

It works best in pairs. Physically step forward to the future-base and record what happens there on large sheets of paper. Have separate sheets for each academic term, working back to the present. Act as if success has been achieved. Write the date and the successful outcome down. 'It is . . . and we have . . . all students are . . .' and continue building-up a picture of success. With the partner writing down the outcomes, everything is described in terms of success. Somehow it creates an energy and the positive and desired outcomes flow out! Then, for each written success, project back down the time-line. Ask questions which continue to keep you in the future-base and presume success. Work hard at this. Questions like, 'Do you remember when we had the previous system? What was the first thing we did back then to change it? What happened as a consequence? Then what happened? How did we overcome that difficulty?' Stay in the future-base literally looking back! Build up a sequence of actions and consequences for each itemised success outcome. Gradually come forward, itemising each action as you come. Once the process is complete, then and only then do we step out of the future-base and critique what is written. At this point logistical detail is added and the timescales can be shifted up or down.

143

Templates such as those provided in Section Four work best in situations where they are a prompt for speculation and reflection. They are a prompt for dialogue and where they are 'real' they are highly motivational. The speculation comes with projecting forward, 'What do I want? What would a successful outcome look and feel like? How would I know I had achieved it? How would others know?' The reflection is part of assessing the resources – inner and outer – the learner has for working towards the goal. Goals which are written and discussed become more concrete when they are described in specifics. The brain identifies and recognises concrete images more easily than abstract 'desires'. Get the students to conceptualise their desired outcomes in VAK. It is brain-compatible!

We have all got successes in our lives which when remembered seem to evoke a 'warm glow of satisfaction'. Why is this? Why should our physiology change at the point of recapturing that earlier experience? The NLP technique of anchoring does not come with an explanation of the neurological phenomenon but it does operate on the principle that we can access positive states of mind as and when we need them.

Anchoring involves choosing a particular state you wish to access and then using the technique with such effectiveness that you can access that state of mind at any time and under any circumstances. Let us say that the state of mind the student desires is 'confidence'. Firstly we ensure that everyone in the group is relaxed and comfortable, working in pairs and with the physical surroundings. Then we invite each student to think of a state of mind which would be helpful to them – give examples – then have them think about a moment in their lives when they felt that way. For our student he or she accesses a time in his or her life when they were confident. Then with their partner alongside as observer at the point when they begin to feel a 'state change' – feeling slightly more positive and perhaps experiencing a physical warmth – they step forward into the magic circle and as they do so they say one word that is significant for them – 'yes!' or 'now!' or something similar – whilst at the same time squeezing a finger or clenching a fist or some other easily replicable gesture. This is repeated again then again. The observer can give feedback on anything they observed. Eventually, with this tool it is possible just to make the gesture and the associated feeling of confidence and control comes. The gesture and the state of mind have become anchored. This technique will work with young children and can be particularly useful when anxieties are beginning to inhibit performance.

Affirmations are sometimes described as 'brain convincers'. The process of affirming the positive is a direct intervention to counter the little voice which comes with limiting personal beliefs. Repeated sufficiently, affirmations are intended to confuse and contradict our internal belief systems and eventually displace negative and limiting beliefs with more positive ones. It is a method used in counselling and in NLP. It is particularly powerful when used alongside positive personal goals and anchoring.

Encourage the students to re-frame negative and limiting beliefs they may have about themselves into positive beliefs. Positive, unconditional statements in the present tense repeated regularly especially in moments of self-doubt such as: 'I am good at . . .' and 'I will . . .'. They need to be said aloud or listened to. Get students to repeat these positive messages to themselves regularly. The Arsenal and England soccer player, Ian Wright, uses a specially recorded tape with positive affirming messages from friends and family interspersed with his favourite pieces of music. The purpose of the tape is to get him into the correct mental state before important matches.

144

It's all about putting the power of positive thinking into my game. I've had a special compilation tape made up of things that are designed to make me feel positive and encourage me to concentrate on the good aspects. The tape includes some of my favourite bits of music and messages from one or two people close to me . . . it's all about surrounding myself with positive things and shutting out the negative vibes.

IAN WRIGHT interviewed in *The Daily Mirror* by Mike Walters, August 1997

Wright is Arsenal's all-time top goal scorer.

The combination of a stated positive personal outcome with anchoring and affirmations can provide the 'mind technology' to make a lifelong difference!

4 INPUT VIA VAK

Learning first comes in through our senses. As we explore and experience our material world, initial sensory patterns are laid down on elaborate nerve networks. These initial sensory patterns become the core of our free-form information system that is updated and becomes more elegant with each new novel experience. These initial sensory patterns become our reference points and give us the context for all learning, thought and creativity. From this sensory base we will add emotions and movement in our lifelong learning dance.

C. HANNAFORD, *Smart Moves: Why Learning Is Not All In Your Head*, Great Ocean Publishers

To understand human beings, even at a very elementary level, you have to know the limitations of their sensory input.

G. BATESON, *A Sacred Unity: Further Steps to an Ecology of Mind*, Ballantine Books

To ENSURE THAT THE INFORMATION you present has the most impact, use VAK.

An airline pilot explains how he learns complex sequences of drills and checks. Each six months his licence, and therefore his living, depends upon him being able to remember all these drills in sequence and apply them in a test situation. In this case the test situation is in a simulator and amongst the many compulsory drills to be

145

tested is a simulated engine failure during take-off. It is a situation, imagined or real, of high stress. Some 70% of all airline accidents occur as a result of human error. Lives depend not only on his ability to remember, but also on his ability to perform the remembered tasks in sequence whilst accounting for other, unanticipated, variables. Does he remember and learn to perform to this level by being told about it as he sits at a desk and takes notes? Does he remember by reading and re-reading the manual? Does he remember by sitting a written exam? Completing a multiple choice paper? Writing an essay on the psychology of human response? The answer in every case is no.

The flight deck of a modern airliner is organised so that the systems controlling the aircraft can be managed effectively and systematically. You would expect it to be so. Flight instrumentation gives visual feedback on all operating systems. The crew are required to talk through agreed procedures and affirm their completion: it is aural. As they engage a control or operate a switch, the pilots point to or physically touch the instrument: it is physical. In the unlikely event of a stall or being too close to terrain, a warning system operates. Lights flash, a loud warning signal repeats and a recorded voice warns of the danger, the control column 'shakes'. It is visual, auditory and kinesthetic.

How does a pilot learn the complex systems? Yes, there are manuals. Yes, there are updates and briefings. Yes, there are simulator courses, feedback from supervisory captains working with you on the job and regular tests. But, ultimately, it requires the individual on his or her own to learn the mass of material.

So, the airline pilot explains how he does it. Firstly, he takes the systems notes provided by the official manual and, for learning purposes, reconstructs the essential areas into his own notes. These are more maps than notes. Comprising flow charts, highlighted keywords, and the actions sequenced and attached to a mnemonic. Each complex procedure is broken down into structured elements following the same formula. Each separate 'map' is referenced to others and placed in a file. A summary map is placed on the wall above the study desk. Alongside the summary map is a black and white layout plan of the controls in the airline flight deck. To learn the drills, the pilot looks at his flow chart, says the action described there aloud as he reaches forward and touches the switch or control as suggested by the layout plan on the wall. It is visual, auditory and kinesthetic. It is rehearsed until there is no need for the props and prompt cards. Finally, he is able to say the action described, see – in his mind's eye – the position of the switch or control, move left or right hand and operate the switch or control before moving onto the next action. Again, it is visual, auditory and kinesthetic. The learning is being rehearsed in three different sensory modalities. The new knowledge is reviewed formally and informally and at regular intervals to keep the retention high.

The significance of visual, auditory and kinesthetic learning has become more than just common sense in recent years. The discipline of NLP (Neuro Linguistic Programming) concerns itself with observing the subtleties of human behaviour and particularly how we communicate with others and ourselves. The work of the pioneers of NLP, Richard Bandler, John Grinder and Michael Grinder has now been progressed to such a degree that we are able to identify three distinct communication and learning preferences. Because we take in data about the world around us through our senses it makes 'sense' to pay attention to those senses and our modes of utilising them.

In any communication, the spoken or written language, called the surface structure, provides the listener with a rich variety of information about the speaker. It indicates how that person makes sense of the world, how he distorts his perceptions, and when and where these distortions occur. Predicates, for example, may indicate his preferred representational system. The surface structure can also indicate when and what kinds of experience the speaker systematically leaves out of his representation of the world.

B. A Lewis and F. Pucelik, *Magic Demystified: A Pragmatic Guide to Communication and Change,* Metamorphous Press

 Visual

29% OF US PREFER TO LEARN BY SEEING. We will enjoy communicating through pictures, graphs and visual artefacts. We may at an early age show an ability to visualise remembered or constructed scenes. Our spelling and memory strategies may utilise pictures rather than sounds.

Auditory

34% OF US ENJOY COMMUNICATING WITH AND LEARNING BY SOUND INCLUDING THE SPOKEN WORD. Discussion, audio tape, radio programmes, lectures, debates, orals, spoken language exercises will suit those of us with an auditory preference. It may also be that we remember names rather than faces and we spell by recalling the patterns of sounds. When we remember our telephone numbers we will chunk it into three and repeat and become familiar with the pattern of sounds.

 **Kinesthetic**

37% OF LEARNERS PREFER TO ENGAGE WITH THE EXPERIENCE PHYSICALLY. In communication we will model our point with our hands and bodies and become animated as we do so. We learn through experience, movement, modelling and feel frustrated more readily with other forms of learning. Learners of this sort are most critically disadvantaged by schooling which requires physical stasis for extended periods of time.

We do, to some extent, utilise all three. But just as we each have a hand preference, an ear preference, an eye preference and a brain hemisphere preference, we also have a representational system preference.

The leading practitioners in NLP have spent many years characterising the 'typical' attributes of visual, auditory and kinesthetic learners. This work is not research based. It is pragmatic and based on detailed elicitation and modelling. It also recognises that in using language we select and describe the world and our experiences in it, based on that process of selection. The language we use therefore reflects the way we make sense of everyday experience.

 147

Visual Learners

I use pictures and the visual dimension in work more readily now. I also use the visual dimension for note-taking and it frees up associations and ideas which linear note taking cannot do. The students work better in this format too.

ANDREW DUNCAN, TECHNOLOGY TEACHER

Visual Learners . . .

◆ will have very good visual recall and be able to visualise remembered scenes, objects or faces many years later

◆ will enjoy and benefit from visually presented information such as graphs, charts, peripheral posters, keyword display, memory and concept mapping

◆ will utilise a visual spelling strategy and thus 'see' the words, their letters and constituent shapes as they spell them

◆ will look upwards when accessing remembered information

◆ upward eye movements to the left indicate the access of remembered sights or scenes; upward eye movements to the right indicate the access of constructed visual scenes – what an imagined scene may look like

◆ visualisation is characterised by shallow breathing high in the chest

◆ visual learners will speak rapidly, possibly with high-pitched tonality

◆ will use lots of pointing gestures with hands outlining or describing the imagined shape or outline of the argument or information presented

◆ prefers to 'map out' instructions using a layout plan; when giving directions will make lots of references to what you will 'see'

◆ will use visual predicates: 'I see what you mean', 'it looks good to me', 'just imagine', 'I can't quite picture it', 'let's shed some light on this', 'it has the appearance of being right', 'it's not a view I share', 'the future looks hazy', 'someone to look up to', 'do I make myself clear?', 'it has all the signs of success', 'there's light at the end of the tunnel', 'I'm still in the dark', 'she's very bright' and 'look at it from my perspective'.

Auditory Learners

I have always used short role-plays but I now tend to use it more and with a better awareness of sound as a stimulus for learning – e.g., reading Macbeth with half the class emphasising the reading of verbs and the other half the reading of adjectives in a soliloquy. This helps to highlight keywords in an auditory context and stimulates understanding. It also helps them remember it better.

MANDY REDDICK, ENGLISH TEACHER

Auditory Learners . . .

◆ will have good auditory recall and be able to rehearse or anticipate situations by 'hearing' them played out in one's head

◆ will enjoy and benefit from discussion activity, lectures, orals, interviewing, reading and hearing stories, sound recordings and language games

◆ use an auditory spelling strategy which involves remembering the patterns of sounds made as words are spelled

◆ when accessing auditory information will often adopt a 'head-cocked' position accompanied by eye movements which are level

◆ level eye movements to the left indicate the access of remembered sounds; level eye movements to the right indicate the access of constructed sounds – how to say things, anticipating what they may sound like

◆ even breathing in the diaphragm or with the whole chest and with a typically prolonged exhale indicates auditory accessing

◆ auditory learners will utilise an even, rhythmic tempo when speaking with skilled patterning and modulation of sounds to clarify and enhance meaning

◆ the use of accompanying hand gestures to emphasise meaning – counting out points on the fingers, chopping the air for emphasis – is typical of auditory learners

◆ prefer to give and receive instructions verbally with emphasis on sequence, repetition and summary;

149

◆ Will use auditory predicates: 'I hear what you are saying', 'it sounds great to me', 'alarm bells started sounding for me', 'it has the ring of truth about it', 'suddenly it clicked', 'everyone's talking about it', 'this idea has been rattling around in my head', 'let me sound you out', 'I'm in tune with your thinking', 'something tells me not to', 'it struck a chord', 'a resounding victory' and 'I don't like your tone'.

● Kinesthetic Learners

"I use the idea of writing in the air ... and I get the class to repeat words and phrases as they do so with their eyes shut. We use shouts and whispers and high and low voices. I use large cards with questions written on and we physically move them around – blu-tacked to the board – to make matching pairs. I also used cards with sentences summarising a literary text which had to be physically moved around to make sense, thus instilling a 'picture' of the sequence of events in the students' minds."

SUSAN SHORT, LANGUAGES TEACHER

Kinesthetic Learners . . .

◆ will remember events and moments readily and will also recall their associated feelings or physical sensations

◆ will enjoy and benefit from physical activity; modelling; body sculpture; field trips; visits; learning by 'doing'

◆ may spell best when able to replicate the physical pattern of the letters of the words either by writing or by moving the writing hand or by rehearsing such movements as the letters are spelled out

◆ may be characterised by use of accompanying hand and body gestures whilst talking but not to reinforce meaning; often it will be a physical and repetitive patterning of small movements as one talks or listens

◆ will fidget and need regular breaks when learning

ACCELERATED LEARNING IN PRACTICE — brain-based methods for accelerating motivation and achievement

◆ will give instructions by demonstration or modelling with the body or with gestures; when giving directions would be more inclined to take you there.

◆ Will use kinesthetic predicates: 'It feels good to me', 'Can you handle this?', 'I feel touched by what you say', 'she's got a solid understanding of this material', 'I've changed my stance on this', 'does this grab you?', 'I don't follow', 'it was a deeply moving experience', 'it's a weight off my mind', 'I felt backed into a corner', 'we are making great strides together'.

Teachers can dramatically increase their impact by exploiting opportunities for their input to be visual, auditory and kinesthetic.

Some examples of visual input include:

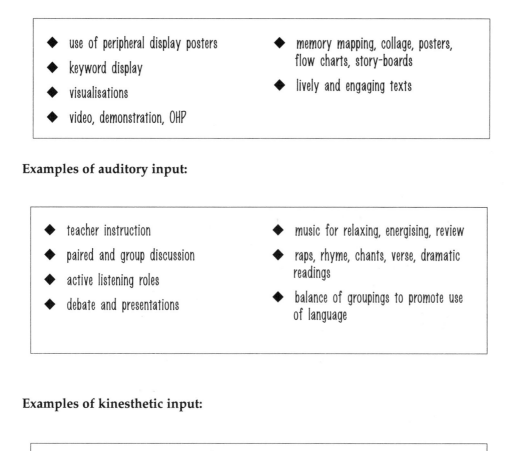

◆ use of peripheral display posters

◆ keyword display

◆ visualisations

◆ video, demonstration, OHP

◆ memory mapping, collage, posters, flow charts, story-boards

◆ lively and engaging texts

Examples of auditory input:

◆ teacher instruction

◆ paired and group discussion

◆ active listening roles

◆ debate and presentations

◆ music for relaxing, energising, review

◆ raps, rhyme, chants, verse, dramatic readings

◆ balance of groupings to promote use of language

Examples of kinesthetic input:

◆ design and make activities

◆ continuity lines

◆ physical modelling

◆ visits, field trips

◆ body sculpture, mime, learned gestures

◆ accompanying learned physical movements

◆ regular break-states and brain gym

5 ACTIVATING THROUGH MULTIPLE INTELLIGENCES (7 PLUS 1)

> *Ultimately, a full understanding of any concept of any complexity cannot be restricted to a single model of knowing or way of representation.*

H. GARDNER, *The Unschooled Mind, How Children Think and How Schools Should Teach*, 1991

IN THE ACCELERATED LEARNING IN THE CLASSROOM CYCLE we build on our VAK input of new information by 'activating' the student understanding of that information. The activation stage allows the learner to develop further a full understanding of the significance of the new information, how it integrates with what is already known and how it may be applied in a wider variety of contexts. The activation stage draws on recent work on multiple intelligence.

Using the most recent understanding of intelligence – what it is, how it can be accessed, developed and applied – will help in organising accelerated learning experiences. This chapter uses Howard Gardner's model of multiple intelligence as a way of identifying, accessing and developing different sorts of talents and abilities in each of our classrooms. It offers seven (plus one) different doors into the same house.

Gardner, interviewed in September 1997, was asked, 'how should thoughtful educators implement the theory of multiple intelligences?' His response is a good jump off point for thinking about our own teaching. . .

> Although there is no single MI route, it's very important that a teacher takes individual differences amongst kids very seriously. You cannot be a good MI teacher if you don't want to know each child and try to gear how you teach and how you evaluate to that particular child . . . linking the multiple intelligences with a curriculum focused on understanding is an extremely powerful intellectual undertaking. When I talk about understanding, I mean that students can take ideas they learn in school, or anywhere for that matter, and apply those appropriately in new situations. We know people truly understand something when they can represent the knowledge in more than one way. We have to put understanding up front in school. Once we have that goal, multiple intelligences can be a terrific handmaiden because understandings involve a mix of mental representations, entailing different intelligences.

H. GARDENER, *Educational Leadership*, ASCD, VOL.55, No.1,1997

We use the model of multiple intelligence to structure different sorts of lessons. We can teach for each intelligence as a subject in itself. This requires not only broad subject knowledge but also an understanding of process, the developmental stages of each intelligence and the cultural context in which that intelligence operates. We can teach with the intelligences to acquire knowledge. We can teach about each intelligence and thus enter into the realms of meta-cognition or knowing about one's own learning.

The model offered in this chapter will allow the reader to:

◆ understand the stages in the development of an intelligence

◆ utilise these stages to teach via multiple intelligence

◆ audit their existing provision to achieve a 'balance' across the different intelligences

◆ promote understanding amongst learners of their different intelligences

◆ take and use at least seven classroom strategies for each intelligence

Understanding the stages in the development of an intelligence

In the development of an intelligence, four different stages are passed through (based on work by David Lazear).

◆ **STAGE ONE: STIMULATION**

In stage one the young child begins to encounter in everyday experience the required stimulus to enable the development of his or her balance of dominant intelligences. Sensory stimulation ensures that dendritic branching begins to take place and the more the stimulus is repeated, the more connections in the brain become permanent. This is the encounter theory. In a home where there is a lot of talk, discussion and debate, where the child is talked to and with and where his or her views are given status, the linguistic intelligence is developed. In childhood, if music is part of the environment, if the mother sings to her child and pleasure is associated with different types of musical arrangements, then it is more likely that this child will assign value to such experiences and the scope for development of the musical intelligence will be created. Impoverishment of early experience does not preclude its elaboration at a subsequent date but from what we know about 'trimming' and the developmental windows of the brain it may became more challenging.

◆ **STAGE TWO: AMPLIFICATION**

As the child begins to interact with others around her and becomes aware of the community in which she assumes roles, opportunities to amplify the dominant intelligences occur. This will be through 'modelling' the behaviours she observes. It may be in a domestic context through observing parental figures, in play with peers and gradually where genuine responsibilities are taken on. Different cultures will assign value and significance to such early responsibilities in different ways. In the west our concept of childhood and what it means to be a child enforces a delay in some children accessing 'adult' experiences. Rehearsal and regular practice amplifies the intelligence area.

◆ **STAGE THREE: LEARNING AND UNDERSTANDING**

From modelling and rehearsal in interaction with parents or peers, the developing intelligence is refined through problem-solving encounters and structured learning.

153

Challenging tasks are encountered or are set for the learner. In classrooms the young learner refines her creativity and problem-solving skills, becoming more autonomous as she trusts her ability within that intelligence or combination of intelligences area.

◆ **STAGE FOUR: TRANSFERRING AND EFFECTING**

With the basics in place for problem-solving, for identifying and making meanings, the individual can now begin to effect 'transfer'. This means that the skills and abilities associated with a given intelligence or combination of intelligences can be applied in a wide variety of contexts including non-classroom and non-domestic contexts. Transfer is at first 'near' then 'far'. Near transfer means that the learner can solve problems in the same discipline. For example, a maths student can compute statistically within the framework of classroom exercises but is not yet able to apply the techniques in another context. The student who achieves far transfer can appreciate the underlying principles behind the technique and apply them in a variety of real-life contexts. This student can apply knowledge of statistics to bus timetabling or crime statistics or readership surveys.

Utilising the four stages to teach via multiple intelligence

In structuring our teaching we can use a simple structured model to work through the developmental stages. It is called **SALUTE** so I hope it catches your attention.

◆ *Stage one: Stimulation* **(S)**
Here we activate the senses and turn on the brain. We raise general awareness of this intelligence by exercises and activities which require listing and sorting, observing and describing, demonstrating and showing.

◆ *Stage two: Amplification* **(A)**
This involves practice for expanding, deepening and nurturing a stimulated intelligence. It means practice in strengthening the intelligence capacities as well as working with the different sorts of outputs the intelligence generates. Students need to be introduced to the specific learning tools they will be using during the lesson as well as having an opportunity to practise with them.

◆ *Stage three: Learning and Understanding* **(LU)**
This is where we teach for and with the intelligence. By doing so we make learners more familiar with learning tools, interpretation of task and structured problem-solving approaches.

◆ *Stage four: Transferring and Effecting* **(TE)**
This is about the integration of an intelligence and its associated problem-solving tools into the world beyond the classroom. The goal of this stage is 'mastery' to the extent that it becomes part of the learner's cognitive, affective and sensory life.

For each of the seven plus one intelligences described on the following pages the reader is taken through each of the four stages in turn.

Interpersonal

> **Whenever two people meet there are really six people present. There is each man as he sees himself, each man as the other person sees him, and each man as he really is.**

WILLIAM JAMES, *Bloomsbury Dictionary of Thematic Quotations*, Bloomsbury Publishing

The interpersonal intelligence is that ability to understand and work with others. It necessitates an ability to enter into the 'map' of another, make sense of the world from their viewpoint and adjust behaviour accordingly. An individual who shows this talent will be able to observe and respond to subtle changes of mood, and behaviour, motivation and intention, amongst others.

Daniel Goleman points up the significance of the interpersonal intelligence when describing the consequences of what he calls 'emotional illiteracy'. Quoting research which suggests that the school drop-out rate is between two and eight times greater for children who are rejected by their peers than for those who have friends, he goes on to suggest that the emotions can be 'schooled'. Two research projects he cites demonstrate a 50 to 60% success rate in 'raising the popularity of rejected children' (*Emotional Intelligence*, pp. 250–2).

For Goleman, many children who become 'rejects' socially are those who have not learned the interpersonal skills and are unable to read the emotional cues of others. He demonstrates connections between the popularity with peers of children at the age of seven and the incidence of mental health problems in adult life. Popular children, children who can interact positively with others, fare better.

155

A person with a well-developed interpersonal intelligence will be able to:

- ◆ identify the emotions of others
- ◆ see issues from different perspectives
- ◆ form, build and maintain a variety of social relationships with others
- ◆ work in small groups and in teams
- ◆ listen, acknowledge and respond to the views of others
- ◆ influence others

To develop and access the interpersonal intelligence:

◆ STAGE ONE: STIMULATION

Exercises which involve listening to others and acting on what is heard. Attributes listing or brainstorming: 'What are the qualities of a good communicator?' 'What makes a good communicator popular?' Discussion and agreement on class guidelines for effective communication. Games which require teamwork for a successful outcome. One such example is 'the knot'. In groups of about seven or eight a circle is formed, each person holds hands across the circle with two others. Across the circle everyone is now holding hands with two others. The challenge is to undo the knot without letting go of the hands.

◆ STAGE TWO: AMPLIFICATION

Exercises which require the participants to empathise or to see things from a variety of different and alternative perspectives or to reach towards consensus in a situation which requires them to give something up. The balloon game is a classic example. A better one is the desert island consensus game. The teacher provides a list of ten items which may or may not be of use on a desert island. Each individual ranks their selection and records it on a sheet. Having done this, the small group agree amongst themselves which priority order is best. They do this by discussion and consensus decision-making. Their agreed rank order is recorded and they compare with other groups until a whole class ranking is established.

I taught 'A Day in the Life of a Monk' as part of Year 7 history in silence! Using bells and plain chant and gesture to indicate how they should conduct themselves as monks. The follow-up writing was pleasing. I also presented the 'slave trade' as a hearing in court. In groups of five with the pros and cons discussed. The class then listened to the offerings according to criteria previously agreed by the class – content, technical knowledge, interpretation of events, passion – and judged them. I would like to do more of this, although I haven't got the follow-up right yet. I am planning the 'Treaty of Versailles' along similar lines.

ANN NASH, HISTORY TEACHER

◆ STAGE THREE: LEARNING AND UNDERSTANDING

Working with others where success depends on collaborative input. Structure exercises which require the participants to describe an experience from a point of view other than their own. Exercises which require the participants to adopt a chosen character role and immerse themselves in it. Mock collaborative exercises which require empathy, for example, UN Security Council meetings, an environmental enquiry, a committee meeting to discuss a complex decision, a press conference to explain some 'academic' topic such as the workings of the digestive system.

◆ STAGE FOUR: TRANSFERRING AND EFFECTING

Describe how practising the mental rehearsal of the outcomes of the attributes listing exercise described above in everyday situations or before potential interpersonal conflicts will help achieve a more positive result. Identify these qualities in personalities whom you know and perhaps admire.

In class teaching, insist on a regime of mixed groupings from the earliest. By the end of each term all students should have worked with everyone else in the class. As you introduce a learning activity, explain why you have chosen to group in the way you have. Departments ought to have agreed protocols for groupings and discuss these protocols with students as you use them. Move from the 'safe' to the 'challenging'. A model could be built around the following: single-sex, friendship groups to single-sex, non-friendship groups to mixed gender groups. Boy/girl pairings offer a greater diversity of language intervention than boy/boy pairings in addition to different preferred participation strategies. From time to time look to set up boy/girl pairings and again explain the logic of doing so.

Use the individual, pair, share, present model. Start with the individual and give him or her something which he or she can achieve. It may a piece of research or an item of information gleaned from a text. Then go to pairs and have each partner exchange their information. Individuals can now go to group working with something to contribute in every case. In groups, give feedback, summarise and prioritise the contributions before sharing with the whole class.

Use pairs, small group activity and collaborative learning – also empathising, conflict management, team problem-solving, interviewing others and active listening.

Templates which encourage deliberate consideration of the point of view of others and templates which require assembling a range of alternative positions before choices begin to be made will develop the vital lifelong learning skill of empathy.

Intrapersonal

I think somehow we learn who we really are and then live with that decision.

ELEANOR ROOSEVELT, *Bloomsbury Thematic Dictionary of Quotations,* Bloomsbury Publishing

In a sense we have two brains and two minds – and two different kinds of intelligence: rational and emotional. How we do in life is determined by both – it is not just IQ, but emotional intelligence that matters. Indeed, intellect cannot work at its best without emotional intelligence.

D. GOLEMAN, *Emotional Intelligence – Why it can matter more than IQ,* Bloomsbury Publishing

'Intra' means 'within'. The intrapersonal intelligence relates to an understanding of oneself and the ability to access one's own feelings and emotions, judge and make sense of them and act on those judgements. Those with a strong intrapersonal intelligence will be self-motivated, have a high degree of self-knowledge and a strong sense of values.

I first became aware of the ability to judge and make sense of one's own feelings and then manage behaviours based on that process in Strangeways Prison, Manchester, England in 1983. For a short time I had the opportunity to observe the work of the prison education unit there. Many of those who were incarcerated in the adult prison were under the age of 25 and within that age group there was a high degree of recidivism.

Truancy and exclusion are also associated with crime. A survey for the recent UK Audit Commission study 'Misspent Youth' indicated that 65% of school-age offenders sentenced in court had also been excluded from school or were persistent truants. In the UK the cost of juvenile crime is £7 billion a year. In their 1995 book, *A Mind to Crime*, Anne Moir and David Jessel explain why biological factors contribute to the fact that 89% of all crimes are committed by men. Amongst the factors they identify are biological differences between male and female brains which lead to males being less attuned and less in control of their emotions.

The work I saw in one or two of the classes at Strangeways involved helping individuals use structured tasks to reflect on significant moments in their lives, behaviours around those moments, feelings about the behaviours categorised as positive or negative and the consequences of those behaviours. The participants charted out the sequence of events using what looked like a doctor's chart of highs and lows with each significant moment marked in order. What became apparent was that these men had very little skill in being able to make sense of their feelings. They were unable or unwilling in some cases to relate behaviour to outcome. What they were working on in the class was the development of the intrapersonal skill. One could argue that the lack of it had contributed to the situation in which they then found themselves.

A person with a well-developed intrapersonal intelligence will:

◆ be aware of their thoughts, feelings and emotions

◆ find appropriate outlets for expressing those thoughts, feelings and emotions

◆ attempt to find solutions to philosophical questions

◆ be self-motivated

◆ be consistent in living to and applying a set of personal values and beliefs

◆ value personal growth and development

To develop and access the intrapersonal intelligence:

◆ **STAGE ONE: STIMULATION**

The intrapersonal intelligence will be stimulated when we are in situations – which require introspection. Heightened awareness means that we move through different emotional states and that these differences are reflected in how we act – the ability to reflect not only on outward actions but also on the thinking patterns which led to those actions. This is the beginning of metacognitive development. Use the 'Personal Readiness for Learning' templates and others such as the 'Feelings Inventory' (see p.224).

◆ **STAGE TWO: AMPLIFICATION**

Encourage discussion and analysis of things which help learning and things which hinder, by introducing circle time. Circle time is a way of describing a class or smaller group working together in a 'safe' situation where there are agreed rules, usually sitting in a circle, usually working on personal contributions, affirmations, active and reflective listening and celebrations. It is used in one form or another in many primary and junior schools. Content is less important than process and it is within the affective domain that most interventions take place. Students will offer personal contributions when they wish to and for younger students, each will have a turn for a special day – perhaps a birthday – on which they will be able to assume a role of their choice or have some music of their choice or a reading of their choice.

Use SWOT analysis and PMI. SWOT involves analysing the 'strengths', 'weaknesses', 'opportunities' and 'threats' presented by an issue, challenge or problem. Students are encouraged to balance out the differing views which impact on a given situation. PMI means Plus Minus Interesting and, again, is used to balance out arguments relating to a problem. Use feedback games to get an immediate quantification of how students feel they are doing. 'Fingers in the air' is a good example. 'On a scale of none to five, with five being fully understood and none not at all, put your fingers up in the air to rank how well you understood this last point. Explain your scoring to your neighbour. What would you need for a higher score?' Utilise student interest surveys to encourage discussion about interests and motivation. When introducing memory or concept mapping, start with examples the students complete by themselves.

> One recent lesson worked particularly well. The aim was to raise pupil motivation regarding coursework by helping towards their own understanding of what aspects constitute good coursework. Pupils were in pairs and had a mark-scheme in 'pupil-speak'. Extracts from four different pieces of coursework from a previous year were distributed and pupils had to mark an extract. Then As paired with Bs and Cs with Ds. Pupils had to mark the second extract and compare marks. The reasons for each mark had to be given. They had to list what they felt was suitable criteria for obtaining the marks available. Feedback from groups was listed. All were on task and debates broke out over certain pieces.

JANE RHODES, GEOGRAPHY TEACHER

◆ **STAGE THREE: LEARNING AND UNDERSTANDING**
Monitoring personal responses. Use Text and Context note-taking methods and create opportunities for students to explain their notes to others. Do SWOT or PMI analyses of famous historical decisions. Provide essay titles which develop the intrapersonal: 'Mistakes I won't repeat', 'My life in the future', 'How I'd be different if I'd grown up in a different culture', 'How a Martian might explain me', 'Myself from different angles', 'How music affects me'. Work with younger students, especially boys, on encouraging the use of affective language and other reflective tools.

◆ **STAGE FOUR: TRANSFERRING AND EFFECTING**
Use exercises to track thinking – particularly those which apply the 'pole-bridging' technique. 'Pole-bridging' is the self-conscious and deliberate act of describing what you are doing as you do it, drawing attention to the circumstances in which notes are taken or an experiment is conducted or a mathematical computation is made. Use the 'Personal Readiness for Learning' templates (see p.223) or strategies which add language to doing. Use SWOT or PMI for everyday problems. Use goal-setting activities, diaries, learning journals. Discuss moral and ethical issues. Encourage students to set personal targets for improvement which they then monitor. Teach and practise assertiveness skills.

 **Linguistic**

 Words are, of course, the most powerful drug used by mankind.

RUDYARD KIPLING, *Bloomsbury Dictionary of Thematic Quotations*,
Bloomsbury Publishing

The linguistic intelligence includes a sensitivity to the meaning of words, to their order, to the sounds, rhythm and inflection of words and to their capacity to change mood, persuade or convey information.

"F Y WNT T TLK RLLY WLL, Y'LL HV T LRN VWLS"

A capacity for linguistic expression will not necessarily be evident in an ability with formal, examinable English. Many children who delight in the sounds of language, its flexibility and variety, who can mimic the linguistic idiosyncrasies of their friends and others, who manage their own street argot and who can develop their own linguistic patterns may do so without parallel development in formal language.

In 1982 I travelled from Washington DC to North Carolina by Greyhound bus. Sitting opposite were two teenage American girls who looked like twins. When they chose to, they adopted a private language which, no doubt, they had developed and which allowed them to speak freely without anyone around understanding what they were saying. They added nonsense sounds before and after longer words to disrupt the recognisable pattern of language. To me, sitting opposite, it was gibberish. To them it was not only fun, it was exploratory and their own. Fifteen years later, I have no idea whether they were accomplished in formal English or whether they would have secured examination passes but it did seem they had a natural facility or talent – what Gardner calls an 'intelligence' – for language. In every classroom in the country there are young people who have such latent talents yet where they are not able to access and utilise formal language they can become increasingly disenfranchised from the curriculum as they grow older.

The UK the Government White Paper 'Excellence in Schools' (DFEE 1997) introduces a national literacy strategy which describes national targets and which provides case studies of existing good practice. One such case study from Summerhill Junior School builds on two key structures – the framework for teaching and the literacy hour – which is helping *'shift the emphasis of their planning from what they should be teaching to how they should be teaching literacy'* (their emphasis).

This is how it is described.

The teaching objectives set out in the National Literacy Project framework are implemented through a daily dedicated hour for literacy. Typically the teacher will spend:

10 – 15 minutes – on whole class work from a text which all pupils share
10 – 15 minutes – whole class work or sentence work
25 – 30 minutes – group activities
5 – 10 minutes – whole class review to share, present, revise and evaluate work

The school places emphasis on careful classroom organisation and on training pupils to work independently. This enables the teachers to devote almost all of their time to teaching literacy and not managing the lesson.

DFEE, *Excellence in Schools*, 1997

Whilst the prescriptive nature of this can be challenged, the underlying intention is positive. It can be seen that as well as learning the content the students are learning through processes about language and about working with others and are applying the language in a wide variety of contexts.

A person with a well-developed linguistic intelligence will:

◆ learn through listening, writing, reading and discussion

◆ imitate or mimic the linguistic idiosyncrasies of others

◆ develop their own application and understanding of language

◆ be a better than average communicator

◆ have a predominantly auditory representational system

All teachers are language teachers. Use these outline activities and adapt them for your subject area.

To develop and access the linguistic intelligence:

◆ **STAGE ONE: STIMULATION**

Use these warm-up activities which require students to use and develop language through individual and small group activities. 'Dangly Bits' are riddles which demand co-operation, discussion, analysis and speculation. They are good for initiating group activity and for developing active listening and questioning skills. You can get groups of three to work on the possible solutions with the class teacher handling clarifying questions or, better still, have groups of four with the fourth person knowing the answer and the others having to co-operate together and ask him or her the agreed clarifying questions.

Examples include:

Q. Which one is the odd one out? GS GA WA C G D R GK

(A. R is the only one which is not a position in netball!)

Q. Two look-alike boys were at a party and a stranger said, 'You two must be twins.' The boys laughed and said, 'We have the same parents and were born on the same day in the same year, but we're not twins.' How come?

(A. They were two of triplets!)

Q. What belongs to you but others use it more than you do?

(A. Your name)

Q. Some pieces of coal, a carrot and an old hat are lying in the middle of a lawn. Nobody had put them on the grass, and they didn't fall out of a plane. How did they get there?

(A. The remains of a snowman after a thaw!)

Q. A man was shot to death in his car. There were no powder marks on his clothes showing that the killer must have been outside the car. All the windows were closed and the doors were locked. There were only bullet holes in his body. How was he murdered?
(A. He was in a convertible and the roof was down!)

'Building Blocks' are exercises which reinforce the use of keywords, key concepts or any list which can be recalled in sequence. An added refinement is to build the list alphabetically. Examples include an alphabetical list of excuses for not coming to school that day. 'I couldn't come to school because I had an allergy'; 'I couldn't come to school because I had an allergy and bulimia'; 'I couldn't come to school because I had an allergy and bulimia and constipation . . .'.

Words in sequence which begin with the last letter of the previous word. Keywords related to a subject. For example KS2 Science Materials and their Properties with the materials listed in any order – 'the scientist was made of wood'; 'the scientist was made of wood and paper'. The list could include any or all of the materials worked on in the class and others besides.

◆ STAGE TWO: AMPLIFICATION

By using key vocabulary flash cards and distributing them around the class so that each pair of students has at least one card we initiate discussion. The cards when chained together in sequence should cover the key areas of the unit being worked on. Nominate a pair to start. They hold up their card, explain it and answer any questions which arise. The next pair do the same but explain the relationship between this new card and the previous. The process builds so that the entire unit is covered.

This can be developed by encouraging small groups to construct a continuous narrative in sequence using all the key words. In addition, the class teacher can 'pre-figure' the work by introducing his or her own narrative which embeds all the words.

Activities such as 'Making a Case', which requires pairs or groups to argue for a desired outcome or defend a position, can benefit from the use of structured problem-solving and thinking tools and templates such as the 'fishbone diagram'. Have these placed in the classroom so that all can see them and follow the prompts in sequence. Other good 'tricks' to aid linguistic development include the 'handy story helper' and the 'handy writing helper'. On the left hand we have the 'handy story helper' which consists of a palm with the title of our story written on it, then a thumb with 'place' followed by fingers with 'people', 'problem', 'action' and 'ending'. The child learns this sequence on their left hand and on their right we have a palm with 'subject' written on it, then a thumb with 'paragraphs' followed by fingers with 'capitals', 'punctuation', 'neatness' and 'checked'.

Any activity in any subject which encourages experimentation with language and provides different contexts for such experimentation to take place or demonstrates that language can be fun as well as a powerful tool will serve the amplification stage. Use puns, poems, rhymes, plays-on-words, word games, story-telling, active listening roles, metaphor in story-telling, puzzles and anagrams, written and spoken language exercises.

ERIC (Everyone Reads in Class) Project at Firth Park School, Sheffield where periods have been changed to a 30 period week of five times 55 minute lessons with one 25 minute lesson for whole school reading time. Peer tutoring for students needing reading practice. Also at Kingsdon Manor EBD Special School, Somerton.

◆ **STAGE THREE: LEARNING AND UNDERSTANDING**
Three simple types of language activity demonstrate the ways in which all teachers can access and develop this intelligence.

Active listening and hot-seating. Active listening strategies encourage students to listen for different types of information from the same source. At any time you can encourage the development of active listening skills by assigning different listening roles to different groupings within the class. Ways of assigning the groupings could include by row or table grouping within the class – 'the front row will listen for . . .', or by month of birth or by first letter of name or any other way which is simple. Assign a listening role from any of the following suggested roles:

'the three most important things'

'three practical applications for this information'

'what would you teach to a Martian?'

'how might you apply this information in your own life?'

'three things you didn't know before'

'how might this information have helped someone living 100 years ago?'

'what evidence of the application of this information is there in the outside world?'

'what are the essential key words to know?'

Students can then be re-grouped in a way which requires them to listen actively to what each new group member has to contribute. If you had assigned four listening roles then each group of four would have four different types of contribution to listen to in addition to four different perspectives on the same input. Hot-seating involves using three roles – an observer, an interviewer and an interviewee – and encouraging rotation around those roles so that each student gets a different perspective on the same issue.

Adding language to doing. By carefully structuring situations where students describe aloud what they are doing as they do it, we develop not only language skills but also thinking skills. Ways of maximising purposeful language exchange, the use of keywords, structured problem-solving using templates and self-questioning tools are described in detail elsewhere in this book.

Research using primary and secondary sources. An understanding of the difference and relative significance of primary and secondary source information is easily demonstrated, though perhaps difficult for younger learners to grasp. When they are able to do so, then the application of this understanding beyond formal education will be an enabling and lifelong personal skill which will open up new perspectives on everyday events.

◆ STAGE FOUR: TRANSFERRING AND EFFECTING

All teachers are language teachers, irrespective of subject specialism. Activities which encourage different types of listening, which encourage purposeful talk, which nurture and develop an enthusiasm for the written word and which provide opportunities for mechanical, informational, personal and imaginative written response will all contribute to the development of lifelong learning skills.

 Mathematical and Logical

 Equations are just the boring part of mathematics. I attempt to see things in terms of geometry.

STEPHEN HAWKINGS, *A Brief History of Time*, Bantam Books

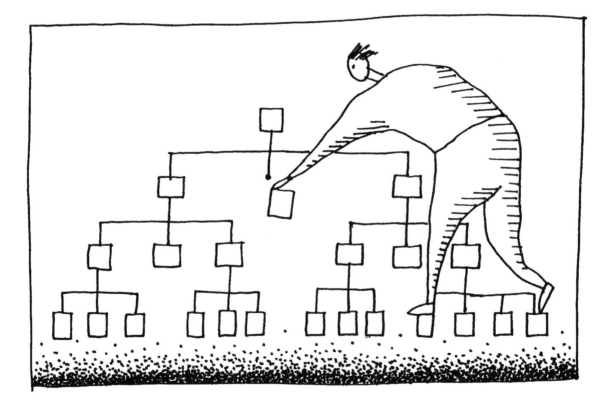

> You mentioned your name as if I should recognise it, but beyond the obvious facts that you are a bachelor, a solicitor, a Freemason, and an asthmatic, I know nothing whatever about you.

SIR ARTHUR CONAN DOYLE, *The Norwood Builder* from
The Memoirs of Sherlock Holmes

Individuals with a mathematical and logical intelligence are problem-solvers who can construct solutions non-verbally. They delight in sequence, logic and order and can readily discern patterns and relationships in the world around them. The mathematical and logical intelligence was an area of interest for Jean Piaget's work on human development starting with manipulating and ordering objects in the nursery and gradually developing to higher and more abstract levels until it becomes more internalised and more detached from the everyday world of physical objects. In *Frames of Mind,* Gardner explains the process.

> It is in confronting objects, in ordering and re-ordering them, and in assessing their quantity, that the young child gains his or her initial and most fundamental knowledge about the logical-mathematical realm. From this preliminary point, logical-mathematical intelligence rapidly becomes remote from the world of material objects ... Over the course of development, one proceeds from the realm of the sensori-motor to the realm of pure abstraction - ultimately, to the heights of logic and science.

Imagine a child who exhibits an early fascination with the mystery of numbers. This child not only wants to know what toys are in the toy box but also what quantity. Later they are ordered by size and then by colour; her toys are separated from her brother's. There are afternoon toys and morning toys; toys for 'just me' and toys that can be shared. Quantity and category are followed by concepts of time. 'If I'm allowed to spend one hour watching my favourite videos how many can I see?' The fascination begins to extend beyond the home. 'How many lamp-posts are there between home and school? How many steps does it take?' And then into activities. 'What steps do I need to follow to open the computer game?' 'If I throw this ball against the wall can I do so while adding up?' 'Can I do it by adding in twos or threes?' Then it gets taken to school. Number sequences and patterns, estimation, fractions, percentages, painting by numbers, different ways of classifying leaves, the pattern of dance steps, what happens next in the story, cause and effect in history, the Periodic Table. The world we grow up in is surrounded by opportunities to see patterns, to classify, to speculate and predict and to begin to detect the rules which underlie everyday events.

167

A person with a well-developed mathematical and logical intelligence will:

◆ be familiar at an early age with the concepts of time, space, quantity, number, cause and effect

◆ understand and be able to manipulate abstract symbols to represent concrete objects and concepts

◆ discern the pattern in relationships

◆ construct hypotheses and test them, collect data, formulate models, develop counter-examples and build a detailed rationale based on this process

◆ be capable of 'mathematical thinking'

◆ seek to find order and harmony in the immediate environment

To develop and access the mathematical and logical intelligence:

◆ STAGE ONE: STIMULATION

Games which encourage the identification of patterns and require actions based on observation and application of those patterns. Examples include 'Dingbats' . . .

OHOLENE

HOLE IN ONE

TIME TIME

TIME AFTER
TIME

KNEE
LIGHT

NEON LIGHT

EZ
iiiiiiiiiiii

EASY ON
THE EYES

◆ STAGE TWO: AMPLIFICATION

Activities which require new information to be organised, reflected upon and then applied will nurture the mathematical and logical intelligence.

Avoid putting students into situations where the absorption of information is a passive experience. In classroom teaching stimulate and engage thinking by using the following structured questions.

Accessing

◆ **Recalling** – what three things of significance can you recall about this topic?

◆ **Comparing** – what are the positive and negative attributes of each?

◆ **Identifying attributes and components** – can you list the key attributes of . . . and the most important component parts of each attribute?

Organising

◆ **Establishing criteria** – how do you decide what is significant or of importance? Would your criteria be the same as someone else's?

◆ **Classifying** – in what different ways might you re-organise the material? Might your classification differ for different audiences?

◆ **Ordering** – can you sequence the key points in order of importance?

◆ **Identifying relationships and patterns** – using a concept map organise the key topics on the page and between each listed topic explain the connection, its nature and significance

Reflecting

◆ **Identifying main ideas** – which ideas would you teach first? What would you draw attention to in your explanation?

◆ **Identifying errors** – which ideas would you teach first? What would you draw attention to in your explanation?

Projecting

◆ **Predicting** – as a result of organising the information, what outcomes seem most likely? For each outcome specify the clues that lead you to reach that prediction

◆ **Elaborating** – go back over your conclusions. What further information would be useful to a reader?

◆ **Summarising** – provide a synopsis in five or seven bullet points

◆ **Verifying** – how might you confirm the accuracy of your conclusions? How might someone else do it?

169

Use sequencing activities, work with number, measurement and estimation; prediction, speculation and hypothesising; syllogisms and analogies; problem-solving. Encourage brainstorming information before ordering and organisation. Find and use codes. Use the descriptive – reflective – speculative (DRS) sequence and encourage students to provide descriptors of the steps in any sequence.

◆ STAGE THREE: LEARNING AND UNDERSTANDING

When Reuven Feuerstein developed his programme of Instrumental Enrichment he recognised the need to start from establishing *'what cognitive structures lead to problem-solving and thinking'*. He spent 25 years developing what he now calls the 'Learning Potential Assessment Device' – a set of psychological test procedures to determine where the deficiencies in cognition are. The identification of the deficiencies then leads to 'mediation' wherein the teacher uses instruments or teaching tools to teach and develop the missing competencies. Many adolescents, for example, are weak in skills of planning, systematic searching for and collection of data, perceiving relationships among and between various school experiences and real life. Many are impulsive in problem-solving approaches, fail to make comparisons or connect to previous experience and some have an episodic grasp of reality.

Feuerstein listed three levels of cognitive functioning necessary to achieve efficient thinking. We can use these to guide us in developing the mathematical and logical intelligence.

- **Input.** The quantity and quality of the information gathered by the student when confronted by a given problem or experience.

- **Elaboration.** The efficient use of available information and cues.

- **Output.** The student's ability to communicate his or her thoughts and thinking processes to others.

The following prompt derived in part from Feuerstein's will help in developing the building blocks of thinking. In each stage, the student:

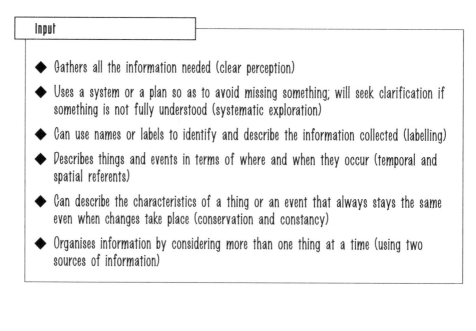

Input

- ◆ Gathers all the information needed (clear perception)
- ◆ Uses a system or a plan so as to avoid missing something; will seek clarification if something is not fully understood (systematic exploration)
- ◆ Can use names or labels to identify and describe the information collected (labelling)
- ◆ Describes things and events in terms of where and when they occur (temporal and spatial referents)
- ◆ Can describe the characteristics of a thing or an event that always stays the same even when changes take place (conservation and constancy)
- ◆ Organises information by considering more than one thing at a time (using two sources of information)

Elaboration

◆ Defines what the problem is, what we are being asked to do (analysing disequilibrium)

◆ Uses only that part of the information gathered that is relevant and ignoring the rest (relevance)

◆ Has a good concept of a final outcome or of what has to be done (interiorisation)

◆ Makes a plan that includes all the steps needed (planning behaviour)

◆ Compares objects and experiences to see what is similar and what is different; what belongs to the past, the future and the present (comparative behaviour)

◆ Finds the class or set to which the new object or experience belongs (categorisation)

◆ Works out different possibilities and the consequences of choosing one or another (hypothetical thinking)

Output

◆ Is clear and precise in using language to describe the problem and the solution. Is able to 'see things' from the point of view of the listener (overcoming egocentric communication)

◆ Thinks things through before giving an answer (overcoming impulsivity)

◆ Pauses before responding but is able to start again if a considered answer or response is mistaken (overcoming trial and error)

A key part of Feuerstein's work was the concept of 'bridging'. Bridging means taking the skills developed in exercises and applying them to the real world. We do this through the sorts of questions we ask in classrooms, the examples and case studies we provide and the problems we ask students to wrestle with.

◆ STAGE FOUR: TRANSFERRING AND EFFECTING

The thinking skills developed and practised using some of the techniques above can be applied to real-life situations using problem-based learning. The Summer 1997 Curriculum Update of the ASCD is devoted to problem-based learning. Here are some of the real-life problems that some of the students it describes are working on:

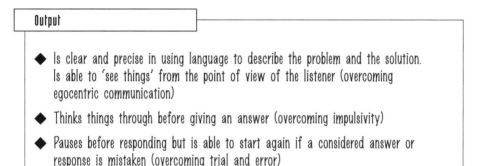

Medical students who, instead of receiving a lecture with notes on the brainstem are organised into teams to work on a simulated patient case where the symptoms described in the notes suggest that something was wrong with the brain stem. Students now have to provide a diagnosis, generate multiple hypotheses, determine what they

171

did and what they didn't know about the brain stem and then find more information.

Students in KS3 worked on an ill-structured problem to do with the environment. In the scenario a large oil company wants to dispose of an abandoned oil rig by towing it to the Atlantic and sinking it in deep water. Activists, concerned by such an action's effect on the environment occupy it and are now living there. Students have to act as mediators and present their case to resolve the problem. In doing so they have to consider how toxic substances are typically disposed of – oil at sea, oil from a car, medical supplies, spent nuclear fuel rods – and consider things from a number of perspectives.

A large volcano in the centre of the country is threatening to erupt. If it erupts a third of the country will be wiped out. In response, students work in groups to study volcanoes, determine the probability that such an event would occur, and describe the effect a major natural disaster would have on jobs and politics in the region. They present back their findings which range from drilling into the volcano to reduce the pressure and developing the evacuation plans, to not telling the public because, as they reason, the volcano is unlikely to erupt, there is no way to predict or prevent an eruption and widespread panic would lower property values and scare industry and income away from the area.

Curriculum Update, ASCD

In working this way students learn not only the immediate content, but the interconnectedness of all disciplines whilst simultaneously applying their mathematical and logical intelligence.

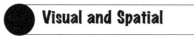

● Visual and Spatial

Every child is an artist. The problem is how to remain an artist once he grows up.

PABLO PICASSO, *Bloomsbury Dictionary of Thematic Quotations*, Bloomsbury Publishing

From the eye to the visual area of the brain, the system functions much like a complex switchboard or computer ... it follows from this that all people need to experience is an image for the right neuronal pathways to fire. It does not matter whether they fire because of stimulation to the retina or other sense organs, or because of an internal stimulus.

SAMUELS AND SAMUELS, *Seeing with the Mind's Eye, the History, Techniques and Use of Visualisation*, New York, 1975

Those with a well-developed visual and spatial intelligence will be readily able to create or re-create images of scenes or objects. They will be able to visualise objects manipulated through three dimensions and through space and time. They may be able to recognise the relationships of objects moving in three dimensions and in time. Their preferred learning methods will include seeing and observing, visualising desired outcomes and some of the stages seen in working towards the successful achievement of that outcome.

In the spring of 1997 I spent an afternoon working with the special needs staff of a large comprehensive school in Bristol, England. They had asked me to come and work with them on ways to help students improve their memory. I discovered on arrival that three Yr 10 students who allegedly had the worst memories were going to help me. One of them, I'll call him Peter, was following GCSE courses in Language and Literature. He could not remember the name of the play he had studied the week before nor the author nor the characters in the play. He had difficulty accessing large areas of the curriculum but apparently was 'good' at spelling. I was curious about this and began to ask him about it. We chose some difficult words and tried them out. What we discovered was that he had a very good visual memory and when given time and a method, he could picture the words, separate them into little chunks and then repeat back the letters he saw there. He would look at the written word, shut his eyes and then 'see' each chunk as a complete bold, hand-written image set against a coloured background and located in the centre and slightly up and to the left of his field of vision. When we used this method and he was given time to rehearse it mentally, his spelling success rate soared. Peter may or may not have had a visual intelligence; he certainly had an effective visual strategy which he had only limited opportunities to use in school.

A person with a well-developed visual and spatial intelligence will:

◆ learn through seeing and observing

◆ be able to visualise imagined scenes easily

◆ interpret and construct graphs, maps and other visual media

◆ be able to construct, build or conceive three-dimensional objects or imagine their 'unfolded' construction

◆ be proficient in design activities including abstract or representational or both

◆ be good at manoeuvring when this involves manipulating self or body through space

Whilst none of Gardner's categories of intelligence are claimed to be complete, perhaps the visual and spatial intelligence more than any other current category is susceptible to further examination. The ability to visualise and the ability to discern patterns and relationships between objects in space seem in some practical instances to be unnaturally harnessed together, particularly as spatial intelligence seems to be an underlying human survival need.

To develop and access the visual and spatial intelligence:

◆ STAGE ONE: STIMULATION

The Bulgarian educationalist Georgi Lozanov uncovered the way that learners took in information on the periphery of the senses. Using visual stimuli above eye-level which summarises the key content – known as peripherals – we can improve recall dramatically. We seem to have a remarkable capacity to recall and spatially organise visual information. So that learners can 'see' in their mind's eye the information as it was. When we observe the eye patterns of learners as they recall and describe visually stored information, there is a conformity of pattern. Eyes move up and around. Visually reconstructed scenes have a corresponding pattern of movements up and to the left; visually imagined scenes have an eye movement pattern of up and to the right. Useful information when, on a Saturday morning, you ask a teenage son or daughter where they stayed the night before!

Sometimes a different seating position will encourage learners to take a different view (literally) of the information displayed in the classroom and initiate the unconscious processing described by Sternberg.

Information presented or encoded in primary colours seems to be more readily memorable than in black and white.

◆ STAGE TWO: AMPLIFICATION

A top Olympic swimmer describes how he uses visualisation for performance improvement.

> I started visualising in 1978. My visualisation has been refined more and more as the years go on. That is really what got me the world record and the Olympic medals. I see myself swimming the race before the race really happens ... About 15 minutes before the race I always visualise the race in my mind and 'see' how it will go ... You are really swimming the race. In my mind I go up and down the pool, rehearsing all parts of the race, visualising how I actually feel in the water.

HARDY, JONES & GOULD, *Understanding Psychological Preparation for Sport: Theory and Practice of Elite Performers*

Whilst we don't all have the natural ability to visualise imagined or reconstructed scenes readily, it can be developed. A guided visualisation to assist in finding out about learning preferences was described in *Accelerated Learning in the Classroom* (see p.183), Network Educational Press Ltd.

'As you listen to the music I'd like you to relax. Feel the soles of your feet on the floor, settle down and prepare to enjoy a journey. You may close your eyes if you wish. Breathe deeply. As you listen to the music relax from the top of your head to the soles of your feet. Enjoy the feeling. . . . Pause. . . We are about to begin a journey to explore how you enjoy learning best. When we return you'll know all you need to know to help you begin to learn successfully. . . .Pause. . . As you relax your eyes and your mouth

and your ears and your neck continue to breathe deeply and enjoy the music.

Take yourself to a place where you enjoy learning. Enjoy the sights and sounds of being there. As you continue to relax and listen to the music, enjoy the sounds as you learn successfully, whether your place is light or dark or warm or cool, you can feel success as a learner when you are there. When you are being even more successful as a learner enjoy the experience, continue to relax, asking yourself what is it that is making me so successful here? Is the learning fun? What is making it fun? Is it useful? In what ways is it useful? . . . Pause. . . As you continue to relax and see and hear and feel yourself being a successful learner, how are others helping you be successful? Breathe deeply, listen to the music . . . And as you enjoy being in your perfect learning place, ask yourself what's the best time of day for me to be learning? And how do I like to eat when I'm learning?

As you enjoy the music, continuing to breath deeply, you may like to think a little more about how you learn best . . . what sort of things are you enjoying doing as you learn best? Think of the subject where you learn best. What is it you do in that subject that helps you more than anything else? And as you continue to breathe deeply, enjoying the music and your successes in learning spend some time there . . . Pause . . . before preparing to come back with all the secrets of your learning successes. And as the music fades and my voice rises, be aware of being back here (in the classroom) and of those others around you. Gently stretch out as the music stops.'

The text should be read with the voice at or just below the level of the music. The language is intended to be *suggestive*. In other words you engage the students in asking questions for themselves. This works at an unconscious level. By saying 'you may like to think about what makes your learning so easy?' rather than 'what makes you a good learner?' you are engaging a deep thought structure and not foreclosing on any possible answers. Visualisations, such as this one about learning preference or about exam preparation, not only develop a state of relaxed alertness but also begin to develop the ability and confidence to visualise. Visual recall strategies are very effective in remembering large amounts of information. But it may need practice.

> **Imagery can be developed, however, in most non-imagisers, although this gets more difficult with age. It takes regular and devoted practice since it literally involves an activation of electro-chemical circuitry in the brain.**

J. HOUSTON, *The Possible Human: A Course in Extending Your Physical, Mental and Creative Abilities*, J.P. Tarcher.

◆ STAGE THREE: LEARNING AND UNDERSTANDING

To develop the visual and spatial intelligence of learners, check that your classroom and the learning environment is visual. Is learning reinforced through visual display? Do students learn in the corridors and public areas? Do you, in your classroom teaching, use visual reference materials? Can you use your own physical presence to assist learning – by, for example, accompanying gesture or movement? Can you place the key words relating to the topic you are teaching above eye-level so they can be seen from all parts of the room?

175

Other visual strategies include:

◆ **Highlighting in primary colours.** Colours can be used to assist in learning the steps in a given process. For example, the stages in long division or the constituent parts of a word.

◆ **Learning posters.** Students who construct free-form learning posters and then introduce those posters to the rest of the class or the rest of the group or to a video camera.

◆ **Continuum lines.** A visual record of a sequence of events drawn as a series of points on a continuous line. Used a lot in primary and junior schools not only to convey a sense of sequence but also to indicate timescales.

◆ **Storyboards.** Best used as a proforma with the space for the camera shot above and the descriptor and dialogue below. The best encourage a sense of narrative structure but also show how the movement, position and proximity of the camera shapes meaning. A wonderful introduction to narrative and camera convention is to have students video record a TV commercial then count the number of cuts, record the type of camera shot — long-shot, medium close-up, close-up, big close-up — and whether and how the camera was moving — tracking, panning, climbing, dropping. Each shot is drawn and described on the storyboard. TV commercials have a completely different meaning after this!

◆ **Flow charts.** A simple method of structuring a sequence of actions, cause and effect.

◆ **Topic webs.** A method of building out patterns of connections around a central idea. Like the web everything has a connection with ideas which lead back to the centre.

◆ **Memory maps.** An extension of topic webs and learning posters, memory maps are described in full later in the book.

◆ **Templates.** With the continued use of different types of template, the method of thinking which they encourage begins to be part of the learner's mind-set. In the very early stages, working through with the template used as a writing prompt soon becomes unnecessary; the learner assimilates the prescribed sequence as part of a mental repertoire.

◆ **STAGE FOUR: TRANSFERRING AND EFFECTING**

Encourage visualisations of solutions prior to discussion or description. A capacity to visualise desired outcomes and to develop the visual memory is of lifelong benefit.

Kinesthetic

> I can feel the quality of a note by what I feel, I can sense musical sound through my feet and also through my hands. I can identify the different notes as I press the pedal according to which part of my foot feels the vibrations and for how long, and by how I experience the vibrations in my body.

EVELYN GLENNIE, International percussionist who went deaf at the age of eight

If you could only dance all that you've said, then I would understand.

Zorba the Greek,
NIKOS KAZANTZAKIS,
The Saviours of God,
Simon & Schuster

Those with kinesthetic intelligence will have the ability to use the body in highly differentiated and skilled ways. To work with objects and manipulate them with finesse. They will learn best by doing where physical movement aids memory.

Kinesthetic learning has traditionally been downgraded as something that is done in primary and junior schools – 'we don't have time for that here in secondary school' – and is often associated with special learning needs. This tendency not only undervalues the real and powerful impact physical reinforcement has on learning but also forgets that physical co-ordination is a highly desirable, lifelong skill which is learned and which can attract high salaries! One would hope that your dentist would combine a knowledge and understanding of dentistry with a high degree of manual dexterity and particularly so once inside your mouth! You would want your children's bus driver to have good hand–eye co-ordination. It is best that the pilot who flies the plane taking you on holiday can combine hand and feet movements as well as visually monitor data and listen on the headset and talk to the others around; if not, that week in Skegness begins to look more attractive.

Physical movement aids learning. It can help in neural networking, supply oxygen to the learning instrument – the brain – to keep it in the best state for learning and it can also help imprint information through associated motor movements. It is also a talent or an intelligence in itself. Why pay a very large sum of money to witness adults in tights and short skirts dancing to pieces of classical music? Why pay money to observe a man hit a ball 300 yards with a piece of metal whilst simultaneously applying spin and fade and allowing for wind and the surface it will land on? A top professional footballer may not be able to string a series of well-rounded sentences together but is there not an intelligence of some sort in being able to run, hit a ball with the inside or outside of either foot, apply spin and swerve and land it on a another moving target forty yards away?

A person with a well-developed kinesthetic intelligence will:

◆ enjoy exploring through touch, movement, manipulation and physical experience

◆ learn by doing

◆ show dexterity in fine and gross motor movement

◆ remember most clearly what was done rather than what was said or seen

◆ be concerned over improvement in physical performance

◆ benefit from frequent physical breaks

◆ demonstrate creativity through construction, physical movement and expression

◆ show co-ordination, sense of movement, timing, balance, dexterity

To develop and access the kinesthetic intelligence:

◆ STAGE ONE: STIMULATION

Brain gym activities such as those described in *Accelerated Learning in the Classroom* and in *Brain Gym for Teachers* (Dennison, P. & Dennison, G. E.), will not only energise by providing co-ordinated physical movement leading to increased blood flow, but will also provide a means of increasing neurotrophins (natural neural growth factors), connecting the hemispheres and improving hand–eye co-ordination and fine and large motor control. A well-timed combination of brain gym exercises will also offer an opportunity for the classroom teacher to change the 'physical state' of the learners in his or her charge. Should the class come in having witnessed an 'incident' in the school yard or be 'high' for some other reasons, then a carefully chosen brain gym activity such as alphabet edit will immediately displace all those other preoccupations.

Guided visualisations or classroom yoga can also have the desired effect of taking the learners to the desired physical state of readiness for learning you want them to be in before starting other work.

◆ STAGE TWO: AMPLIFICATION

Simulations, design and build activities, the enactment of scenes from an excerpt from literature or the rehearsing of a moral dilemma through a short role-play offers learning which is not only memorable and engaging but also physically active.

The human body – on its own or in combination with others – offers a cheap, easily resourced and instantly powerful route into learning. Obvious examples include modelling of the workings of the digestive tract or the inner ear; the differences in structure between solids, liquids and gases modelled by students locked together or bumping around; the movement of the planets in relation to each other; the effect of erosion on rivers; bar graphs and charts; driving and resisting forces.

> There's a lot in maths that I try and teach using physical examples. We get students outside to build models and take part in demonstrations involving different types of mathematical concepts. The other week I was teaching about parabolas using a water rocket.

HEAD OF MATHS, FROME COLLEGE, SOMERSET

◆ STAGE THREE: LEARNING AND UNDERSTANDING

The model of learning advocated throughout the *Accelerated Learning in the Classroom* approach is that of connect – preview – focus on task – diffuse – focus on task – diffuse – focus on task – diffuse – review and, for kinesthetic learners especially, this patterned structure with opportunity for reflection or review alongside some physical activity, say, stretching or movement of some sort, goes a long way to reducing tension and helping them stay within the learning experience.

In summary, use role-play, drama, physical movement, body sculpture, class group games, field trips, visits, design-and-make activities. Provide support and praise for extra-curricular involvement in 'physical' activities. Utilise regular break states and focus-diffuse-focus strategy. Build in regular review to lessons.

◆ STAGE FOUR: TRANSFERRING AND EFFECTING

Mind and body are one system. Mental state and physical performance are intertwined. Correct mental attitude will enhance physical performance and correct physical state will improve mental performance. David Hemery, prior to his World Record and Olympic-winning 400 metres hurdles run at the Mexico Olympics in 1968, describes how he attuned himself physically and mentally to win. His account brings together some of the significance of affirmations, outcomes thinking, of focusing on one's own performance not those of others and of mental rehearsal of physical performance. . .

> I was on the track watching Jeff Vanderstock who was the expected winner of the games. He did a start out of the blocks and I felt my throat constrict and recognised that my mind was on him, and I knew that I could not control how fast he ran and that I had to come back inside myself. I left my shoes and spikes on the side and used the in-field to simulate going back to my very early training days where I had been in the situation of running on very firm sand at the low water's edge. I just ran down the field imagining the feeling I had at that stage, with the sun on my back, feeling the warmth, the power, the strength, the fluidity ... recalling this one day I had run on the beach ... I just kept on running and running, lifting up faster and faster, and there didn't seem to be any fatigue. It was just an unbelievable flowing feeling. Eventually, I slowed down and jogged back. It was enough to come back into my senses, of what it felt like to be strong and flowing ... it took my awareness back inside. By the time I had done that I was back inside me and Jeff Vanderstock could do his own thing.

DAVID HEMERY, 1990

179

● Musical

" I haven't understood a bar of music in my life, but I have felt it. "

IGOR STRAVINSKY, *Bloomsbury Dictionary of Thematic Quotations*, Bloomsbury Publishing

" At the suggestion of the school site manager we introduced music in the general areas around the school. We had a large foyer area and children would arrive early and mill around. The site manager put up speakers and he played music of his own choice which was easy on the ear. The change in atmosphere and to the start of the day was remarkable. Children were generally quieter and we seemed to have more settled and prompt start to our day. Punctuality actually improved! "

PAT COLLARBONE, Director, London Leadership Centre and former Headteacher, Haggerston School, London from a speech at a Leicestershire Headteachers' Conference

For many with a musical intelligence tones, rhythms and larger musical patterns are constantly in their consciousness. They will listen to and respond with insight to a variety of sounds including environmental sounds, music and the human voice, and be able to interpret patterns in such sounds and create their own using instruments, voice or technology. By recognising and discussing different types of music, genres and cultural variations, they will demonstrate their interest in the role music plays in human lives.

I listened to a story recently which suggested the possibility that listening to music may have an impact on our physical and emotional response which we cannot yet fully explain. The speaker, a specialist in the training of music teachers, told how he and his wife shared their home with his elderly mother-in-law. For many years his mother-in-law had suffered from Alzheimer's disease, a degenerative brain condition which leads to physical deterioration in the brain with consequent profound and traumatic loss of memory. This woman, a widow who with her late husband had been a ballroom dancer, was so enfeebled by this condition that she was unable to bring herself to leave the house. As her condition worsened, she became trapped in one room. In her state she was unable to discern whether the change in the colour and texture of the carpet represented a drop of one-quarter of an inch or one-quarter of a mile. Her daughter and son-in-law struggled to persuade her to leave her room. By chance the speaker happened to be playing the piano in an adjacent room early one evening. The sound of the piano must have filled the house because shortly after starting a piece with which the elderly woman would have been familiar from her ballroom dancing days, he was startled when she 'waltzed' into the room. She had left her own room for the first time in months. As the music continued, she continued on her own to move around in what was a parody of the dancing which she once had practised to perfection.

What was happening when that music played? Was there some neural patterning which fired the memory? Was there an area of the brain in which the patterns of sounds were recognised? Why did the pattern of sounds stimulate the movements of the dance? Why did the music produce a dramatic change of response when all else had failed?

Millions of neurons can be activated in a single (musical) experience. Music has an uncanny manner of activating neurons for purposes of relaxing muscle tension, changing pulse and producing long-range memories which are directly related to the number of neurons activated in the experience.

D. CAMPBELL, *Introduction to the Musical Brain,* Richardson

The subject of music and learning is a fascinating one. We do know that in our classrooms there are children who can describe the colours in pieces of music, who are moved emotionally by pieces and who are able to articulate their creative response through movement and dance.

A person with a well developed musical intelligence will:

> ◆ discern patterns in sounds and enjoy experimenting with them
>
> ◆ show sensitivity to mood changes in sounds
>
> ◆ have a sense of rhythm and be able to respond to music artistically
>
> ◆ be curious about music and seek to develop their own categories and preferences
>
> ◆ enjoy improvising and experimenting with sounds of different sorts

To develop and access the musical intelligence:

◆ STAGE ONE: STIMULATION

Be flexible, be sensitive, be aware of the outcomes you seek and be aware of the potential pitfalls.

Flexibility in how and when you choose to use music is important. As the class teacher you choose the occasions when the use of music will enhance the learning in your classroom. On some occasions it is to set a mood prior to work; on others it is to evoke a theme and encourage listening; it can be used to arouse, demarcate time on task or assist in review. Avoid using music as wallpaper; avoid personal stereos; you choose the music, preferably without lyrics. Demonstrate sensitivity to different categories and musical genres so that over time students are learning about music as well as with music. Explain why you choose to use music. If in doubt go to an expert! Use the experience of the trained music specialist on your staff.

◆ STAGE TWO: AMPLIFICATION

Recognising that music can alter mood and that there is an obvious link with the sound of strong rhythmic beating and collective physical action, music can be used to arouse and learn content to a strong repetitive beat. Music can also be used for the opposite effect. Calming music can create a space in the classroom for reflection and relaxation.

> I have a bottom set in Year 10 for Science. When we're doing discussion work in pairs or in groups or we're writing up assignment work I use music. At first they thought I was mad. This is a difficult school and these are challenging kids. Gradually they got used to it. I explained why I was using it and why I chose the music – often classic pieces without words and with a regular and slowish beat – and they began to respond positively. Now when I turn the volume of the music down the noise level in the class goes down too. I know they're on task. It seems to have helped our relationship as well.

CHRIS WARDLE, SCIENCE TEACHER

◆ STAGE THREE: LEARNING AND UNDERSTANDING

Here are some suggested specific strategies for classroom use.

Beginnings. Use music to welcome students into the class and to begin to direct attention towards the learning task.

Demarcation of time on task. Short, lively pieces, which are of a known duration, can be used to provide a frame against which to undertake, for example, a review task or a series of brain gym exercises. Because everyone concerned knows the length of the music there is an in-built expectation about how long the task takes and therefore the transition to the next stage is easier to manage.

Authentication of a mood or evocation of a theme. It may be that you seek a particular atmosphere in which to introduce a new theme or topic. A study of the Tudors would no doubt be enhanced by the use of music from the period – 'La Volta', 'Greensleeves', 'The Agincourt Song' for example. Similarly, work on the poetry of the First World War may be enhanced by the use of popular music hall songs from the time, from the some of the works of Elgar and Delius or music such as *Il Cavatino* which evokes a sense of despair or futility.

Energiser or relaxer. Music can raise the blood pressure and pulse rate or, conversely, lower the blood pressure and pulse rate. Energising may be the last thing you wish to do, but if you should find yourself in an airless classroom on a hot summer's afternoon it may be appropriate. Music will help take the students to a state of relaxed alertness which is the best state of mind for assimilating large amounts of new information. This is the essence of claims made for Baroque music and intelligence. There is no worthy evidence that Baroque music will make you more intelligent! What it may do is encourage a physical state of relaxed alertness which may induce an Alpha wave state in the brain. The Alpha level is characterised by an accompanying sense of 'letting go' where we are more holistic and open to multiple perspectives beyond the rational. Our intuitive sensibilities are high and keen in this state. We are more receptive and open to new information.

Music for guided visualisations. Guided visualisations (see *Accelerated Learning in the Classroom*, Network Educational Press, 1996) are used to make the learner feel relaxed and positive about themselves and their learning. The teacher guides the listener into a visualised mental world whilst the music provides a background.

As an aid to discussion. There is no doubt that laying a piece of music under a discussion activity promptly moves the group onto task and allows the classroom teacher to manage the noise levels by varying the volume of the accompanying music up or down.

Active concert and Passive concert. These methods, which derive from the work in suggestopaedic language learning of Georgi Lozanov, are used to powerful effect in accelerated languages learning. The active concert creates an emotional association with a dramatic piece of music. The voice introduces the new language material whilst surfing the music. As the music rises and falls so the voice goes with it. As the active concert continues the students follow the text using a brightly coloured memory map. The experience is designed to be multi-sensory and whole-brain. The passive concert works in a different way. With accompanying music with an insistent 60–70 bpm – often Baroque – the student listens to the same language text but this time in a 'passive' state. The voice lies under the music and the student is asked to listen to the music and not the voice. The idea is that the voice will engage the unconscious mind whilst the music fully involves the conscious mind.

Stimulant for hemispheric connection. Some of the possible uses include material learned to raps, rhymes, songs, jingles, choral readings, dramatic readings. In English language and in languages generally, collective reading or chanting of narrative verse or rhythmic texts is powerful in recall as well as being fun and encouraging the skill of collective participation.

◆ STAGE FOUR: TRANSFERRING AND EFFECTING

Students encounter music every day of their lives in one format or another. The music they encounter may be deliberately chosen by them, associated with another medium such as television or cinema, be incidental or be deliberately chosen by someone else to shape an experience – in a supermarket or on a telephone answering system for instance. It is very difficult to turn it all off! Just as we encounter music in different ways so too do we listen in different ways. We learn about and with music in different ways. Focused and attentive listening is one way to interact with music. It should be fostered and encouraged as a special skill throughout learning but it is not the only way to interact with music. Some music teachers and others have commented on the use of music as a learning tool offering the view that it devalues the integrity of the listening experience. I argue that by explaining how we use music as we use it, we not only shape thinking about different possibilities and pose underlying questions such as 'in what way is this helping me?' we also increase the range and variety of the types of music learners encounter. They are learning with and about music as we go.

● Naturalist

MARIE CURIE, *Bloomsbury Dictionary of Thematic Quotations*, Bloomsbury Publishing

For many with a naturalist intelligence they will be at home in and delight in the natural environment. An ability to describe the features of a natural environment and classify species will often be accompanied by a sense of elation at being there. Gardner says of the naturalist intelligence that it *'refers to the ability to recognise and classify plants, minerals, and animals, including rocks and grass and all variety of flora and fauna ... there are particular parts of the brain dedicated to the recognition and the naming of what are called natural things'.*

The best examples I can give of an obvious display of the naturalist intelligence are those individuals who show a sensitivity to the natural rhythms of the environment around them – farmers, fishermen, stalkers and beaters, coastguards, game wardens – with an ability to make sense of it. This intelligence is there in the writings of such diverse characters as Gertrude Bell, T.E. Lawrence, Lawrence Durrell and Wifred Thesiger. The American poets Carl Sandburg and Walt Whitman and the English 18th Century poet William Wordsworth are other excellent examples who articulated their response on our behalf.

Wordsworth displayed a precocious sensitivity to the natural world at an early age and this in a historical period where the countryside was viewed partly with disdain and partly with horror and fear. His poetry combines a sense of awe and wonder with reverence for something only partly understood. In this excerpt from his poem *The Prelude* he describes his emotions after stealing a boat and rowing it at night,

> *With trembling hands I turned, and through the silent water stole my way*
> *back to the cavern of the willow tree: there in my mooring place I left my bark,*
> *and through the meadows homeward went, with grave and serious thoughts;*
> *and after I had seen that spectacle, for many days, my brain*
> *worked with a dim and undetermined sense of unknown modes of being; in my thoughts there*
> *was a darkness, call it solitude or blank desertion. No familiar shapes*
> *of hourly objects, images of trees, of sea or sky, no colours of green fields;*
> *but huge and mighty forms, that do not live like living men, moved slowly through my mind*
> *by day, and were the trouble of my dreams.*

In every classroom in the country there are youngsters who may be weak academically but can, nevertheless, manage the care and welfare of a pony or know every dog and its history in the local kennels or describe the best site in a national park to do a grade three climb, what to take and how to do it once you get here. Others will know every site for catching perch within an hour's cycle ride of their home or show a seemingly dramatic and positive personality change in the presence of whippets, ferrets or pigeons!

◆ be attuned to the natural environment and be sensitive to harmony and disharmony there

◆ be able to categorise species and discern significance in patterns of relationships within and between species

◆ show awareness of the interrelatedness of environment, change and time

◆ be comfortable in different types of natural environment

◆ demonstrate concern about the impact of human intervention in the natural environment

◆ understand the significance of environmental and perhaps social 'balance' and have a sense of fairness

To develop and access the naturalist intelligence:

◆ STAGE ONE: STIMULATION

When teachers encourage alertness in learners to their immediate environment and the natural world beyond, it very soon becomes apparent that some students are more attuned and more observant than others. In one primary school a Yr 6 class had planted some saplings in the school grounds. Some noticed that those planted near a fence were dying whilst others planted throughout the grounds were doing much better. In class they agreed that because a neighbour had cut back his trees by the fence there was no shade and so the saplings were exposed to too much sun. Classes with environmental interest walls where children bring in and read cuttings of topical interest and held observation quizzes help to put emphasis on caring for the class and school environment.

◆ STAGE TWO: AMPLIFICATION

Local councils are often good starting points for advice about accessing and using the local environment as a learning resource. In 1995 I was a member of a team who worked on a project for the County of Avon with the City of Bath Council. The title of the project was 'The City of Bath as a Learning Resource' and aside from the obvious projects about and around the significance of the city as a tourist centre, there were supported self-study materials produced in topics such as 'designating a nature reserve', 'pollution and its impact on buildings', 'the protection of canal towpaths', 'flora and fauna in churchyards', 'traffic calming measures', 'social housing in Bath', 'cycle routes through Bath'. The study packs were designed to stimulate enquiry and develop research skills, interview skills, skills of observation, analysis and classification. Each provided access to quality information generated by the local council.

We used to take them in Years 7 and 8 to the Lake District and spend four days on an integrated project. We did work on streams and the speed of water flow at different points in the stream; settlement patterns in and around the village of Hawkshead; traffic and usage surveys; creative writing up on the fells. In the evenings we'd do some abseiling or river walks or orienteering. All the time they were making connections. Some of these kids had never been away from Carlisle to the Lakes and it was only twenty miles away. It was the best thing I've ever done. Even now, I meet some of them in the street, fifteen years later, with their own children and they still want to talk about it.

JR McLean, English Teacher

◆ STAGE THREE: LEARNING AND UNDERSTANDING

Field trips, environmental projects, species counts, the planned management of, and responsibility for, the upkeep of given areas, traffic surveys, pollution surveys. All these activities can develop the key naturalist skills of empathy and sensitivity to the environment, detailed observation, classification of information and conservation. Design projects involving considerations of the environment and the users' integration and use of it – the design of a public play area or of a social space within the school – will also develop the naturalist intelligence.

◆ STAGE FOUR: TRANSFERRING AND EFFECTING

The outdoors can become the classroom. In an article entitled 'The Greening of Learning: Using the Eight Intelligence', published in *Educational Leadership*, Maggie Meyer lists a number of easily replicable activities which she uses. Here are examples:

◆ water-quality monitoring project which includes visualisation of the forested area adjacent to most rivers, kinesthetic simulations of water going down a storm drain, chemical monitoring tests, breathing rates of feeder-fish in different water temperatures, mock presentations to community users groups

◆ on hikes, natural objects that start with different letters of the alphabet are recorded

◆ groups with designated 100 square inch rectangular plots for ecology studies; contents are observed, drawn, recorded and itemised

◆ visits to landfill sites, water treatment plants, open-cast quarry areas

◆ visits from wildlife biologists, parks and recreation manager, the person at the council who designs the play parks, a local farmer

◆ designing a puppet play to teach 5 and 6 year olds about the environment and how to look after it

◆ a video survey of locals and what they know about water supply

IN ORDER TO ASSESS YOUR OWN BALANCE OF INTELLIGENCES AS YOU PERCEIVE THEM AT THIS POINT IN TIME YOU CAN USE THE FOLLOWING SELF-PERCEPTION QUESTIONNAIRE

Please complete the following questionnaire by assigning a numerical value to each of the statements which you consider represents you. If you agree that the statement very strongly represents you, assign a 5. If the statement does not represent you, assign a 0. Use the numbers 5–0 to grade each statement.

On the following pages, transfer the outcomes to the seven (plus one) intelligences listing and then complete the sectioned wheel.

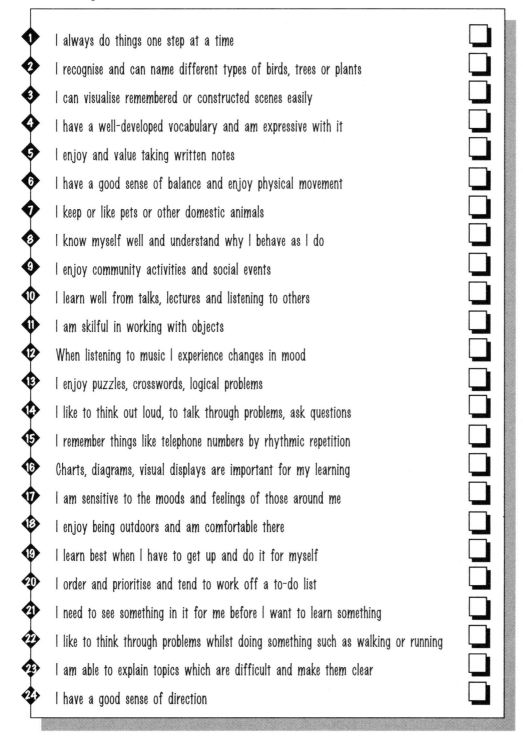

1 I always do things one step at a time

2 I recognise and can name different types of birds, trees or plants

3 I can visualise remembered or constructed scenes easily

4 I have a well-developed vocabulary and am expressive with it

5 I enjoy and value taking written notes

6 I have a good sense of balance and enjoy physical movement

7 I keep or like pets or other domestic animals

8 I know myself well and understand why I behave as I do

9 I enjoy community activities and social events

10 I learn well from talks, lectures and listening to others

11 I am skilful in working with objects

12 When listening to music I experience changes in mood

13 I enjoy puzzles, crosswords, logical problems

14 I like to think out loud, to talk through problems, ask questions

15 I remember things like telephone numbers by rhythmic repetition

16 Charts, diagrams, visual displays are important for my learning

17 I am sensitive to the moods and feelings of those around me

18 I enjoy being outdoors and am comfortable there

19 I learn best when I have to get up and do it for myself

20 I order and prioritise and tend to work off a to-do list

21 I need to see something in it for me before I want to learn something

22 I like to think through problems whilst doing something such as walking or running

23 I am able to explain topics which are difficult and make them clear

24 I have a good sense of direction

187

25. I have a natural ability to sort out arguments between friends ☐

26. I can remember the words to music easily ☐

27. I can take things apart and re-assemble them easily ☐

28. I enjoy games involving other people ☐

29. I like privacy and quiet for working and thinking ☐

30. I can pick out individual instruments in complex musical pieces ☐

31. I can discern patterns and relationships between experiences or things ☐

32. In teams I co-operate and build on the ideas of others ☐

33. I am interested in psychology and human motivation ☐

34. I am observant and will often see things others miss ☐

35. I get restless easily ☐

36. I enjoy working or learning independently of others ☐

37. I enjoy making music ☐

38. I am angered by environmental neglect or obvious pollution ☐

39. I have a facility with numbers and mathematical problems ☐

40. I am an independent thinker and I know my own mind ☐

MULTIPLE INTELLIGENCES: SCORING

Intelligence	Statements	Total score
interpersonal scoring	9, 17, 25, 28, 32	....
intrapersonal scoring	8, 21, 29, 36, 40	....
linguistic scoring	4, 5, 10, 14, 23	....
mathematical and logical scoring	1, 13, 20, 31, 39	....
visual and spatial scoring	3, 16, 24, 34, 27	....

Intelligence	Statements	Total score
kinesthetic	6, 11, 19, 22, 35	
scoring	....	....
musical	12, 15, 26, 30, 37	
scoring	....	....
naturalist	2, 7, 18, 33, 38	
scoring	....	....

Multiple Intelligences wheel

By taking the numerical score against each intelligence from the questionnaire, plotting it on the wheel and shading each segment you will get a visual representation of your balance of intellgences according to Howard Gardner's theory. Shade to the approximate position within each segment – e.g., if you scored 16 shade to a position just into the 15–20 space.

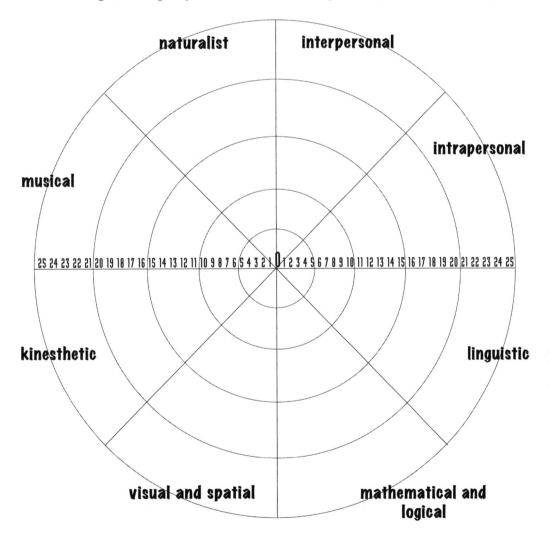

6 DEMONSTRATING THE NEW UNDERSTANDING

> *X is really good because you get varied but structured lessons. We do lots of different things but they all relate to the topic. Then at the end of the lesson we pack up early and just sit and go over what we've done. We talk about it and then the teacher explains how it fits into the next lesson's work. The course is like a jigsaw and the teacher fits the bits together for us.*

South Bristol Secondary Pupil,
Bath University, *Departments Adding Significant Value,* **1994**

ON VISITING A SURREY SCHOOL IN LATE SPRING THIS YEAR I was surprised to find that all those students who were in Year 11 were gathered in the main hall sitting behind examination desks. This was prior to their leaving to go on 'study leave' before sitting GCSE examinations. The Headteacher was well into thanking them effusively for having worked so hard up to that point. She went on to encourage them to continue to work hard in the period left to them prior to sitting the exam. The Deputy then took over and began to guide them through a visualisation exercise. As he did so, Bach's Double Violin Concerto in D minor was playing in the background.

With the students behind the desks where they would sit their exams, he began by encouraging them to relax, listen to the music, place their feet flat on the floor, close their eyes and continue to relax. The music continued, he paused before going on to ask them to remember an experience where they had been successful and, in remembering it fully, to recall just how they had felt, what others had said to them and what they saw themselves doing. Again, he paused, asked them to continue relaxing and then invited them to think of their best piece of schoolwork, what they had done and when and how they had felt about completing it. He asked them to remember what it felt like to be successful and to recall it for a minute or so. Then he got them to think ahead to their first exam when they would be sitting at that very desk and asked them to imagine similar success.

As the music continued to play, he asked them to continue relaxing and to anticipate sitting down, opening the exam paper and feeling good about it; looking through the paper, recognising the questions, already thinking about good answers and then carefully beginning to work through the paper, checking as they went, completing each question well, checking for accuracy and moving on, eventually sitting back feeling very positive about completing the whole paper. He went quiet and the music continued. Slowly he invited them back, caught their attention as the music faded and wished them well before sending them off home.

What was the point of all this? The school in question recognised that just as the thought of spiders provokes panic in some adults and the thought of school and school-days provokes anxiety in some parents, so too can the thought of exams and the exam hall induce stress in students. In a process we are not entirely sure of, the exam hall can, for many, become anchored to feelings of stress and inadequacy. Think of the exam hall, its desk, its clock and all the other paraphernalia, and the anxiety comes. With anxiety comes deterioration in performance. Better to anchor the associations with the hall and exams to more positive experiences. Better to get students to rehearse mentally the exam secrets which will help them succeed. This was what the school was attempting to do. The Headteacher created a positive start, the desks were already beginning to feel familiar, the Deputy helped create a positive connection. When the GCSE examinations started it was their intention to play the music again as students arrived and sat around waiting in the first nervous minutes.

Many students – young and old – never get the chance to 'demonstrate the new understanding' because exam nerves paralyse them into underperformance. The positive management strategies described throughout this book go some way to alleviating this condition.

> *At one Stanwell primary school, achievement levels in the two Yr 6 groups rose dramatically in six months after the introduction of a structured accelerated learning programme. KS2 SATs scores in Science went from 27% at Level 4 and above in 1996 to 100% at Level 4 and above in 1997. The Year group included several children with statements of Special Educational Needs. The Deputy Head described the results as 'absolutely amazing'. The class teachers now use visual learning display on every wall and ceiling, direct interventions to raise self-esteem, learning posters for every unit, rehearsing new learning kinesthetically (lessons on gases and the ear drum being the most successful examples), memory maps, frequent review including every Friday afternoon making posters of what has been learned that week, regular quizzes and informal tests, competitive tests with scores shouted out, new information learned to rhyme.*

> *Describing the success brought by the changes, Yr 6 teachers . . . said, 'they were different children after two terms'. Self-belief had shot up. Every child had affirmation adjectives which they felt described them, tacky-backed to his or her desk. At first some children didn't want the words or rejected them. Eventually, they were all keen. Words like 'outstanding' and 'brilliant' could be seen stuck down on some desks. Children wrote in their profiles of 'enjoying the SATs'.*

When you visit the Yr 6 classrooms at this school what you see is effective use of colour and of space. Children 'show they know' through the creation of their own learning posters. Some of the posters made about gases were in 2-D and were so elaborate they included flaps opened by tiny springs, which the children found at home to make points about pressure. One teacher said that when the class sat their science SAT test *'you could see the children looking around the wall to where the learning posters I made had been. I had taken everything down before the test and I apologised to them beforehand about this. One girl said to me afterwards,* "don't worry Miss, when I looked up I could see where the poster was and wrote it all down . . . I got it all right." *Although the information was no longer on the wall, they saw it as if it was there!'*

This school, which does not want further publicity as a result of an overwhelming demand for visits, would seem to have gone some way to overcome anxieties about testing. Indeed, the teachers said their own anxieties were higher than the children's! Success in testing has spread to Yr 3 where the class now can spell words which previously comprised the Yr 6 test. *'We've just shifted our expectations up and the children followed'.* They achieved 100% success in 20 word tests which included words like: 'voice', 'irritating', 'because', 'constantly', 'extremely', 'allowed', 'square', 'area', 'joint', 'skeleton' and 'muscle'. The teachers I talked to, without directly articulating it, seemed to have adopted the view that there was no failure. The experience of failure was framed as a temporary hiccup and, with the right strategies and time, eventually everyone would be successful: *'there is no failure, only feedback'.*

By using different tools which learners can utilise, adapt and then begin to apply for themselves in a variety of contexts we begin to develop transfer. Regular opportunities to 'perform understanding', combined with the use and subsequent acquisition of problem-solving tools will contribute to all-round performance.

> **Those that have succeeded in raising pupils' levels of thinking across a range of reasoning patterns have done so not by trying to teach the reasoning patterns directly, but by putting their pupils in a position where they must construct the reasoning pattern for themselves, to solve new problems.**

P. ADEY, M. SHAYER AND C. YATES, *A Teacher's Guide to Thinking Science, The Curriculum Materials of the Cognitive Acceleration through Science Education Project, Second Edition*, Nelson

Here are some further positive strategies to allow students to demonstrate the new understanding or 'show they know'. I have organised them into five family groupings – maps, templates, sequences, demonstrations and collaborations.

Maps

Topic webs. Topic webs take the key topic and place it in the centre of the page. The key topic is then connected to related sub-topics in a pattern which looks like the branches of a tree. As each sub-topic branches further from the centre, a pattern of connections emerges. To ensure that the topic web is used to develop thinking about patterns of connections, insist that students specify what the connection between each topic is by writing it onto the branch which links it. A further 'pole-bridging' improvement can be made by structuring an activity where students describe the construction of their topic web aloud to a partner or audience of fellow students.

Memory maps. Memory mapping takes the principles of whole brain learning, the basic architecture of topic-webbing and applies colour, shape, iconography and reflectivity. The illustrator's eight-year-old son's memory map for a talk 'all about me' shows how he understands the architectural and hierarchical principles of webbing.

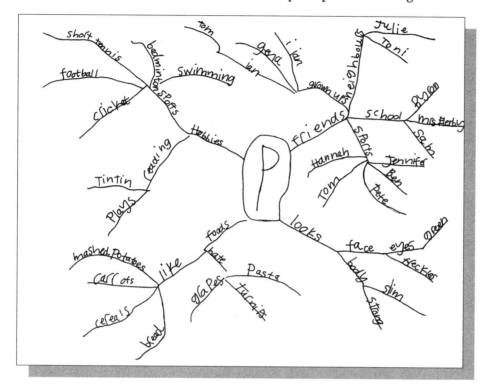

His father helped him prepare for a talk on the Romans for his schoolwork by adding visual icons and selected images to the hierarchy of categories.

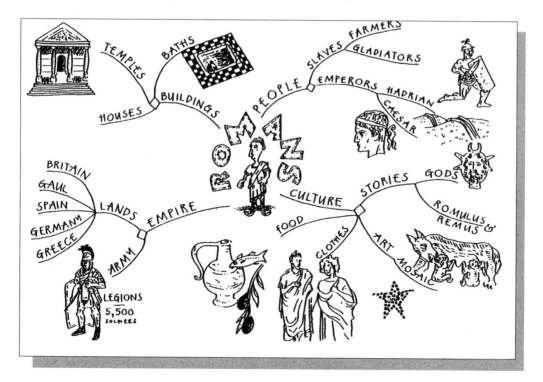

His father, through a memory map on memory mapping, shows us how it is done.

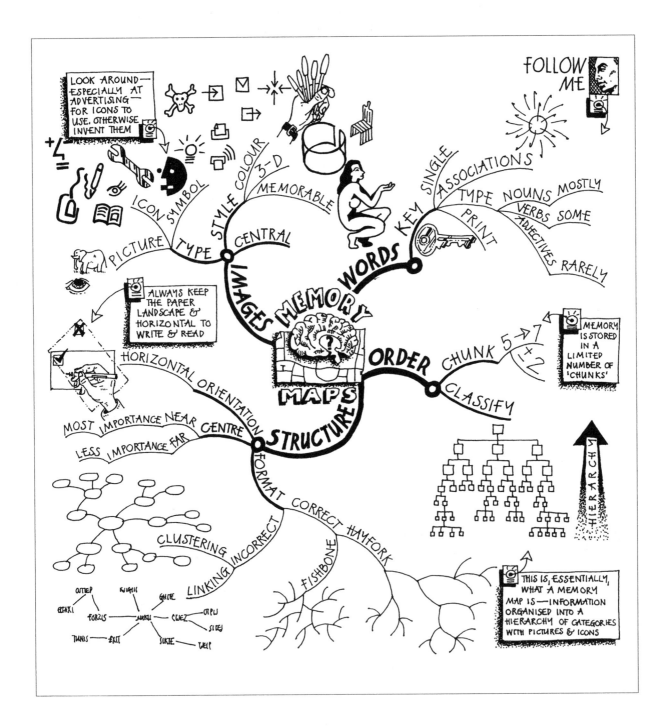

Memory mapping only works when the learner generates his or her own maps. This will require practice in the techniques but do remember it is not an art test! It is the quality of thinking and the degree of interaction with the subject which matters. Some basic tips to help your students include:

194

◆ practise from what is already well known and understood, for example, a memory map about 'me'

◆ start with the architecture – best learned through topic-webbing

◆ build out and from the centre, spatially organising as you go

◆ print the keywords, saying them aloud as you go

◆ add visual icons which capture the essence of the concept and make these icons meaningful to you personally

◆ emphasise the central topic by isolating it

◆ emphasise related key topics by use of bright primary colours

◆ continue to step back from the construction of the map to survey the overall pattern of shapes and connections as you build them

◆ reinforce understanding and recall by explaining it to others, turning it over and quickly sketching out the key patterns and words, physically modelling it on the floor by walking it – move up and down the branches explaining aloud as you go

Text and context notes. Linear notes can be dramatically enhanced by using the text and context method. In addition to taking structured, indented and highlighted linear notes, leave a space at the side of the page for context. In this space record any questions or thoughts – however bizarre and seemingly irrelevant – which arise as the notes are taken. Include in the space the context in which the notes were taken: Where were you? what was happening? What time of day was it? What distractions did you encounter? What personal observations occurred to you about the process of note-taking? A further enhancement is to add essential vocabulary into the context space. Code them by using colours. Link them to the original source in the body text.

Freenoting. In his excellent book *The Einstein Factor*, Win Wenger describes how freenoting works. *'It simply means writing down, on the spot, whatever thought pops into your head as you listen in class, meeting, lecture or even as you read a book.'*
He goes on to point out some of the significant differences between this and conventional note-taking, *'you make no attempt whatsoever to capture the facts that the lecturer is imparting . . . on the contrary you allow your scribbles to range as far and wide from the speaker's topic as your mind carries you, writing constantly and rapidly, so that it is virtually impossible to follow the lecture material.'*
Explaining that the intention is to allow the lecture material to enter the mind subliminally rather than consciously, Wenger points out that freenoters have found that they retain more of their freenoted lectures than they do of lectures to which they tried their best to pay attention. Moreover, *'their scribblings are found to contain brilliant insights that integrate the subject material far more intimately and practically with their own private interests and situations than would normally be the case.'*

195

Templates

When designing worksheets leave 'white space' for note-taking. Use calming colours such as light blue for ease on the eye. Frame the contents. Use a large font and no more than two different fonts in all. Be aware that the top third is read most, the middle third least and the bottom third second most. Guide the eye down the page starting from the top left by using discreet visuals, bullet points – no more than five – and space for a participative reader response such as: 'the three most important points are', 'the best three ideas I can use are', 'the key things I must remember'.

Templates, writing frames and structured problem-solving tools help learners structure a response to any given learning task set. For many, there is nothing more terrifying than a blank sheet of paper. The template can take them out of that funk.

Simple, well-documented, study maxims include the guidelines contained in:

◆ **KWPL** – *Know, Want, Predict, Learn*

◆ **3S TN (Qs)** – *Survey & ask questions as you survey, Skim a small section at a time & ask questions as you skim, Take Notes & ask questions as you take notes, Study your notes & ask questions & answer the questions verbally*

◆ **Memory – intent, file, recall**
Intent – make up your mind that you intend to learn it, use your best methods to **file** *it, test yourself so you can* **recall** *it*

◆ **Be a 'STAR' at tests**
Take the test and be a 'STAR' – Survey all the test questions first, Take time to read all the questions carefully, Answer the easy ones first, Relax and re-read the questions and your answers

Templates can help prepare for learning, encourage breadth of thinking and take the learner into the heart of a task. Some examples are provided in Section Four. Their application is summarised below:

Personal readiness for learning

Self-review. Designed to encourage self-reflection and to further thinking about what helps and hinders personal learning.

Looking after my learning. Helps structure any task by setting a positive and desired outcome then uses a checklist to help the learner stay positive.

Personal learning goals. Designed with structured approaches to tasks in mind.

Behaviour change plan. Helps alleviate entrenched thinking by helping manage problematic behaviours.

Two sides to the problem. Encourages empathy and provides a mechanism for shaping a positive solution.

Why be angry? Ten tips for keeping cool . . .

Connecting the learning

Thinking prompts. Simple tools for thinking around a problem.

Predictions. Develops speculation and reflection skills whilst utilising the magic numbers.

Making careful decisions. Does just that!

Problem solving. A tightly structured catechism for working through any problem.

Learning tools

Homework assessment tool. Helps make explicit what successful homework outcomes may look like.

Story map. Requires the story-writer to think of the audience, purpose and construction of the story before writing it!

Character map. Develops more subtle characterisation.

Project planner. Helpful in independent project work such as that required by GNVQ.

Scientific research planner. Reduces the tendency to 'do' without thinking and organising beforehand.

Spelling styles chart. NLP's greatest, some say only, practical learning tool. Advocates a VAK approach to spelling.

Sequences

Sequencing exercises which use props or artefacts as learning aids to physically manipulate, hide, reveal, re-organise and comment upon can liberate inhibitions in demonstrating understanding. Use postcards, index-cards, post-its or anything which is easily manipulated and on which information can be recorded. Encourage the learners to talk through it aloud as they go. Flow charts, timelines and fishbone diagrams are best used in a similar fashion. Don't overlook the real learning and motor memory recall which is enhanced by connecting physical manipulation with language. Before the separate recording of steps in a flow chart, get them up out of their seats and, as a team, physically walk through it.

Demonstrations

Articulation. The activity of externalising an internal thought process whilst either undertaking an activity or the contemplation of that activity powerfully develops learning and understanding. Wenger, rather controversially argues that we *'consciously think and perceive at the speed of the language we use'*, and so the encouragement of spontaneous, rapid and sensory-rich responses to internal stimuli will engage more areas of the brain. Encourage students to start to notice detail, observe and record that detail and ask questions of it to expand thought structures. For example, can you explain this idea to yourself in your own words now? Can you further explain any images which came into your head as you did so? What was happening? What sense do you make of those images? Is there any emerging pattern of connections? By increasing the proportion of ideas and perceptions that we respond to we alter the signification of importance and reinforce creativity.

Mental rehearsal. Encourage students to rehearse mentally a process or activity before beginning to write about it. For example, 'take 45 seconds to visualise yourself going through each stage of the chemistry experiment . . . now write about what was happening'. 'Before describing the process of photosynthesis in plants, take a minute and no more to rehearse mentally what happens . . . see the plant absorbing light . . . where is the light coming from? . . . what is beginning to happen in the plant? . . . what changes do we see? Now write about that process'. For probability, 'see yourself throwing a sequence of two dice . . . do it one, two, three times . . . what do you observe happening? . . . Now write about it'.

Testing yourself by performing your understanding. Frequent informal testing – particularly self-testing – takes some of the anxiety out of the idea of a test. As a teacher you should encourage self-testing and provide regular opportunities to do it, or, if it happens out of class, to de-brief and learn from the outcomes, from the mistakes. 'Performance of understanding' can be done via the multiple intelligences. A real audience or an audience of one's peers can help by requiring a consideration of presentation factors – attention span, likely interest, key learning points, best medium for the message.

Collaborations

Study buddies. In pairs students discuss and agree the questions which anyone should be able to answer by the completion of the unit, then they compare with others and agree a shared list, then they model the answers broken down into key points and then they test each other.

Each one teach one. When we are required to explain something to another party or, better, to teach something, then we really begin to demonstrate our understanding. Paired shares are good for this provided we give learners strategies to build from what they know and recognise what they don't yet know. Exchanging information previously recorded on a memory-map, before updating the map; agreeing points of agreement, points of difference and points of uncertainty before sharing with others. Some place their faith in the principle that we learn . . .

- ◆ 10% of what we read
- ◆ 20% of what we hear
- ◆ 30% of what we see
- ◆ 50% of what we both see and hear
- ◆ 70% of what is discussed with others
- ◆ 80% of what we experience personally
- ◆ 90% of what we TEACH to someone else

REVIEW AND RECALL FOR RETENTION

> *Doctor, doctor, I can't remember . . .*
> *When did this first happen?*
> **When did what happen?**

WITH THE CORRECT STIMULUS, our brains are perfectly able to access memories. In Section One we looked at prevailing models of memory and certain principles of recall. In this chapter we explore the best practices for storing and retrieving via this perfect memory.

It is important to recognise that with memory it is better in every way to work smarter than to work harder. Strategies which are unsuccessful for learners in a classroom environment will not become more successful for them when they get home. Doing the same thing but doing it with more intensity and for a longer period of time will not work.

In a 1996 research study 85% of the sample of 12 year olds asked, did not know what the word 'revise' meant! One student said it was the 'word teachers used when they couldn't think what to give you for homework'! Yet how often do teachers send students home with that very instruction: 'revise for your test'? One popular Geography GCSE syllabus suggests that 26% of marks are awarded for recall. Teachers must provide their students with tools for revision and recall.

Certain principles of memory can be used to guide us to useful review and recall tools for students. They are best summarised as the **SCOTS CLAN MAPS** model of memory.

<u>S</u>ensory	<u>C</u>hunked	<u>M</u>nemonics
<u>C</u>olourful and visual	<u>L</u>ocated	<u>A</u>lliteration, rhythm, rhyme
<u>O</u>utrageous	<u>A</u>ssociated	<u>P</u>ersonalised
<u>T</u>hematic or topical	<u>N</u>umbered	<u>S</u>hared
<u>S</u>equenced		

Where several principles can be applied in the same activity the results are better.

Multiple memory locations and systems are best for learning and recall. Any system utilising two or more of the brain's natural memory processes is considered a complex and therefore, successful, learning strategy.

SCHACTER, D.L., *Understanding Implicit Memory*, American Psychologist 47, 4, 1992

Teach your students the following principles and techniques and model them yourself . . .

Sensory

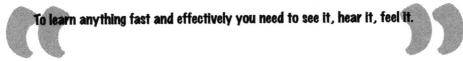

To learn anything fast and effectively you need to see it, hear it, feel it.

T. STOCKWELL, *The Learning Revolution*

Information learned with a physical reinforcement is more readily retained. Organise review activities which necessitate physical modelling:

◆ For younger learners, practising spelling by tracing words in sand or onto sandpaper, or onto a partner's back and he or she guesses the word.

◆ Physical sequencing activities using post-its or index cards laid out in order: learning twenty items of German vocabulary by writing each item and its translation on a post-it and placing them around the room, going to each in turn, practising there and then taking the post-its down and placing them on a sheet of paper and working through them in sequence, finally doing it without looking at the post-its — visualising the original layout as you go. . .

◆ Each student is allocated or selects at random a given part of speech in the foreign language they are learning. This could be a noun, verb, adjective, pronoun or adverb. They then organise themselves into sentences and shout out the string of words in turn. At a prompt they reassemble into different sentences and repeat the process.

◆ Creating a flow-diagram on the floor using both students and props.

◆ Bar graphs using chairs to mark different responses and students as the units of response.

◆ Creating a body sculpture with students modelling 'functions' — e.g., forces in science, the function of red and white blood cells, the condensation cycle, atomic structure and the Brownian motion.

◆ Role-plays.

◆ Constructing a 2-D model of a sequence on the floor with students positioned to replicate stages in a process — for example: the movement of the planets around the Sun, or the spread of a contagious disease, or the importance of feedback in electronic systems or effects of migration, or identifying 2-D shapes and patterns or rotational symmetries or reflective symmetries.

Colourful and visual

Our memory for images is better than our memory for words.

TONY BUZAN, *Use Your Perfect Memory*, Fontana

Colourful images and imagined, brightly coloured scenes are more readily recalled than monochrome equivalents. Visual information is more readily recalled than semantic information – pictures more readily than words. Help learners practise spellings by saying the word aloud first, then chunking them into smaller units of sound, highlighting each unit or underlining each unit in a different colour, and then looking at and storing the brightly coloured image in the upper left field of vision, shutting the eyes and seeing it there before saying out the letters in each chunk.

◆ Use review posters in bold, primary colours and for a specific audience or purpose in mind.

◆ Coloured highlighters can be used to associate related topics or keywords.

◆ Use coloured highlighters to review vocabulary in modern foreign languages or classics – look for different colours for adjectives, verbs and nouns.

◆ Complete topic webs, concept maps and memory maps in bright, patterned colours.

Outrageous

I suppose the high water mark of my youth in Columbus, Ohio, was the night the bed fell on my father.

JAMES THURBER, *Bloomsbury Dictionary of Thematic Quotations*, Bloomsbury Publishing

Experiences which are different and disrupt an expected pattern are distinct and easier to remember. In memory tests where lots of information is presented, items which are different are readily recalled and the greater the difference from the 'norm', the more immediate is the recall. Other examples could include:

◆ Have students rehearse a speech in the most outrageous voice manageable

◆ Construct 'outrageous applications' for new information. How might you teach this topic to a Martian? How might a creature who had never been to this planet view the information? What might be the essentials that a Martian would need to know? *At Brislington School in Bristol, one of the teachers has created a character he calls 'Robot Moron' and the pupils love to teach the Robot Moron.*

◆ List the key learning points from a unit of work (3 or 5 or 7 points), now think of some very famous people, or people you know well, and have them tell you one of the points each; imagine them saying the points, one each, in order, whilst sitting round a table, or singing at a concert, or going round a roundabout.

201

Thematic or topical

> They say that most adults over the age of forty can remember where they were and what they were doing when Kennedy was killed. My memory on this one's pretty hazy – all I can remember is being on top of a book depository in Dallas, Texas and then these policemen chasing me down the street . . .

US Comedian

Where possible new learning should build on what is already known and understood. A powerful way of making connections is to integrate learning through themes. Themes which relate to, and build out from, the 'world' which the learner knows and understands and which can be accessed by examples from that world will help. If these 'themes' can have a dimension which, for the learner, is topical and which can be readily conceived, then so much the better. A radio programme which described the disappearance of 17,000 hectares of forested land annually left me baffled because I could not relate it to anything which readily invited comparison: 'an area the equivalent of . . .'. Encourage thematic and connective thinking by the use of topic webs, concept-mapping, freenotes and memory maps.

Topicality provides a 'hook' onto which learning can be hung. 'What would contemporary characters do in a historical situation?' 'How would a time-traveller understand this?' 'What questions would a time-traveller ask?'

◆ Teach chronology by starting with the chronology of the young learners' lives – which family member lived where? And when? And with whom? And what did they do? And how are they related? And how do we know?

◆ Use the theme of 'all about me' in Yr 7 to allow students to describe themselves in different media and in different subject areas.

◆ Encourage students to make and use analogies.

◆ Use concept mapping to encourage identification of associations, common themes and connections.

◆ Use concrete examples: the Tyrannosaurus Rex was 4.1 metres high, 'that's about the height of the ceiling here'; an acre is 4,840 square yards, or 'about the size of a soccer pitch'.

◆ Teach settlements, or eco-systems, or census data, or population change, by starting with the immediate environment or community the learners know best and building out.

Sequenced

> Though I do not deny that memory can be helped by places and images, yet the best memory is based on three important things: namely study, order and care.

ERASMUS, 1512, *Bloomsbury Dictionary of Thematic Quotations*, Bloomsbury Publishing

◆ Learners use index cards and detail the stages of an experiment on the back. Mix the cards up, turn them over and explain each stage in turn. Events in a play or novel, historical events, laws and principles of maths or science can all use sequencing activities.

◆ Use the descriptive-reflective-speculative strategy.

◆ Use flow charts (modelled large-scale on the floor) clock face diagrams (each hour has an event in the sequence).

◆ Templates for structured thinking, structured written or oral response.

◆ Fish-bone diagrams; flow charts.

◆ Chained reviews

Chunked

Groups of seven occur throughout history – the Seven Wonders of the World, the Seven Deadly Sins, the Seven Ages of Man, seven days of the week – interestingly the Australian aborigines have only seven words for numbers, equivalent to one, two, three, four, five, six and seven. Another word simply means more than seven.

PIERCE, H., *The Owner's Manual for the Brain – Everyday Applications from Mind-based Research*, Bard Press

The maximum units of information an adult will recall without 'chunking' is 7 plus or minus 2. The general rule is the younger you are, the fewer chunks you can remember.

◆ Encourage learners to chunk by teaching them how to make 'family trees' of information using key words; each family is given a title or name which describes their generic grouping and then a mnemonic is devised using the sequence of first letters of each family. Whole units of work can be remembered this way.

◆ Students should use the magic numbers 1, 3, 5, 7. What is the most significant learning point here? What are the three essential pieces of information a learner would have to know? Identify five questions that you want to be able to answer by the end of this piece of work. What seven 'bullet' points must be included on a revision précis for fellow students?

◆ Concept mapping where keywords are grouped together around a key theme and on the connecting lines the 'link' between the word is explained. The map is then described aloud to a partner.

203

Located

 In one research study, subjects memorised a list in the basement of a building and were tested. They then moved to one of the upper floors of the building and were given the same test but scored poorly. When they were asked to visualise the basement which the memory task occurred, their scores improved, and when they were returned to the actual basement room where they had memorised the list their scores improved even more.

P.J. HOWARD, *The Owner's Manual for the Brain – Everyday Applications from Mind-based Research*, Bard Press

Ensure that groups who are sitting public examinations or tests visit the room in which they will sit the examination beforehand. If possible, have them sit at the very desk they will sit at when they complete the exam. Ideally, conduct subject revision programmes in that room with them at that desk!

By creating an association with a place which is familiar, information can be easily recalled. Learn key information in different rooms in the house. Visualise the key facts brought to life as characters and 'locate' them in order in a place with which you are very familiar.

Associated

You can remember any new piece of information if it is associated to something you already know or remember.

LORAYNE AND LUCAS,
The Memory Book, Ballantine Books

Where connections or associations with what is already known can be made, meanings are more readily generated. A good way of beginning foreign language learning is to make connections with words already known and understood in English and whose foreign language equivalents are either the same or very similar in construction and sound.

Numbered

Moriarty. How are you at mathematics?
Secombe. I speak it like a native.

SPIKE MILLIGAN, *The Goon Show*

To remember dates use words to represent figures. Thus 186,282 miles per second becomes 'a dazzling sunray is flashing by' with 1 8 6 2 8 and 2 letters for each separate word. Number key points and attach the number to your notes – e.g. 'the 5 causes of the First World War'.

 204

Mnemonics

> The one-l lama
> he's a priest.
> The two-l llama
> He's a beast.
>
> And I will bet
> A silk pajama
> There isn't any
> Three-l lllama

OGDEN NASH, *Bloomsbury Dictionary of Thematic Quotations*, Bloomsbury Publishing

Mnemonics are best when invented by the learner! Creating it is part of learning it. A number-rhyme system known as the peg-mnemonic can help remember lists of items, dates or ideas. First introduced in England in 1879, the nouns rhyme with the numbers. The system works by learning the 'pegs' and making connecting associations with items in the list you have to remember.

0	= **pill**	*nil replaced by pill*
1	= **sun**	*think of a comic sun with a yellow smiley face*
2	= **shoe**	*one of your own shoes is best*
3	= **tree**	*a fully grown tree in leaf that you are familiar with*
4	= **store**	*as in 'superstore' selling everything*
5	= **jive**	*moving to a rhythm*
6	= **bricks**	*hear the sound they make as they are stacked*
7	= **heaven**	*pearly gates and all*
8	= **crate**	*a wooden box for storing*
9	= **line**	*a railway or even a clothes line*

Any list can be remembered very effectively this way. Simply take the item on your list to be remembered and make a conscious link with the appropriate visual association for that number. An improvement on the basic 'peg' method, and one of the better ways of remembering complicated numbers and data with numerical associations, is to utilise a mnemonic alphabet system. This system was pioneered by Harry Lorayne and involves turning the ten digits 0–9 into sounds. The associations work like this.

0	= **Z, soft C, S**	*zero meaning nothing and beginning with a soft hissing sound*
1	= **T or D**	*where the letters have a single downstroke*
2	= **N**	*where the letter has two downstrokes*
3	= **M**	*where the letter has three downstrokes*
4	= **R**	*where the dominant sound is the 'rrrr' sound at the end of 'four'*
5	= **L**	*The roman letter L was used for 50*
6	= **J, soft G,CH, SH**	*J looking like a reversed 6*
7	= **K, hard C & G,Q**	*K made of two 7's*
8	= **F,V,PH**	*F written in script looks like 8 (F)*
9	= **P,B**	*p is a mirror image of 9*

Alliteration, rhythm, rhyme

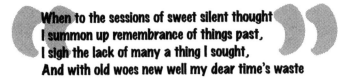

When to the sessions of sweet silent thought
I summon up remembrance of things past,
I sigh the lack of many a thing I sought,
And with old woes new well my dear time's waste

SHAKESPEARE, *Sonnet*

Information carried by a rhythm or tune or learned as the words to a song is not only whole brained but readily accessed. Any topic can lend itself to this approach.

The vitamin called A has important connections
It aids in our vision and helps stop infections.
To vitamin C this ditty now comes,
Important for healing and strong healthy gums.
Finished with both of these?
Here come the B's:
B1 for the nerves
B2 helps cell energise
Digesting the protein's
B6's prize

In geography we can learn the countries of the European Community by creating a sentence using words which begin with the first letters of the countries we want to remember. The countries are – Austria, Belgium, Denmark, Finland, France, Germany, Greece, Ireland, Italy, Luxembourg, Netherlands, Portugal, Spain, Sweden, United Kingdom – and a story chanted in rhythm to remember them could be: '*A Brilliant Device For Finding Good Geographical Information Is Linking Names Properly So Specially United . . .*'

Try remembering geometric shapes to the tune of 'On Top of Old Smoky' or the weather words to the tune of 'Clementine' . . .

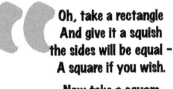

Oh, take a rectangle
And give it a squish
the sides will be equal –
A square if you wish.

Now take a square
And cut it in half
Slice on the diagonal
And you have a triangle

Now take two triangles
And place base to base.
It is a rhombus,
The base line erase

Oh, six triangles
We can take.
Assemble together–
A hexagon shape

Condensation, evaporation
Water cycle, cirrus clouds,
Wind-chill factors, ocean currents,
Trade winds, high pressure zones

Stratosphere and centigrade,
Fahrenheit and barometers
They excite you, they can't bite you
Please make friends with weather words

Strong winds blowing.
Hail, sleet, snowing,
The weather's with us all day long
So look out your window in the morning
Just in case the forecast's wrong

(with thanks to Mary Barrett, child aged ten)

206

Personalised

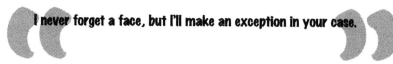

I never forget a face, but I'll make an exception in your case.

GROUCHO MARX

Where the learner has a strong personal connection with the information it is readily recovered. Encourage the learner to consider applications in his or her personal life: how might you apply this? In what ways might you benefit? How might you teach a younger brother or sister?

Where there is an emotional connection the brain 'marks' the information and designates it significant. Alkon, quoted in Kotulak, *Inside the Brain*, suggests that emotion and *'the emotional importance of what has been learned in critical periods in the brain determines its permanence.'* Where there is a real 'or a perceived' personal connection at an emotionally engaging level then the information will be coded for retention.

Personal projects which are on the learner's own chosen theme and which have been individually researched and evaluated; information which is to be presented to a group of peers, where there is a strong personal motivation and where there is an affective interpretation, for example, through creative writing, art or music.

Shared

Many ideas grow better when transplanted into another mind than in the one where they sprang up.

OLIVER WENDELL HOLMES, *Bloomsbury Dictionary of Thematic Quotations,* Bloomsbury Publishing

This is the guaranteed memory method provided the learner is 'actively' participating. Structured opportunities to test understanding are a powerful aid to recall. Use a variety of regular and informal tests. 'Each one teach one', explaining personal notes or memory maps, preparing a lesson-plan for teaching a group of peers and formulating key questions and asking someone else to test you on your understanding of them.

The formula for effective recall is *'motivation plus a clear sense of a positive outcome plus useful strategies plus the correct state'*. The formula is

> *MOTIVATION* – however natural or brain-compatible the system we use is, recall nevertheless requires conscious attention and directed effort. We need to intend to recall the information at the beginning of the 'revision' process.

> Clear sense of a positive *OUTCOME* – an outcome which we can move towards is important. 'Once this is learned what will I be able to do to demonstrate it?'

> Useful *STRATEGIES* – combinations of learning methods, such as those described above – which we can readily use – are imperative.

The correct *STATE* – physical and emotional. Regular breaks, healthy diet and sleep, supportive learning environment and positive state of mind.

Summarise it for your students as **MOSS** and have them use this set of prompts:

MOTIVATION

◆ are you certain about what it is you need to know?
◆ when will you have learned it by?
◆ for what purpose are you learning it?
◆ how will it connect with what you have learned before and what is to come?
◆ how will you reward yourself for having learned it?

OUTCOME

◆ how would someone else know you had learned this material?
◆ give yourself the BIG picture by quickly skimming through the texts or material you need to learn
◆ write out the questions you will be able to answer once this information is learned
◆ visualise yourself having successfully achieved your outcome, listen to what others are saying to you, experience the feeling of success

STRATEGIES

◆ do you have the resources you need?
◆ are the strategies you are using visual, auditory and kinesthetic?
◆ will you combine strategies?
◆ how will you test your recall?
◆ what plans do you have to come back to the material?

STATE

◆ have you set aside an adequate period of time free from interference?
◆ are you in a comfortable space which you can use to help your learning – for example, by sticking up memory maps, posters or post-its onto the wall in front of your table or desk?
◆ is the space warm but not too warm, light, quiet or with music which helps you learn, large enough for you to get up and move around?
◆ will you have regular breaks?
◆ after having a break will you review and preview, before starting again?
◆ remember to reward yourself for application, effort and success!

> We have moved on at quite a pace since February but I haven't forgotten what was a truly memorable day for myself and the staff. The brain and all its working has become the central focus of all my own development and that of the school . . . We have a wide range of exciting developments all around the school and are working on 'optimal learning environments'. We have started action-research projects using brain gym and NLP and introduced Spanish and French this term using the accelerated learning programmes with staff learning alongside the children. I introduced the techniques with a group of 'failing' children focusing on spelling and the results before and after are enclosed. It was the first bit of 'magic' I've ever seen and was unbelievable. I was so impressed we've purchased as many books as we can get, established a new staff library and provided reading time for everyone.

HOWARD KENNEDY, HEADTEACHER, HOLY FAMILY PRIMARY SCHOOL,
letter to the author, September 1997

> The new view, now that we know schools make a difference, dictates a different logic. It requires teachers individually and collectively to review what they do and try to improve it . . . Teachers and schools now believe they can make a difference. They can work towards changes which are achievable and which can be monitored.

MICHAEL BARBER, *The Learning Game – Arguments for an Educational Revolution*, Victor Gollanz

WHEN WE LOOK AT THE OUTCOMES FROM SOME OF THE EXCELLENT WORK DONE HERE IN THE UK AND ABROAD on school effectiveness and school improvement and attempt to place the principles and practices of the accelerated learning in the classroom model into it there is a consistent fit. The Institute of Education, London, produced a valuable summary of the characteristics of effective schools as defined by the prevailing research in 1995. Aside from the impact of leadership, which is outside the scope of this book, the 11 factors align with the emphases given throughout the accelerated learning in the classroom model.

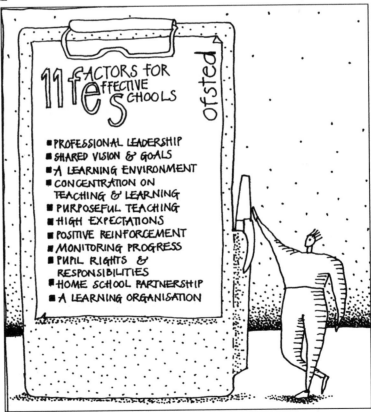

Source: Sammons P et al., (1995) Key characteristics of Effective Schools.
A review of school effectiveness research

209

School effectiveness research suggests that the 'classroom effect is greater than the school effect', in other words, it is easier to precipitate immediate and worthwhile change in individual classrooms than in a school as a whole. It also tends to point up the difficulty of effecting change in schools where there are difficulties. Stoll and Fink (1996) suggest that it is often difficult to focus on teaching and learning in schools where the *'internal capacity to cope with change is missing'*. Quick fixes are impossible. Often the development necessitates the staff and school as a whole questioning their own beliefs about learning, about motivation and about their ability to contribute purposefully to improvement. In 'coasting' organisations, denial of the need for any change is a safe haven to remain in. A good starting point for a reflective practitioner or a reflective school is to question such beliefs and the presuppositions which underlie them. Schools are complex organisations and it is unwise to treat them as entities which will respond in given and thus predictable, ways, so perhaps designations such as 'the reflective school' or 'the learning school' are best avoided, though the tools which educationalists use to apply such labels are of interest and of use.

A tool which is used in counselling and now in management development training is the JOHARI window. Named after its creators Jo and Harry, the JOHARI window reminds us that we are not always best placed to evaluate our own strengths and weaknesses. It looks like this

Know what you know	**Know what you don't know**
Don't know what you know	**Don't know what you don't know**

Sometimes we know what we know. As an English teacher I may know the syllabus I am currently teaching in its present format and the requirements described there. I may recognise that I do not know the contents and requirements of other syllabuses. Perhaps I don't know how imaginative I am at teaching aspects of the syllabus – no one discusses teaching and learning in our meetings, no one observes classroom performance in a supportive and developmental way – I don't know what I know. Perhaps I am oblivious that my assumptions about learning overlook the possibility that learners may prefer to learn and indeed benefit from learning in ways other than those within which I presently operate: I don't know what I don't know and unless I am given a deliberate opportunity to access an alternative possibility, reflect on and assimilate it, then how and indeed why, should I change?

Mechanisms which allow schools and teachers within schools to reflect on and evaluate their own practice in an informed way can be powerful in introducing improvements such as those offered by the accelerated learning methods. The benefit of using checklists of characteristics as a means of self audit is that they can offer the possibility of taking one out of the bottom half of the JOHARI window. Following the work of Peter Senge in the US and

Pedler and Burgoyne in the UK, the concept of the 'learning organisation' has caught the imagination of business and more recently education. Certainly, in my own experience of staff development, if an individual does not perceive him or herself as a learner, exposure to training experiences can at best go no further than the exchange of information stage and at worst consolidate limiting and often cherished beliefs about the status quo.

Schools which exhibit the characteristics of a 'learning school' as exemplified in my list below are perhaps those which are already well positioned to effect significant medium- to long(er)-term improvements. Schools which are struggling with limiting ideas and practices which are institutionalised, and to some extent 'locked in', will tend to go for the cosmetic aspects of accelerated learning and any changes will be short term. The list of 17 ways in which schools have begun to introduce the principles and practices of accelerated learning (overleaf) is not exclusive, nor is it best practice. It reflects the diversity and imagination of the schools which have found the model of value to them.

---

11 Characteristics of a learning school

Self-development opportunities for all

With appropriate guidance and systems, people are encouraged to take responsibility for their own learning and development

Positive learning climate

An internal climate which encourages openness, risk-taking, giving and receiving feedback, learning from successes and failures

Openness to learning

Sharing ideas with colleagues from your own and other schools

Environmental scanning

All staff freely communicate and share information about external factors which contribute to school success

Enabling structures

Appraisal for development. Clarity about roles and responsibilities. Opportunities for career growth

Learning approach to strategy

Whole-school involvement in strategic decision-making, monitoring and evaluation for improvement

Participative policy-making

Collegiate decision-making enabled by supportive management structures

Informating

Sharing of recent, relevant data regarding student performance, departmental and school performance

Formative accounting and control

Regular information about budgets and about spending. Management of budgets delegated out

Internal exchange

Departments talk to and plan with each other. Competition for scarce resources is managed

High expectations

Encourage and foster high expectations of staff and student performance. Monitor strategically, tactically and diagnostically.

adapted PEDLER, BURGOYNE AND BOYDELL, *Developing the Developers*, Henley Management College

---

To ensure that the model has sustained impact it is necessary to plan for a sustained and considered approach which is introduced and monitored over at least a three-year period. The essential dimension to this is to agree a shared vision of what the organisation aspires towards with all 'stakeholders' – students, parents, staff, support staff and governors – and communicate that vision with clarity and consistency. Everyone involved in the education of the learners should be able to say exactly what they will contribute and how they will contribute it.

1 Utilise the school or college development plan to specify targets in terms of benefits to students. Be specific about how all planned activity will relate back to student benefits. Organise the development planning process to engage all staff and involve as many other stakeholders as possible. Everyone should know exactly what they are doing, to what level and why. Plan on at least a three-year cycle. Separate Vision, Goals – Targets and Tasks. Vision – what does the organisation aspire towards? Goals, which are long term – what are the key successes which will help us know we are working towards our vision? Targets – which are medium term – what specific outcomes do we have to achieve to mark the movement towards each goal? Tasks, short term, what do people have to do to meet each of these targets successfully? *Holy Family Primary School, Langley and St James Catholic High School, Hendon*

2 Create and maintain a learning school culture. This cannot be done when staff development is structured around 'events'. Integrate all staff development activity to the agreed school and departmental goals and targets. Review the impact all staff development programmes (not events!) make on student learning as described in your development plan. *Brislington School, Bristol*

3 Ensure all departments are learning departments. Encourage regular review and sharing of teaching and learning successes. Departmental meetings should have a regular slot to focus on teaching and learning. All departments should have an agreed and structured approach to group work. Encourage involvement in variety audits. *Wadham School, Crewkerne.* Set up achievement teams who read key texts related to learning and who summarise and discuss these before trying the ideas out in the classroom. *Sittingbourne Community School.* At Cramlington High School, Northumberland, a research and development 'team' summarise innovations in discussion papers for staff.

4 Introduce a negotiated rolling programme of peer observation and student pursuit to allow staff to observe and share good and different practice. *Stewards School, Harlow.* Reserve a slot at whole-staff meetings for staff to detail recent successes in practical teaching strategies. The last Friday of each month is 'positive Friday' where everyone is positive about their learning – so no put-downs or grumbles about 'unteachable' students. Reinforce it with humour and fines if necessary!

5 Utilise data. A month after an INSET 'event' use a feedback proforma and ask staff to specify in what ways your teaching has changed? How has this impacted on student learning? Do this alongside student research – conduct a variety audit for teaching and learning – to keep momentum up. *Birley School, Sheffield.* Do it again three months later. Share the data. Relate the collection of data to student performance and subsequent mentoring programmes. *Bedminster Down School, Bristol*

6 Monitor the PSHE programme to ensure that the teaching of study and thinking skills is structured for progression and integration into all classroom teaching. *Ralph Allen School, Bath.* Develop a Thinking Skills Curriculum and utilise an agreed understanding of the key issues amongst staff to design programmes and materials for students. 'Sorted – in your exams' at the *Harwich School, Dovercourt, Harwich* includes study and revision packs based on a model which takes the best of accelerated learning and thinking skills strategies. To ensure transfer, involve all staff in the use of such approaches. Re-designate Heads of Year to Year Achievement Co-ordinators and change the emphasis from pastoral support and behaviour management to facilitators of learning. Ninestiles School, Birmingham, have moved from mixed ability teaching to setting but pupils choose which set they wish to be in.

7 Encourage outcomes thinking at all levels – 'what will success look, sound and feel like?' Establish key strategies related to learning and achievement as policy and incorporate into the staff handbook. Utilise templates across the curriculum and put copies of the most important into the student planner.

8 Tall poppies. Observe all prospective appointees teaching and introduce a reference proforma where the emphasis is on teaching and learning. *St John the Baptist School, Woking.* Introduce observation week where informal observation occurs at agreed times. Internally second staff out to learning support. Institute a timetabled rolling peer observation programme supported by an agreed focus between participants.

9 Establish a massive promotion of parents' evening with a shift in emphasis from reporting to target setting. Organise parents' evenings on teaching and learning and the roles of parent, student and school. 'How to accelerate your child's learning evening for parents.' *The Castle School, Taunton*

10 Mentoring. Older students assume a responsibility for helping younger students be familiar with the learning environment and provide an older role-model with whom they can relate and communicate in a difficulty. This can also take place across different age institutions or with different types of school.

11 Introduce study-skills days with mixed age groups learning about a non-school topic via new study skills. Organise study-skills assemblies and put the visual materials up around the school; brain week; memory week; learning corridors with subject-specific keywords.

12 A Baccalaureate system to promote and recognise diversity of talent. Utilise the multiple intelligences model and link to Bronze, Silver and Gold awards in each.

13 Evaluate students' preferred learning styles alongside the students, using inventories and explaining what they mean and how they can impact on learning. *Mallett Lambert School, Hull*

14 Skills of goal and target setting taught and integrated into school planners. Target setting for specific weak areas – e.g., poor organisation, time on task, low work rate. *Crispin School, Somerset.* Teach target setting early and in a

213

non-curriculum context. Short-term targets and their significance, particularly for boys, is recognised and built into curriculum planning and lesson delivery. *Woolwich Polytechnic School, Greenwich*

15 Structure schemes of work to include teaching methodology, what students will know by the end of the unit, pre-processing questions to be signified beforehand and keywords. *Sir William Nottidge School, Kent.* Modularise the curriculum input and provide an introductory briefing booklet for each half-termly module. *Lutterworth Grammar and Community School*

16 Introduce positive belief training programme for staff and for students; letters to parents encouraging high expectations; role modelling of readers and learners; 'it's cool to achieve' celebrations. *Dene Magna School, Gloucester.* Visual records of successes. *Firth Park School, Sheffield*

17 Initiate homework and after-school learning clubs about non-school topics.

Highlights of research on good teaching

Good teaching is fundamental to effective schooling. We have a picture of effective teachers as semi-autonomous professionals who:

◆ are clear about their instructional goals

◆ are knowledgeable about their content and the strategies for teaching it

◆ communicate to their students what is expected of them and why

◆ make expert use of existing instructional materials in order to devote more time to practices that enrich and clarify the content

◆ are knowledgeable about their students, adapting instruction to their needs

◆ teach students meta-cognitive strategies and give them opportunities to master them

◆ address higher as well as lower cognitive objectives

◆ offer regular appropriate feedback

◆ integrate their instruction with that in other subject areas

◆ accept responsibility for student outcomes

Source: David Hopkins, University of Nottingham, *Creating the Conditions for Effective Schooling*, Somerset LEA, 1996

With so much known about the characteristics of effective teaching we can use existing inventories and checklists to audit our own professional practice. I provide one here from the work of David Hopkins and one of my own which relates to the Accelerated Learning Cycle. Feel free to use mine if it will help your thinking about improving the learning which occurs in your classroom.

THE ACCELERATED LEARNING CYCLE

> PRE-STAGE

Create the supportive learning environment

◆ *What strategies are in place to build the self-esteem and self-belief of the learner?*

◆ *How do you communicate positive beliefs about success?*

◆ *In what ways does your classroom space support learning?*

◆ *On entry to your class how might a learner begin to feel positive about learning?*

214

◆ *What do you know about your learners' preferred learning styles?*

◆ *How have you prepared your lessons to accommodate different preferences?*

Connect the learning

◆ *How would a learner know how this lesson connected with what went before and what is yet to come?*

◆ *Do the learners have long-term goals – WIIFM – to help them understand the benefits of this work?*

◆ *Do the learners know – if in outline – the content of the syllabus?*

◆ *Is it in 'their' language or recorded appropriately?*

◆ *Do the learners know their own preferred learning styles and those of others?*

◆ *What knowledge do the learners already have about this topic?*

◆ *What strategies do you use to utilise possible prior knowledge?*

BIG picture

◆ *In what ways can you describe the content of the lesson to access all learners?*

◆ *What do you do to alleviate anxiety about the possible difficulty of the content?*

◆ *How might the learners record the BIG picture for themselves?*

◆ *Can you use the BIG picture as a reference point to record progress?*

Describe the outcomes

◆ *Can you describe what you hope the learners will have achieved by the end of the lesson?*

◆ *Are they able to establish some desired outcomes and short-term, informal targets for themselves?*

◆ *Could they describe these to you?*

◆ *How have you broken down the content?*

◆ *In what ways have you differentiated? To what extent is there choice?*

◆ *Have you anticipated and planned for any extension work or homework?*

STAGE FOUR

Input

◆ *In what ways can your input include VAK?*

◆ *Can you utilise other sources of information and input –*
e.g., guest speaker, video, audio tape?

◆ *Is your input of an appropriate duration?*

◆ *Is the language of any auditory or text of any visual input at a suitable register?*

◆ *Is the language multi-sensory?*

◆ *Do you 'pole-bridge' by adding language to doing?*

◆ *In what ways might the students find the input memorable!*

◆ *How do you check for understanding as you progress?*

◆ *Is your feedback, educative, immediate and developmental?*

STAGE FIVE

Activity

◆ *Which of the 7 plus Intelligences does the activity access?*

◆ *How might the 7 plus Intelligences be balanced over time?*

◆ *In what ways are the learners encouraged to make choices?*

◆ *Do the participants know and understand the success criteria for the activity?*

◆ *Do the activities encourage individual, pair and group work?*

◆ *How are the learners encouraged and supported in the activity?*

◆ *Can all participants achieve in the activity?*

STAGE SIX

Demonstrate

◆ *To whom and at what point will the learners demonstrate their understanding of the new information?*

◆ *In what ways can the demonstration be part of the ongoing learning?*

◆ *Will the learners have opportunities to reflect on and revise understanding as a result of this stage?*

◆ *Is the demonstration differentiated?*

◆ *Is it supportive? Is it safe? How might a weaker student be encouraged to take risks?*

◆ *How will you assure ultimate success?*

STAGE SEVEN

Review for recall and retention

◆ *How often and in what ways do reviews feature in your lessons?*

◆ *Do you apply the 'six times' rule?*

◆ *Have you taught memory techniques and are you using them?*

◆ *Are the learners encouraged to self-review or review in pairs or peer groups?*

◆ *Against what criteria are reviews conducted?*

◆ *How do reviews encourage long-term recall and understanding?*

◆ *At what point do you connect to the goals of the student, the BIG picture and the outcomes for the lesson(s)?*

◆ SECTION THREE: REVIEW

1 For your classroom teaching how can you improve the 'connecting' examples and experiences you provide to accelerate the students' learning?

2 When reading for information how might the principle of the BIG picture help?

3 How might your school or college use the principle of anchoring to help students have more positive associations with public examinations and tests?

4 For a topic which you already teach, describe ways in which you can integrate more visual, auditory and kinesthetic stimulation into the experience for the students. How might this enhance their learning?

5 In what ways could learning experiences within classrooms and across schools be better structured to help access and develop all types of intelligence?

6 Should tests and mock exams be less frequent or more? If more, how can we help students improve their all-round experience?

7 How might schools and classroom teachers best develop memory skills in students? Should there be discreet sessions on memory and recall or should it be integrated into teaching?

8 List five key recommendations for your school or college to begin to utilise the methods described in this book. What first steps need to take place for developments to begin?

Section Four:

Resources and contacts for accelerated learning in the classroom

Preview of Section Four:

Resources and contacts for accelerated learning in the classroom

IN SECTION FOUR YOU WILL FIND:

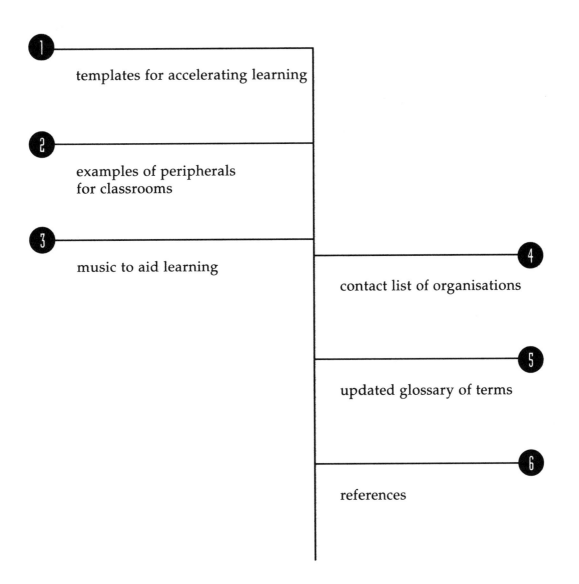

1. templates for accelerating learning

2. examples of peripherals for classrooms

3. music to aid learning

4. contact list of organisations

5. updated glossary of terms

6. references

Section Four:

Resources and contacts for accelerated learning in the classroom

1 TEMPLATES FOR ACCELERATING LEARNING ACROSS THE CURRICULUM

PERSONAL READINESS FOR LEARNING

Self-review

Looking after my learning

Behaviour change plan

Why be angry? Ten tips for keeping cool ...

Two sides to the problem

Personal learning goals

CONNECTING THE LEARNING

Predictions

Thinking prompts

Making careful decisions

Problem-solving

LEARNING TOOLS

Story map

Character map

Homework assessment tool

Five exam secrets

Spelling styles chart

Project planner

Science planner

PERSONAL READINESS FOR LEARNING

SELF-REVIEW

List the three things that make you the world's greatest expert on yourself

....

....

List three difficulties you have overcome in your life

....

....

What sort of person did you need to be to help you overcome the difficulties? List three attributes

....

....

What three things do you most want to get out of school?

....

....

What sort of person will you need to be to help you get what you want in school? List three attributes

....

....

LOOKING AFTER MY LEARNING

My name: ....

Date: ....

Time and place: ....

Unit of work: ....

What do I want to do today (my goal)?

....

How will I do it?

....

Can I close my eyes and see myself doing the task? Can I hear what others are saying to me as I am doing the task? When I am successful what will I have done?

....

When I am successful what will the end product be like? Describe it.

....

STAY POSITIVE CHECKLIST. **As you progress ask yourself these questions . . .** How well am I doing? Am I staying on task? Am I reviewing what I've done as I go along? Could I explain my progress at each stage to someone else? Do I need a break!?

What will my reward for success be?

....

If I don't achieve my goal how will I improve next time?

....

224

PERSONAL READINESS FOR LEARNING

BEHAVIOUR CHANGE PLAN

My name: ....
Date: ....
Time and place: ....

What I wanted to happen	What I did that was wrong	What actually happened
The best outcome would be	To get the best outcome I must avoid	To get the best outcome I need to

WHY BE ANGRY? TEN TIPS FOR KEEPING COOL . . .

◆ Remember no one can make you feel angry; you are the only person who controls your mind; you can choose to be calm

◆ Imagine yourself in the calmest, happiest place on earth; notice what it's like being there

◆ Take the innervoice which is going over and over what is annoying you and reverse it; for example, if someone has said hurtful things to you and you are repeating them in your head try 'reversing' them so they carry the opposite meaning

◆ Remove yourself from whatever or whoever is making you angry

◆ Close your eyes and imagine the other person dressed as a clown, a frog, a muppet character or anything which makes 'them' look silly

◆ Take whatever the other person has said to you and repeat it in as silly voice as you can manage; repeat it five times then ask yourself 'is it really so important or is it silly?'

◆ Use an 'I' message to tell the other person how you feel and what you want them to do in future: 'when you . . , I feel . . , in the future I would like you to . . , how do you feel . . ?'

◆ Try to look at it from the other person's point of view; think of three good reasons why they might have behaved in the way they did

◆ Do some physical exercise

◆ Breath deeply and count slowly as you exhale; repeat

225

PERSONAL READINESS FOR LEARNING

TWO SIDES TO THE PROBLEM

My name: ....
The name of the person I argued with:.................................
Time and place: ....

My explanation	Their likely explanation	How I feel
How they probably feel	What the best outcome is	To get the best outcome I am willing to

PERSONAL LEARNING GOALS

Date: ....
Time and place: ....
Unit of work:...
Time to be spent on it: ....

What will you have successfully achieved in this time?
....

Do you have all the equipment you need?
....

Quickly skim over all the information and then list three things you will do in order
1 ....
2 ....
3 ....

Relax, survey the information again and list five (or more) important questions you need answers to.
....
....

Read the material again. Try to find answers to your questions. Take notes as you read. Tick the type of notes you will take.
Memory Map   Text/Context   Concept Web   Linear

Go over your notes every 20 minutes and on finishing. List what you have to do next...
....

226

CONNECTING THE LEARNING

PREDICTIONS

What might happen? List three possible predictions

....

For each prediction list all the clues that make you think that an alternative might happen.

Prediction one
   clue ···
   clue ···
   clue ···
   clue ···

Prediction two
   clue ···
   clue ···
   clue ···
   clue ···

Prediction three
   clue ···
   clue ···
   clue ···
   clue ···

Look again at each prediction and say whether it is <u>Likely</u>, <u>Unlikely</u> or <u>Uncertain</u>

Which is your preferred choice?

THINKING PROMPTS

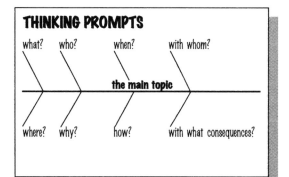

what?   who?   when?   with whom?

the main topic

where?   why?   how?   with what consequences?

THINKING PROMPTS

Linear thinking

'summarise'   'explain in your own words'

'list'   'show how'   'why is that . . .?'

'give three examples of . . .'   'find . . .'

Lateral thinking

       'create'   'based on the evidence recommended . . .'

'contrast'   'classify'   'list similarities and differences'

'imagine'   'make a presentation on'   'analyse'

CONNECTING THE LEARNING

MAKING CAREFUL DECISIONS

What options are available to me?

My chosen option is . . .

Consequences: what will happen if you choose this option?	Explanation: say why you think each consequence will occur	Importance: explain the importance of each consequence

PROBLEM-SOLVING

◆ **Define the problem**

What is the present situation? What facts do we know? What facts might we need? What are the present consequences of the problem remaining? Upon whom or what does the problem impact?

◆ **List the causes of the problem**

◆ **Why is it necessary to resolve the problem?**

What would the benefits of resolving the problem be?

◆ **What are the possible solutions of the problem?**

◆ **What would happen if we adopted these possible solutions**

List the possible consequences and those who would be affected by them. How significant is each consequence?

◆ **What might prevent us adopting these solutions?**

◆ **If we could solve the problem now, using the best of the solutions, would we do so?**

228

LEARNING TOOLS

STORY MAP

Title of my story:...

As a result of reading my story I want the reader to....................

....

....

....

The moral of my story is ....

....

....

....

The other characters are..

The setting for the story is (list three things) ....

....

....

The first decision my character makes is to ....

....

The decision is a good/bad decision because..................................

....

As a result of this decision this happens ....

....

The story ends when ....

....

CHARACTER MAP

The three most important characters in my story are

a ....

b ....

c ....

Three things you would notice about my characters are

a ....

b ....

c ....

Each character is interesting because

a ....

b ....

c ....

Likeable and unlikeable things about my characters

a ....

b ....

c ....

The mistake they make together in the story is..................................

....

As a result this happens to them..

....

This is what they learn from the problem..

....

Likeable and unlikeable things about my characters

a ....

b ....

c ....

229

LEARNING TOOLS

HOMEWORK ASSESSMENT TOOL

Date: ....

Topic: ....

Competency	1 point	2 points	3 points
Is the main idea clear?	Main idea is barely detectable	Main idea is stated Remains clear throughout the work	Main idea is clearly stated. Referred to throughout. Effective beginning and ending of para 1
Are there further ideas?	There are no further ideas	There are further ideas These are detailed and relate to the main idea	There are several further ideas These are all detailed & relate to the main idea
Is there supporting information?	Confusing Some details are not related	Some detail on further ideas Attempts to make connections	Lots of detail on further ideas Outside sources Ideas are connected
Is there a carefully followed plan?	Writing is rambling but some ideas are related	Writer has a plan and follows it	Well-followed plan Good flow between paragraphs
Mechanics	Several grammatical, punctuation & spelling errors	Few grammatical, punctuation & spelling errors	No grammatical, punctuation & spelling errors

FIVE EXAM SECRETS
Before

◆ **Plan.** Plan your revision ahead and write down your plan. Stick to your plan and give yourself a reward each time you complete it.

◆ **Review.** Go over the material a little and often. When you review write up some short notes as a memory map then test yourself on it. Make sure you list all the important key words — correctly spelled — down the side of your map. Test yourself on these too.

◆ **Anticipate.** Before you go to sit the exam imagine yourself being successful. Remember a time when you were successful (in anything) and say quietly to yourself that 'I have everything I need to succeed', say it again as you relax and think about being successful. Do the same as soon as you sit down at the exam desk on the day of your exam.

During

◆ **Tip out.** Open the exam booklet and on a fresh page quickly dump your memory map of the topic onto the page. Spend no more than five minutes doing this. Add to it later if you remember details.

◆ **Survey.** Take five minutes to look at the whole exam paper and identify all the things you can do well in. Look at all the sections and check back to your memory map as you go. Have an outline plan of how much time to spend on each question based on how many marks they are worth. Then begin with the easier questions.

LEARNING TOOLS

Spelling Styles Chart ✔

VISUAL

- ◆ Look at the word; say it aloud pronouncing all the sounds
- ◆ Close your eyes and see the letters as you spell the word
- ◆ Open your eyes and write the word
- ◆ Check for accuracy and write it again
- ◆ Look up to the left, close your eyes, and see the word in a bright colour
- ◆ Hide your original; write it again and check for accuracy and write it again in another colour
- ◆ Do it again three times . . .

AUDITORY

- ◆ Say the word
- ◆ Sound it out saying each letter or blend or syllable
- ◆ Spell it out aloud
- ◆ Spell it out aloud and write it as you say it
- ◆ Check for accuracy and write it again; check again
- ◆ Hide your original and spell it out aloud again but this time in a funny voice or to a tune
- ◆ Try it again this time speeding it up or slowing it down
- ◆ Write it out; check for accuracy

KINESTHETIC

- ◆ Look at the word; trace it with your index finger as you say the letters
- ◆ Close your eyes and feel the letters as you trace the word with your index finger
- ◆ Write the word; check for accuracy
- ◆ Try the same but with your other index finger, then both at once — this is hard! Write it in the air
- ◆ With a partner trace a word onto their back; then they guess the word . . . swap
- ◆ Walk the word in the playground
- ◆ Movement, write it, check it . . .

MULTI-SENSORY

- ◆ Use strategies from the other three boxes
- ◆ Close your eyes and see the letters as you say the word and trace the shape out onto the desk, your partner's back or in the air in front of you
- ◆ Open your eyes and write the word
- ◆ Check for accuracy and write it again
- ◆ Look up to the left, close your eyes, and see the word in a bright colour and say each letter
- ◆ Do it again three times . . .

231

LEARNING TOOLS

PROJECT PLANNER

My goal stated: ....
My goal in the form of a question:......................................
....

Three sources of information I will use	The steps I will use to achieve my goal	Five concepts or ideas I will consider in my research
The three methods of presentation I will use	The project timeline Wk. 1 .... Wk. 2 .... Wk. 3 .... Wk. 4 .... Wk. 5 .... Wk. 6 .... Wk. 7	How I will know if I have been successful

SCIENCE PLANNER

Date: .... Lesson: ....
Unit of work: ....
Title of experiment: ....
What will you prove with this experiment ....
....
List the equipment needed...
....
1. What is the first thing you do?...
....
What happens?...
....
2. What do you do next? ....
....
What happens?...
....
3. What do you do next? ....
....
What happens?...
....
Read through 1, 2 & 3.
What is your scientific explanation for what happened?
....
....
....

ACCELERATED LEARNING IN PRACTICE — brain-based methods for accelerating motivation and achievement

❷ THE GREAT AND THE GOOD: PERIPHERALS FOR CLASSROOMS

'There is nothing good or bad, but thinking makes it so.' WILLIAM SHAKESPEARE, *Hamlet*

'Difficulties are opportunities to better things; they are stepping stones to greater experience.' BRYAN ADAMS, rock musician

'We all have the ability to shape to some extent the way our lives will turn out.' TREVOR MCDONALD, news presenter

'Whatever you can do or dream you can, begin it. Boldness has genius, power and magic in it. Begin it now.' JOHANN WOLFGANG VON GOETHE

'We are disturbed not by things, but by the views we take of things.' EPICTETUS, *The Encheiridion*

'It is through education and learning that we can ultimately achieve all our goals and desires.' COLIN JACKSON, world record holder

'If you can dream it, you can do it.' WALT DISNEY

'The future belongs to those who believe in the beauty of their dreams.' ELEANOR ROOSEVELT

'Be not afraid of growing slowly, be afraid only of standing still.' Chinese proverb

'Always remember that your own resolution to succeed is more important than anything else.' ABRAHAM LINCOLN

'Education means never having the feeling of inadequacy. . .' DUNCAN GOODHEW, Olympic medalist

'Macho does not prove mucho.' ZSA ZSA GABOR

'Imagination is more important than knowledge.' ALBERT EINSTEIN

'Imagination is the highest kite one can fly.' LAUREN BACALL

ACCELERATED LEARNING IN PRACTICE — brain-based methods for accelerating motivation and achievement

'If it's not going to matter in five years it doesn't matter now.' CHER

'The world of the future will favour intellectual properties of invention, creation and understanding. Imaginative thinkers will be the ones working in the 21st Century. Only education can provide the training for those who will do this work.' GRIFF RHYS JONES, broadcaster

'Tens of thousands of people never find out where their talent is. Where else are they going to find out but at school?' TERRY PRATCHETT, author

'In the long history of humankind (and animalkind too) those who learned to collaborate and improvise most effectively have prevailed.' CHARLES DARWIN

'The turtle only makes progress when its neck is stuck out.' ROLLO MAY

'There's a thin line between being a leader and a ring leader.' SUSAN KOVALIK

'The mind can also be an erogenous zone.' RAQUEL WELCH

'If you learn from your mistakes, you become a better person. If you don't learn from what you've done wrong, then you're defeating the purpose.'
WAYNE GRETZKY, Canadian hockey player,
only man in NHL history to score 2000 points

'Genius is one per cent inspiration and ninety-nine per cent perspiration.' THOMAS ALVA EDISON, US inventor

'The one who has the most things when he dies wins.' T-shirt, London, 1997

'No truly educated person can ever be bored.' ARTHUR C. CLARKE, science fiction author

'A problem is a chance for you to do your best.' DUKE ELLINGTON, jazz musician

'Education can open doors and the more doors open to you the more chance you have in life.'
SHARON DAVIES, Olympic silver medalist and Gladiator

'Don't listen to anyone who tells you that you can't do this or that. That's nonsense. Make up your mind you'll never use crutches or a stick, then have a go at everything. Go to school, join in all the games you can. Go anywhere you want to. But never, never let them persuade you that things are too difficult or impossible.' DOUGLAS BADER, British WW2 fighter pilot, speaking to a 14-year-old boy who had lost his leg in a motor accident

3 MUSIC TO AID LEARNING

The following selections of music have all been successful in classrooms or adult training. Timings are approximate.

The following ten CDs are recommended to get you started:

> *Pure Classical Moods – Tranquillity*. EMI Records 1997 7243 5 66356 2 3
> *Pure Classical Moods – Power*. EMI Records 1997 7243 5 66357 2 2
> *Pure Classical Moods – Dreams*. EMI Records 1997 7243 5 66358 2 4
> *The Best Classical Album in the World!* – EMI Records 7243 8 44161 2 6
> *That's Jazz – Simply the Best of Jazz*. EMI Records 1995 7243 8 36436 2 2
> *Senses 20 Contemporary Moods and Themes*. Polygram 1994. 7 314516 627 2
> *Gypsy Kings Greatest Hits*. Columbia 1994. 14 477242 10
> Kenny G, *Montage*. Arista 1990. 260 621
> Mike Oldfield, *Tubular Bells*. EMI 1973
> *This is Cult Fiction: 28 Cult TV and movie classics*. Virgin 1995. 7243 8 40867 2 5

Companies which produce specialist tapes for learning are listed on page 239.

The piece of music which caused a sell-out in the USA when researchers demonstrated improvements in maths scores when learners listened to it beforehand (not during!) was Mozart's *Sonata for Two Pianos in D Major!*

Beginnings

Beethoven, *Symphony no 5 in E minor – Allegro con brio* (6.32)

Verdi, *Brindisi* – from *La Traviata – Libiamo ne lieti calici* (3.10)

George Frederick Handel, *Hallelujah Chorus* – from *The Messiah*. (4.25) The best known oratario ever written.

Prokofiev, *Montagues and Capulets* from *Romeo and Juliet*. (1.57)

Jeremiah Clarke, *Trumpet Voluntary*. (2.13) A popular choice for weddings and other joyous occasions.

Mark Knopfler, *Going Home*. 1983. From the film *Local Hero*.

Weather Report, *Birdland*

Iggy Pop, *Lust for Life*. 1996. From the sound track of the film *Trainspotting*. A great sound but the lyrics need checking out first.

Demarcation of time on task

Chopin, *Waltz no 6 in D flat* – the 'minute waltz'. (1.59) Lasts more than a minute! Light, rippling and good for short review tasks which require movement.

Ravel, *Bolero* – conclusion. (c.5.26) Insistent piece which builds and builds. Schoolchildren may be familiar with it as the theme tune to the film *10*.

Mozart, *Eine Kleine Nachtmusik – Allegro*. (5.48)

Blues Brothers, 'Rawhide'. *The Best of the Blues Brothers*. (2.43) A great album for plucking tracks from.

Authentication of a mood

Edward Elgar, *Cello Concerto in E minor. Adagio – Moderato* (3.20) A powerful and uplifting piece. Perhaps the Jacqueline du Pre version is best known.

Gustav Holst, *The Planets* – Jupiter suite. (4.47) Contains the rousing hymn tune *I vow to thee my country*.

Albinoni, *Adagio in G minor*. (5.48) A haunting piece which has subsequently been popularised by its use in a TV commercial.

Bach-Gonoud, *Ave Maria*. (2.43)

Giorgio Moroder, *Love's Theme*. 1978. Taken from the film *Midnight Express*.

Ella Fitzgerald, *Every Time We Say Goodbye*.

Louis Armstrong, *We Have all the Time in the World*.

Energising

Rossini, *William Tell Overture*. (2.42) The classic get-them-out-of-their-seats piece. Brain gym is never the same without this!

Bach, *Brandenburg Concerto no 1*. 1st Movement. (4.45)

Carl Off, *Carmine Burana* – O Fortuna (2.45) A stirring piece for chorus and orchestra. Play it loud and stand well back!

Vivaldi, *The Four Seasons* – Concerto no 4 in F minor (Winter). (3.26) Likely to be well known amongst schoolchildren as a result of Nigel Kennedy's version and its popularity for television pieces.

George Frederick Handel, *The Arrival of the Queen of Sheba*. (3.04) The music describes the hustle and bustle of activity as the queen is about to arrive.

Edward Elgar, *Pomp and Circumstance no 1* Op 39 (6.42) The long-gone British Empire in all its 'glory'.

Gipsy Kings, *Greatest Hits*. Particularly *Bomboleo* and *Medley*. A favourite in Pizza Hut but high energy nevertheless!

Relaxing and as music for guided visualisations

Debussy, *Clair de lune*. (4.55) An atmospheric piece with emphasis on atmosphere and colour.

Rachmaninov, *Rhapsody on a Theme of Paganini* – variation 18 (3.19)

Vaughan Williams, *Fantasia on a Theme by Thomas Tallis*. (16.30) Based on a metrical psalm by the Tudor composer. Nostalgic and highly evocative of an English landscape.

Burgon, *Nunc dimittis*. (2.42) Originally written as the closing theme music to the TV adaptation of John Le Carre's thriller *Tinker, Tailor, Soldier, Spy* and now in the repertory of many cathedral choirs

John Williams, *Schindler's List* – theme tune. (5.02) Tasmin Little on violin. Theme tune to the deeply moving film about one man's attempt to save victims of the holocaust.

Mozart, *Concerto for Flute and Harp in Il Andantino*. (8.14) Amongst Mozart's loveliest. Slow, delicate and serene.

Stanley Myers, *The Deerhunter* – theme tune Cavatina. (3.36) John Williams on guitar. A delicate and floating piece.

'Ambient' music to manage noise levels and to lay under discussion and group activity

Mike Oldfield, *Tubular Bells*. A modern popular symphony inspired by Ravel and written by Mike Oldfield who also plays all the instruments.

Eric Satie, *Gymnopedies etc*. Delicate, soft and dreamlike with some little ironies hidden within.

Vangelis, *Love Theme*. 1989. Instrumental taken from the film *Blade Runner*. Also recommended is the album *Pulstar – The Hits of Vangelis* which includes *Chariots of Fire*.

Jean Michel Jarre, *Equinoxe Part 4*. 1978. Many of Jarre's better known pieces are ideal for classroom use. Try *Oxygene Part IV* played by Hank Marvin.

Bjork and David Arnold, *Play Dead*. 1993. Contemporary music featuring vocalist Bjork with Jah Wobble. Slow, insistent and heavy beat.

Evocation of a theme

Edward Elgar, *Introduction and Allegro for Strings op 47*. (13.12) Captures a long-vanished picture of England and particularly the Worcestershire countryside.

Art of Noise, *Robinson Crusoe*. 1989. The quirky pop version of a well known theme tune. A classic!

Incantation, *Cacharpaya*. 1991. Andean pipe music.

Nicolas de Angelis, *Concerto de Aranjuez – Rodrigo's Guitar Concerto. Rodrigo Vidre*. 1982. Guitar and strings with a spaghetti western 'feel'. See also music by Enrico Morrone, Angelo Badalmenti *(Twin Peaks)* and Julian Bream's *Ultimate Guitar Collection*.

Capercaillie, *Coisch A Ruin*. 1992. Taken from the TV series *A Prince Among Thieves*. In Gaelic. Many of the Capercaillie albums lend themselves to classroom use.

Jeff Wayne, *Eve of the War*. 1978. Brilliant! Stirring instrumental taken from the album *The War of the Worlds,* based on the HG Wells' novel and with a Richard Burton narration.

Clannad, *Robin (The Hooded Man)*. 1984. More Gaels! Mellow and calming with harmonies on top of an instrumental piece.

Salif Keita, *Folon – The Past*. 1995. Internationally known albino vocalist from Mali. Other recommended African artists include Baba Ma'al, Youssou N'Dour, Miriam Makeba and the Bhundu Boys.

Active concert

Michael Nyman, *The Piano – theme tune.* The heart asks pleasure first. (1.37)

The Edge, *Rowena's Theme*. 1986. Taken from the film *Captive*. An instrumental arrangement for piano and guitar.

Billy Taylor Trio, *I Wish I Knew (How it Would Feel to be Free)*. Better known as the theme music for Barry Norman's *Film 97*.

Horace Silver, *Song for my Father.*

Dave Brubeck, *Take Five.*

Passive concert review

Bach, *Double Violin Concerto in D Minor – Il Largo ma non tanto*. (7.38) One of Bach's finest melodies: the two soloists imitate each other seamlessly and the music 'rolls over the listener in waves'.

Mozart, *Concerto no 21 in C Major – Andante.* (7.15)

J.S. Bach, *Orchestral Suite no 3 in D – Air on the G String.* (4.19) Another piece which has become part of the repertoire of accelerated learning trainers for concert review because of its regular beat.

Beethoven, *Piano Concerto no 5 in E flat Adagio un pocco mosso.* (7.25)

Pachelbel, *Canon in D.* (4.54) Highly structured piece with a regular beat which has meant it is popular with those producing review and relaxation tapes. Also available with background sea sounds!

Vivaldi, *Flute Concerto no 3 in D major – Cantabile.* (3.14)

Marcello, *Oboe Concerto in D minor – Andante e spicatto.* 1982. Theme from the film *'The Firm'*.

The companies below specialise in music to aid learning

LIND Institute, PO Box 14487, San Francisco, CA , USA, 94114

Lifesounds, PO Box 227, Kalispaell, MT, USA, 59903
music@digisys.net

OptimaLearning, 885 Olive Avenue, Suite A, Novato, CA, USA, 94945-2455
barzak@optimalearning.com
www.optimalearning.com

4 CONTACT LIST OF ORGANISATIONS

The 21st Century Learning Initiative (UK)
(formerly Education 2000)
Letchworth Garden City Heritage Foundation Offices, Broadway,
Letchworth Garden City, Hertfordshire, SG6 3AAB
(tel: 01462 4811107/fax: 01462 481108

Accelerated Learning in Training and Education, (ALiTE), 24 Abbotsford Road, Cotham,
Bristol, BS6 6HB, UK
(tel: 0117 9743669 fax: 0117 9742589)
alite@demon.co.uk
www.alite.co.uk
Training in school and classroom approaches described in this book.

Accelerated Learning Systems Ltd, 50 Aylesbury Road, Aston Clinton,
Aylesbury, Bucks, HP22 9AH
*Suppliers of excellent Accelerated Learning publications especially in early years education and
in languages.*

Anglo-American Books, Crown Buildings, Bancyfelin, Carmarthen, SA33 5ND
(tel: 01267 211880)
*Importers of the most comprehensive selection of books, tapes and videos related to Accelerated
Learning, NLP and self-esteem. Mail order only.*

Association for Neuro-Linguistic Programming, PO Box, 78, Stourbridge, West
Midlands, DY8 2YT
*Attracts a membership from business, counselling and education and training. Produces a
quarterly journal called 'Rapport' as well as a members directory. Organises two conferences a
year on aspects of NLP. Promotes NLP and related disciplines. NLP training is powerful in
work on belief systems and how to change them, utilising language with precision and
outcomes thinking.*

Association for Supervision and Curriculum Development, 1250 N. Pitt Street,
Alexandria, VA 22314, USA
*The professional development and support organisation for US teachers. Organises excellent
training events and circulate useful booklists and regular newsletters. Useful for information on
multiple intelligences, thinking skills and brain-based learning.*

British Institute for Brain-Injured Children, Knowle Hall, Bridgwater, Somerset, TA7 8PJ
Does pioneering practical work based on patterning exercises with parents of brain injured children.

The British Society for Music Therapy, 25 Rosslyn Avenue, East Barnet, EN4 8DH
(tel: 0181 368 8879)

Edu-K, contact Kay McCarroll, 0181 202 0747
Provides training in kinesiology and brain gym are held each January in the United States.

Exeter Extended Literacy Project (Excel). Contact David Wray, University of Exeter School of Education, Heavitree Road, Exeter, EX1 2LU
A range of strategies has been developed to extend children's use and control of literature. Includes use of writing frames – templates, work in a range of genres and linking ten teaching strategies with ten process strategies.

First Steps. Contact Alan Howe, Consultant for English, Wiltshire County Council, Professional development Centre, Drove Road, Swindon, SN1 3AH
Wiltshire LEA language and literacy programme. It is developmentally based and uses diagnostic frameworks which link assessment to teaching.

Hermann International, 794 Buffalo Creek Road, Lake Lune NC 28746, USA
thinking@hbdi.com
www.hbdi.com
Design and distribution of the Hermann Brain Dominance Profile.

The Institute for Transactional Analysis, 37 Prebed Mansions, Chiswick High Road, London, W4 2LU
The national co-ordinating organisation for transactional analysis in the UK.

International Alliance for Learning, 10040 First Street, Encinitas, CA 92024-5059
info@ialearn.org
The international umbrella organisation for promoting accelerated and brain-based learning. Conferences are held each January in the United States.

International Council for Self-Esteem, c/o Daniels Publishing, 38 Cambridge Place, Cambridge, CB2 1NS
Co-ordinates conferences and some training events relating to self-esteem as well as publishing materials on topics such as circle time.

Learning Strategies Corporation, Wayzata , Minnesota, 55391-1836, USA
info@learningstrategies.com
www.learningstrategies.com
For information on photoreading and related products to do with 'whole-mind reading'.

London Leadership Centre, 10 Woburn Square, London WC1H 0NS
Contact Pat Collarbone
University of London Institute of Education centre focusing on the professional development of school leaders and offering a network and exchange between practitioners and researchers. Publishes a termly journal.

Model Learning Ltd, PO Box 5346, Brentwood, CM14 5RW
(tel/fax: 01277 202812)
info@modellearning.com
www.modellearning.com
Memory maps and illustrations in this book by Oliver Caviglioli of Model Learning, a company that produces and leads transformational courses in the area of individual and organisational learning.

NASEN, National Association for Special Educational Needs
Contact Sue Panter, 18 Thornton Court, Girton, Cambridge, CB2 0NS
A membership organisation for teachers and others involved in teaching children with Special Educational Needs. Organises conferences and training events.

Project Intact, The Binoh Centre, Norwood House, Harmony Way, Victoria Road, Hendon, London NW4 2BZ
Trains individuals and groups in thinking skills based on Feuerstein's work and that of Vygotsky. Offers accredited training in dynamic assessment, instrumental enrichment and mediated learning.

Project Renaissance, PO Box 332 Gaithersburg MD, USA 20884-0332
http://www.winwenger.com
Leading-edge thinking about intelligence and how to develop it.

SAPERE, Society for the Advancement of Philosophical Enquiry and Reflection in Education, 21 Bramley Road, London, W5 4SR
Offers training in the teaching and delivery of a curriculum known as 'Philosophy for Children'.

Scottish Consultative Council on the Curriculum, Gardyne Road, Broughty Ferry, Dundee DD5 1NY. Contact Ian Smith – ISmith@sccc.ac.uk
A forum for the exchange of the most recent ideas about teaching and learning. Produced a series of discussion documents entitled 'Teaching for Effective Learning' which are available for purchase.

Society for Effective Affective Learning (SEAL), PO Box 2246, Bath, BA1 2YR
An organisation which exists to promote better understanding about varied kinds of intelligence, right and left brain learning, valuing the individual and improving learning opportunities for all. Publishes a regular journal and organises conferences and training events. Has members worldwide. Supplier of LIND Baroque music tapes for learning. Useful contact for suggestopeadia and Lozanov-based language learning. Membership reflects a variety of eclectic interests.

School Improvement Network, University of London, Institute of Education, London WC1H 0AL
A network based at the Institute to promote good practice amongst practitioners and researchers. A termly journal and a members directory outlining case studies and areas of interest are published and conferences are offered.

 GLOSSARY OF TERMS

Active concert

Summary input of new information by reading over music. The reading is deliberately 'dramatic' and follows the pace and intensity of the music. The combination of dramatic music and reading alerts the 'emotional brain' to the significance of the new information.

Active listening

A method of encouraging students to listen for a specific purpose. Students are directed towards a given content area or a given set of questions to 'listen for'.

Affirmation

Sometimes colloquially described as 'self-convincers' for the brain, affirmations involve the repetition of positive and personal descriptors of desired behaviours in order to reinforce the likelihood of their successful achievement. The principle behind this is that the brain will 'learn' the newly introduced belief.

Alpha state

A brain wave cycle of per second which research has shown is the optimum state for learning. Can be induced through the use of some pieces of music which have a beat of 60 to 70 beats per minute. Baroque music is used in language learning for this particular purpose.

Amygdala

An area of the brain within the limbic system which has been the focus of much recent research. Is regarded of significance in attaching and routing emotional associations.

Anchoring

A technique derived from NLP which helps access a desired mental or physical 'state' by anchoring related physical associations to a mental experience.

Attention

The operation by which a person selects information, a limited amount of which we are able to focus on at any one time.

Baroque music

Used in accelerated learning for concert review. Baroque music of 60–70 beats per minute can induce an alpha brain wave pattern and helps to access long-term memory.

BASIS

A mode for building and maintaining self-esteem and self-belief. BASIS stands for Belonging, Aspirations, Safety, Identity and Success. Successful self-esteem programmes contain all of these elements.

BIG picture

By giving an overview, or BIG picture, first, right brain learners can access the material. BIG picture helps alleviate learner anxiety and helps to connect what is to come with what has gone before.

Brain gym

A physical activity which connects left and right brain and is useful for managing the 'state' of learners. The activities either stimulate (laterality dimension), release (focusing dimension) or relax (self-awareness dimension).

Break state

In recognising the optimum time on which a learner at a given development stage can remain on task, 'break states' help keep the learner in a positive physical and mental state for learning.

CAT

Computerised Axial Tomography. A scanning facility which is used to monitor activity in the brain.

Corus callosum

An area of the brain which connects left and right hemispheres of the neo-cortex. There are differences in male and females in the corpus callosum to which scientists attribute significance.

Dopamine

A neurotransmitter now being associated with some motor functions, learning, memory and with feelings of pleasure and elation. Each time a neurotransmitter like dopamine floods a synapse, circuits that trigger thoughts and motivate actions are etched onto the brain. Recent research connects dopamine to addictive behaviours.

Flow

A state described by Csikszentmihalyi wherein an individual is both physically and mentally pre-disposed to be highly and unusually creative.

Hippocampus

An area within the limbic system of the brain associated with long-term memory.

ITI

Integrated Thematic Instruction.

JOHARI window

A quadrant of statements used to encourage self-reflection.

Learned helplessness

A state of mind which is unresourceful and which can lead to a downward cycle of limiting beliefs and underachievement.

Memory map

A non-hierarchical, non-sequential method of taking summary or revision notes. Memory mapping is derived from Tony Buzan's Mind Map technique which links left and right brain and which encourages the learner to discern patterns and relationships in new information.

Metacognition

Essentially, learning about learning-metacognition is the understanding of the nature and purpose of learning and its processes.

Myelination

The sheathing of the axon to improve the effectiveness of communication between brain cells.

Neuron

Containing cells, axons and dendrites, the neuron is a self-contained communication centre which sends and receives messages.

Neurotransmitter

A chemical substance which promotes or inhibits chemical connections between neurons.

NLP

Neuro Linguistic Programming. NLP concerns itself with the difference between competence and excellence in human communication. Sometimes defined as the study of the structure of subjective experience, NLP can be utilised to change unhelpful behaviour patterns and beliefs.

NO LIMIT

An acronym which describes the principles of Accelerated Learning: Know the brain and how it works, Openness and relaxation for optimum learning, Learn to capacity, Input through VAK – Visual, Auditory and Kinesthetic – Multiple intelligence activities, Invest more through BASIS, Try it, test it and review it.

Passive concert or concert review

A summary review to reinforce learning and improve recall. The content is read to music of 60–70 beats per minute. This engages the brain into an alpha cycle appropriate for long-term memory.

Peripheral

Any visual stimulus which reinforces positive messages around learning. Peripherals can be a summary of content, keywords, affirmations or role models.

Positive suggestion

Reinforcement through the learning environment, learning activities and the language and behaviour of the teacher that successful learning will take place and the learner will achieve.

Rapport

The skill of rapport involves the ability to empathise and to enter respectfully into the 'map' of another and thus perceive 'reality' from different perspectives.

Relative lateralisation

The different functions of the two halves of the brain. Certain motor and cognitive functions can be specifically located in the brain though it needs to be acknowledged that the brain can 're-learn' and is to some extent 'plastic', that there are some gender differences and that there are dangers in over-emphasising the isolation of function.

Resilience

The ability to deal positively with adversity: 'there is no failure only feedback'.

Sensory Language

Language, deliberately chosen, which accesses all representational systems.

SQ3R

Survey, Question, Read, Review, Relate.

Serotonin

A neurotransmitter which has became the focus of much recent research into self-esteem, self-concept and physical development. Levels of serotonin vary in individuals and such levels have been associated with improved or retarded physical development and with positive or negative mental states.

Strokes

A unit of attention given or received. Strokes can be positive or negative, conditional or unconditional, real or plastic.

Synapse

The gap between nerve endings and receiver cells the excitation of which arises from connections between neurons.

Template

A structured tool used by a teacher or learner to more effectively engage with a learning task.

Triune brain

A model of the brain, attributed to Paul MacLean, which identifies three distinct functions corresponding to evolutionary stages which significantly impact on learning.

VAK

Visual, Auditory and Kinesthetic. Learners, in receiving information through the senses, will have a preferred sensory or representational system. Research suggests 29% of learners will have a visual preference, 34% will be auditory and 37% kinesthetic.

Variety Audit

A simple means of checking variety of teaching and learning strategies used in the classroom.

Visualisation

A technique for creating or recreating a scene visually. Visualisation can be used to facilitate learning, goal setting or behavioural changes.

⑥ REFERENCES

Abbot, John, *Learning Makes Sense: Recreating Education for a Changing Future*
(Education 2000, London, 1994)

Adey, P., Shayer, M., *Really Raising Standards: Cognitive Intervention and Academic
Achievement* (Routledge, London, 1994)

Adey, P., Shayer, M., and Yates, C., *A Teacher's Guide to Thinking Science, The Curriculum
Materials of the Cognitive Acceleration through Science Education Project*
Second Edition (Nelson, 1995)

Alkon, D., *Memory's Voice: Deciphering the mind-brain code*
(Harper Collins, New York, 1992)

Armstrong, T., *Seven Kinds of Smart: Identifying and Developing Your Many Intelligences*
(Plume, New York, 1993)

Ashman, Adrian, F., Conway, N.F., *An Introduction to Cognitive Education*
(Routledge, London, 1997)

Barber, Michael, *The Learning Game – Arguments for an Education Revolution*
(Victor Gollancz, London, 1997)

Bateson, Gregory, *A Sacred Unity: Further Steps to an Ecology of Mind* , Ballantine Books,
(1991)

Birren, F., *Colour and Human Response* (Van Nostrand Rheinhold, New York)

Black, I. B., *Information in the Brain: A Molecular Perspective*
(MIT Press, Cambridge, MA, 1991)

Bloom, B., *A Taxonomy of Educational Objectives* (David Mackay, New York, 1956)

Bloomsbury Thematic Dictionary of Quotations (Bloomsbury, 1990)

Blum, Deborah, *Sex on the Brain: The Biological Differences between Men and Women*
(Penguin, 1997)

Bolles, E.B., *Remembering and Forgetting: An Inquiry into the Nature of Memory*
(Walker, New York, 1988)

Borba, Michelle, *Esteem Builders* (Jalmar Press, California, 1989)

Boulding, K., *The Image* (University of Michigan Press, 1966)

Briggs, K.C., and Myers, I.B., *Myers -Briggs Type Indicator* (Palo Alto, California, 1977)

Brown, J.A.C., *Techniques of Persuasion* (Penguin, London, 1983)

Bruer, John, T., *Schools for Thought: A Science of Learning in the Classroom*
(MIT Press, 1993)

Butler, K., *Learning and Teaching Style in Theory and Practice*
(Columbia, The Learners Dimension, 1984)

Caine, R.N., Cane, G., *Making Connections: Teaching and the Human Brain*
(ASCD, Virginia, 1991)

Caine, R.N., Cane, G., Cromwell, S., *Mindshifts: A Brain-Based Process for Restructuring
Education* (Zephyr Press, USA, 1994)

Caldwell and Spinks, *The Self-Managing School* (Falmer, 1988)

Calvin, W., *How Brains Think: Evolving Intelligence Then and Now* (Wiedenfield and
Nicholson, The Orion Publishing Group, London)

Campbell, D.G., *Introduction to the Musical Brain* (Richardson, Texas, 1983)

Campbell, K., *Teaching and Learning Through Multiple Intelligences*
(Allyn and Bacon, 1996)

Carbo, M., Dunn, R., Dunn, K., *Teaching Students to Read Through Their Individual
Learning Styles* (Prentice Hall, NJ, 1988)

Carpenter, R.H.S., *Neurophysiology Third Edition* (Edward Arnold, Hodder & Stoughton Educational)

Chapman, Carolyn, *If the Shoe Fits: How to Develop Multiple Intelligences in the Classroom* (Skylight, IL, 1993)

Chesson, D, et al., *Hemispheric preferences for problem solving in a group of music majors and computer science majors* (Instructional Psychology, June, 1993)

Clay, Marie, M., *Reading Recovery: A Guidebook for Teachers* (Heinemann, NZ, 1993)

Claxton, Guy, *Hare Brain, Tortoise Mind: Why Intelligence Increases When you Think Less* (Fourth Estate, London, 1997)

Coleman, J. S., *Equality of Educational Opportunity* (Washington DC, US Government, 1966)

Coopersmith, Stanley, *The Antecedents of Self-Esteem* (W.H. Freeman, California 1967)

Covey, Steven, *The Seven Habits of Highly Effective People*

London Borough of Croydon, *Student Motivation: Findings from Qualitative Research* (BMRB International, 1996)

Csikszentmihalyi, M., *Flow: The Psychology of Optimal Experience* (Harper Collins, New York, 1990)

Damasio, A., *Descartes' Error: Emotion, Reason and the Human Brain* (Grosset/Putnam, New York, 1994)

De Porter, B., *Quantum Learning,* (Piaktus Press, 1993)

Dennison, P., Dennison, G.E., *Brain Gym for Teachers* (Edu-Kinesthetics, CA,1989)

Department for Education and Employment, *Excellence in Schools* (HMSO, July, 1997)

Dhority, Lynn, *The ACT Approach: The Use of Suggestion for Integrative Learning* (Gordon and Breach, MIT, 1991)

Diamond, M., *Enriching Heredity: The Impact of Environment on the Anatomy of the Brain* (Free Press, New York, 1988)

Dilts, R., Epstein, T., *Dynamic Learning* (Meta Publications, New York, 1995)

Dixon, Norman, *Preconscious Processing* (Chichester, New York, 1981)

Druckman, Swets, *Enhancing Human Performance, Issues, Theories and Techniques* (National Academy Press, Washington, 1988)

Dryden, G., Voss, J., *The Learning Revolution* (Accelerated Learning Systems, England, 1994)

Equal Opportunities Commission, *Educational Reform and Gender Equality in Schools* (Equal Opportunities Commission, 1996)

Fisher, Robert, *Teaching Children to Learn* (Stanley Thornes, London, 1995)

Fisher, Robert, *Teaching Children to Think* (Blackwell, London, 1991)

Fullan, M., Stiegelbauer, S., *The New Meaning of Educational Change* (Cassell, London, 1991)

Gallwey, Timothy, W., *the Inner Game of Tennis,* (Bantam Books, New York, 1979)

Gardner, Howard, *Frames of Mind: The Theory of Multiple Intelligences,* (Fontana, London, 1993)

Gardner, Howard, *The Unschooled Mind, How Children Think and How Schools Should Teach* (New York, 1991)

Gardner Howard, *The Theory of Multiple Intelligences,* (Basic Books)

Gates, Bill, *The Road Ahead* (Viking, NY, 1995)

Gazzaniga, M.S., *The Social Brain: Discovering the Networks of the Mind* (Basic Books, New York, 1985)

Goleman, Daniel, *Emotional Intelligence – Why it Matters More than IQ* (Bloomsbury, 1996)

Greenfield, Susan, *The Human Brain: a guided tour* (Science Masters, 1997)

Gregorc, A., *Inside styles: Beyond the Basics* (Maynard, Gabriel Systems inc., 1985)

Gregory, Richard, *The Oxford Companion to the Mind* (OUP, New York, 1987)

Halpern, D.F., *Sex Differences in Cognitive Abilities* (Erlbaum, New York, 1992)

Hannaford, C., *Smart Moves: Why Learning Is Not All In Your Head,*
(Great Ocean Publishers, 1995)

Hardy, Jones and Gould, *Understanding Psychological Preparation for Sport: Theory and Practice of Elite Performers* (Wiley, England, 1996)

Harman, W., and Rheingold, H., *Higher Creativity* (JP Tarcher, Los Angeles, 1985)

Hart, L. A., *The Human Brain and Human Learning* (Addison Wesley Longman, New York, 1983)

Hepper, P., *An examination of foetal learning before and after birth*
(Irish Journal of Psychology, 12)

Herbert, *The Elemental Mind*

Hermann, Ned, *The Hermann Brain Dominance Instrument* (Hermann International 1997)

Higbee, Kenneth, L., *Your Memory: How it Works and How to Improve It*
(Second Edition, Marlowe, New York, 1996)

HMSO, *Discipline in Schools, Elton Report* (HMSO, London, 1989)

HMSO, *Effective Management in Schools: a report for the DFE* (HMSO, London, 1993)

Houston, J., *The Possible Human: A course in extending your physical, mental and creative abilities* (Los Angeles, JP Tarcher, 1982)

Howard, Pierce, J., *The Owner's Manual for the Brain – Everyday Applications from Mind-Brain Research* (Bard Press, Texas, 1994)

Howe, Michael, *IQ in Question* (Sage Publications, London, 1997)

Hutton, Will, *The State We're In* (Jonathan Cape, London, 1995)

Institute of Education, *Accounting for Variations in Academic Effectiveness between Schools and Departments* (Institute of Education, London, 1996)

Institute of Education, *Key Characteristics of Effective Schools*
(Institute of Education, London, 1995)

James, Oliver, *Britain on the Couch – Treating a low Serotonin Society* (Century, 1997)

Jensen, Eric, *Brain-Based Learning and Teaching* (Turning Point, 1995)

Jensen, Eric, *Completing the Puzzle: A Brain-Based Approach to Learning*
(Turning Point, 1996)

Jensen, Eric., *The Learning Brain* (Turning Point, 1994)

Johnson, D.W., Johnson, F.P., *Joining Together: Group Theory and Group Skills*
(Allyn and Bacon, MA, 1994)

Kotulak, Ronald, *Inside the Brain* (Andrews and McMeel, 1996)

Kovalik, Susan, *Integrated Thematic Instruction: The Model*
(SKA, third edition, 1994)

Lazarus, R.S., *Emotion and Adaption* (OUP, New York, 1991)

Lazear, D., *Seven Ways of Teaching: The Artistry of Teaching with Multiple Intelligences*
(Zephyr Press, AZ, 1993)

LeDoux, Joseph, *Emotional Brain* (Simon and Schuster, NY, 1996)

Lewis, Byron A., and Pucelik, Frank, R., *Magic Demystified: A Pragmatic Guide to Communication and Change* (Metamorphous Press, OR, 1982)

London Borough of Croydon, *Pupil Motivation Research* (BRMB International, 1996)

Lothian Regional Council, *Promoting Quality Learning* (Lothian Regional Council, 1996)

MacLean, P.D., *The Triune Brain in Evolution* (Plenum, New York, 1990)

McCarthy, B., *The 4MAT System* (Excel Publishing, Arlington, 1982)

Mehrabian, A., *Silent Messages* (Wadsworth, 1971)

Mirsky, N., *The Unforgettable Memory Book* (BBC Worldwide, London, 1994)

Moir A., Jessell, D., *Brain Sex: The Real Difference Between Men and Women* (Michael Joseph, Penguin Books, London, 1989)

Moir A., Jessell, D., *A Mind to Crime: The Controversial Link Between Mind and Criminal Behaviour* (Michael Joseph, Penguin Books, 1995)

Neubauer, P.B., Neubauer, A., *Nature's Thumbprint: The New Genetics of Personality* (Addison-Wesley, MA, 1990)

Nottinghamshire County Council, *Raising Achievement Checklists* (Notts CC, 1996)

Odam, George, *The Sounding Symbol: Music Education in Action* (Stanley Thornes, 1995)

OFSTED, *Annual Report of Her Majesty's Chief Inspector of Schools 1994/95* (HMSO)

OFSTED, *Subjects and Standards, Issues for School Development arising from OFSTED, Inspections 1994/95 at KS3 & 4 and Post-16* (HMSO, 1996)

OFSTED, *Access and Achievement in Urban Education* (HMSO, 1993)

Oldroyd and Hall, *Managing Staff Development* (Paul Chapman Publishing, 1991)

Ornstein, Robert, *The Right Mind: Making Sense of the Hemispheres* (Harcourt Brace, New York, 1997)

Pedler, Burgoyne & Burdell, *Developing the Developers* (Henley Management College, 1993)

Perkins, David, *Outsmarting IQ: The Emerging Science of Learnable Intelligence* (The Free Press, New York, 1995)

Pinker, Steven, *How the Mind Works* (London, 1998)

Pinker, Steven, *The Language Instinct* (Penguin, London, 1994)

Popcorn, Faith, *The Popcorn Report* (Harper Collins, 1996)

Quality in Education Centre, University of Strathclyde, *Schools Speak for Themselves* (NUT, London, 1996)

Reich, Robert, *The Work of Nations* (Vintage Books, London, 1991)

Restak, Richard, *The Modular Brain* (Touchstone, New York, 1994)

Rogers, C.R., Freiberg, H.J., *Freedom to Learn* (Merrill, New York, 1994)

Rose, Colin and Goll, Louise, *Accelerate Your Learning* (Accelerated Learning Systems, 1992)

Rose, Colin, Nicholl, Malcolm, J., *Accelerated Learning for the 21st Century* (Delacorte Press, NY, 1997)

Rose, Steven, *The Making of Memory* (Bantam Press, London, 1993)

Rosenthal, R., Jacobsen, L., *Pygmalion in the Classroom* (Holt, Rinehart & Winston, New York, 1968)

Sammons, P., Hillman, J., Mortimore, P., *Key Characteristics of Effective Schools: A Review of School Effectiveness Research, International School Effectiveness Centre & Improvement Centre*, Institute of Education, University of London for OFSTED (OFSTED, 1995)

Samuels, M., and Samuels, N., *Seeing with the mind's eye, the history, techniques and uses of visualisation* (New York, 1975)

Scheele, Paul, R., *The PhotoReading Whole Mind System* (Learning Strategies Corporation, 1993)

School Improvement Network *Research Matters, Effective Learning*, Institute of Education, (University of London, Summer 1996)

Schorr, Lisbeth, *Within our Reach: Breaking the Cycle of Disadvantage* (Doubleday, New York, 1988)

Scottish Consultative Council on the Curriculum, *Teaching for Effective Learning* (Scottish CCC, 1996)

Seligman, M.E.P., *Learned Optimism* (Knopf, New York, 1991)

Senge, P., *The Fifth Discipline* (Doubleday, New York, 1990)

Springer, Sally, P., and Deutsch, George, *Left Brain, Right Brain: Perspectives from Cognitive Neuroscience* (Freeman, New York, 1998)

Sternberg, R.J., *The Triarchic Mind: A New Theory of Human Intelligence* (Viking, New York, 1988)

Sternberg, R.J., *Successful Intelligence: How Practical and Creative Intelligence Determine Success in Life* (Plume, New York, 1996)

Stoll and Myers, eds, *No Quick Fixes: Perspectives on Schools in Difficulty* (Falmer, London, 1998)

Sylwester, Robert, *A Celebration of Neurons: An Educator's Guide to the Human Brain* (ASCD, VA, 1995)

University of Bath, *A Study of Departments Adding Significant Value* (University of Bath and Avon TVEE, 1994)

University of Strathclyde, *Schools Speak for Themselves* (Quality in Education Centre, 1996)

Wenger, Win, *The Einstein Factor* (Prima Publishing, California, 1996)

Whitaker, P., *Managing to Learn* (Cassell, London, 1995)

Winebrinner, S., *Teaching Kids with Learning Difficulties in the Regular Classroom* (Free Spirit Publishing, MN, 1996)

ARTICLES, NEWSPAPERS AND PERIODICALS

American Psychologist, D.L.Schoter, 'Understanding Implicit Memory' (47,4,1992)

ASCD, 'Curriculum Update: Problem-based learning – the search for solutions to life's messy problems' (ASCD, Summer, 1997)

Chatelaine, 'Brainstorm' (differences between men's and women's brains) (December, 1995)

Coffield, Frank, *Can the UK become a learning society?* From the text of the Fourth Annual Education Lecture, King's College, (London, June, 1997)

Discover, 'Music of the hemispheres' (brain development in trained musicians), (March 1994)

Discover, 'What happened to Phineas?' (Phineas Gage, historical case of a hole through the brain causing a personality change) (special issue: 1994 – the Year in Science) January 1995)

Discover, 'Kernel of fear' (amygdala in the brain is responsible for association fear with certain stimuli) (June 1995)

Discover, 'S/He-brains' (phonological processing differs between men's and women's brains), (June 1995)

Discover, 'A brain that talks' Neurological evolution of human language, (June 1996)

The Economist, 'Looking at inner landscapes' (brain mapping) (July 3, 1993)

The Economist, 'Thought prints in the sand: brains improve with use' (Science And Technology, February 24, 1996)

Educational Leadership, Doll, W. E., Jr. 'Complexity in the Classroom' (Educational Leadership 4:1, 1989)

Educational Leadership, 'Teaching for Multiple Intelligences' (ASCD, USA, September 1, 1997, Vol 55)

Educational Management, Dimmock, C., 'Restructuring for School Effectiveness: Leading, Organising and Teaching for Effective Learning' (Educational Management and Administration Vol 23, No 1, 1995)

Forbes Magazine, 'Preventing (or at least postponing) brain drain' (how to decrease the effects of ageing on mental ability) (September 25, 1995)

The Guardian Newspaper, 'Lie detection tests shows those who are right are often wrong' (London, September 13, 1997)

The Guardian Newspaper, 'Guru with an axe to grind' (a revolutionary language teacher whose success raises questions about traditional learning) (London, April 29, 1997)

The Independent Newspaper, 'How they made Monica smile again: relaxation techniques have enabled Monica Seles to recover from her stabbing and play in the US Open' (August 25 1995)

Learning and Individual Differences, 'Cognitive Gender Differences: What are They and Why are They There?', Feingold, D., (8, 1996, 25-32)

MacLean's, 'Grumpy old men' (men lose brain tissue three times faster than women as they age), (April 22, 1996 v109 n17 p31)

McFarland, R and Kennison, R 'Asymmetrical effects of music upon spatial-sequential learning' (*California State University Journal of General Psychology*, 1988, 115, July)

Management Today, 'The Next Big Idea: why knowledge management is more than a fad' (London, August, 1997)

Nature, 'Sex Differences in the Functional Organisation of the Brain for Language' Shaywitz, B., et al (373, 1995)

Nature, 'Abnormal Processing of Visual Motion in Dyslexia Revealed by Functional Brain Imaging' Eden,, F., et al (382, 1996)

Neuropsychologia, 'Hemispheric Differences in Global Versus Local Processing of Hierarchical Visual Stimuli' VanKleeck, M, H., (27, 1989, 1165 – 1178)

New Statesman & Society, 'Exorcising the ghost' (differences between the brain and the computer), (March 19, 1993)

Observer Newspaper, 'The blind shall see and the deaf hear – without a doctor' John Illman , (London, May 4, 1997)

Observer Newspaper, 'That winning feeling' Oliver James, (London, June 8, 1997)

Omni, 'An interview with Michael Gazzaniga' (neuroscientist) (Oct 1993)

Psychological Review, 'The Magical Number Seven Plus or Minus Two' Miller, G, A., (63, 1956, 81-97)

Psychology Today, 'Growth spurts mirror mental milestones' (child development) (September 1987)

Science, Barinaga, Michael, 'The Tide of Memory Turning' editorial (June 29, 1990)

Science, 'In vivo evidence of structural brain asymmetry in musicians' (February 3, 1995)

Science, 'Arguing over why Johnny can't read' (learning disabilities), (March 31, 1995)

Science, 'Researchers get a sharper image of the human brain' (May 12, 1995)

Science, 'Common mechanisms of visual imagery and perception' (June 23, 1995)

Science, 'Discrete cortical regions associated with knowledge of colour and knowledge of action' (October 6, 1995)

Science, 'Increased cortical representation of the fingers of the left hand in string players' (October 13, 1995)

Science, 'Central command neurons of the sympathetic nervous system: basis of the fight-or-flight response' (October 27, 1995)

Science, 'Functional brain imaging studies of cortical mechanisms for memory' (November 3, 1995)

Science, 'The brain's visual world: representation of visual targets in cerebral cortex' (November 3, 1995)

Science, 'Activation by attention of the human reticular formation and thalamic intralaminar nuclei' (January 26, 1996)

Science, 'The cerebellum: movement co-ordinator or much more?' (April 26, 1996)

Science News, 'Language without rules; a curious speech disorder raises questions about the genetics of grammar' (May 28, 1994)

Science News, 'The social brain: new clues from old skull' (digital versions of Phineas Gage's skull suggests that iron rod wounded areas of frontal lobe responsible for personal and social behaviour) (May 21, 1994)

Science News, 'Is this the way Bobby Fisher does it?' (computer-generated images of chess players' thinking processes) (May 21, 1994)

Science News, 'Clues emerge on how brain reads, spells' (July 28, 1990)

Science News, 'Brain faces up to fear, social signs' (amygdala involved in emotion and social behaviour), (December 17, 1994)

Science News, 'Brain gets thoughtful reappraisal' (basal ganglia and cerebellum involved both in muscle movement and thinking co-ordination) (Octber 29, 1994)

Science News, 'Images of intellect: brain scans may colorize intelligence' (positron emission topography used to observe brain activity during problem solving) (October 8, 1994)

Science News, 'Making cerebral sense of words' (research on cerebral activity that gives meaning to words) (March 11, 1995)

Science News, 'Brain's singular way with language' (native and second language learning rely on same areas of brain) (April 1, 1995)

Science News 'Viruses reveal the brain's fright circuits' (the location of brain centres controlling the fight-or-flight reaction to fright uncovered by scientists using genetically engineered viruses) (October 28, 1995)

Science News, 'Brain scans set sights on mind's eye' (mental imagery may rely on areas of the brain used for visual processes) (December 2, 1995)

Science News, 'Biomedicine, Imaging hyperactive brains' (brains of children with Attention Deficit Hyperactivity Disorder different from those of normal children) (November 25, 1995)

Science News, 'Brain region linked to conscious memories' (hypocampal formation involved in explicit memory) (January 20, 1996)

Science News, 'Brains hammer home categorical knowledge' (processing of categorical knowledge occurs in specific brain regions) (February 17, 1996)

Shea, T, C., 'An investigation of the relationship among preferences for learning style element of Design and reading achievement at ninth grade' (Dissertation, 1983)

Skeptical Inquirer, 'The belief engine' (May-June 1995)

The Times Educational Supplement, 'Cognitive course boosts exam results' (London November 22, 1996)

Time Magazine, 'Brain bane' (dyslexia linked to abnormality in brain) (August 29, 1994)

Time Magazine, 'How gender may bend your thinking' (research shows physiological differences in the brain related to the thought processes of men and women) (July 17, 1995).

Time Magazine, 'Fertile Minds: How a Child's Brain Develops' (February 10th 1997)

Time Magazine, 'Total Recall: how scientists are uncovering the secrets of memory' (May 5th 1997)

The Times Newspaper, 'Why IQ tests would have derailed a rocket scientist' (London August 24th, 1997)

Whitfield, Richard., *Human Attachment as the Bedrock of Mentalising and Civility,* paper for HMC Annual meeting, Glasgow, October 1996

Acknowledgements

The publishers wish to thank the following people and organisations for permission to use extracts from their material in this book. Every effort has been made to contact copyright holders of materials reproduced in this book. The publishers apologise for any omissions and will be pleased to rectify them at the earliest opportunity.

M. Barber, *The Learning Game*
Reproduced from M. Barber's *The Learning Game* by permission of Victor Gollancz Ltd., Wellington House, 125 Strand, London, WC2R OBB.

I. Black, *Information in the Brain: A Molecular Perspective*
J. Bruer, *Schools for Thought: A Science of Learning in the Classroom*
L. Dhority, *The ACT Approach, The Use of Suggestions for Integrated Learning,*
Extracts reproduced with permission of The MIT Press, 5 Cambridge Center, Cambridge, MA 02142-1493.

G. Claxton, *HARE BRAIN TORTOISE MIND: Why Intelligence Increases When You Think Less*
Reprinted by permission of Fourth Estate Ltd., 6 Salem Road, London, W2 4BU, from *HARE BRAIN TORTOISE MIND: Why Intelligence Increases When You Think Less* by Guy Claxton © 1997 by Guy Claxton.

Crown Copyright is reproduced with the permission of the Controller of Her Majestyís Stationery Office.

B. Gates, *The Road Ahead*, Viking
Reproduced with permission of Penguin Putnam Inc. 375 Hudson St, New York NY 10014.

Susan Greenfield, *The Human Brain*
Reproduced from Susan Greenfield's *The Human Brain,* by permission of Weidenfeld and Nicholson, The Orion Publishing Group,

Ronald Kotulak, *Inside the Brain*, Universal Syndicate Press
Excerpts reproduced with permission from Universal Syndicate Press, an Andrews McMeel Universal company.

P Maclean, *The Truine Brain in Evolution*, Plenum Publishing
Reproduced from P Maclean's *The Truine Brain in Evolution,* by permission of Plenum Publishing Corp. 233 Spring Street, New York, NY 10013.

Nick Mirsky, *The Unforgettable Memory Book*, BBC Worldwide
Reproduced from *The Unforgettable Memory Book* by Nick Mirsky with permission of BBC Worldwide Limited
© 1994 Nick Mirsky

G. Odam, *The Sounding Symbol – Music Education in Action*
Reproduced with the permission of Stanley Thornes Publishers Ltd from *The Sounding Symbol – Music Education in Action* first published in 1995.

C. Rose & L, Goll, *Accelerate Your Learning.*
Material reproduced with permission of Accelerated Learning Systems Ltd., 50 Aylesbury Road, Aston Clinton, Aylesbury, Bucks, HP22 5AH.

P Whittaker, *Managing to Learn*, Cassell
Reproduced from P. Whittaker, *Managing to Learn,* 1995, by permission of Cassell Plc, Wellington House, 125 Strand, London, England.

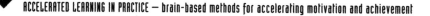

INDEX

Bold page numbers indicate definitions and major references

253

£19.95   42001.   00050944   30.05.01

ACCELERATED LEARNING IN PRACTICE — brain-based methods for accelerating motivation and achievement